Advance Praise for *The Purchasing Machine*

"A compelling business case for why procurement and supply chain management have beome so important for all companies who want to be leaders in their respective fields."
—Helmut F. Porkert, Chief Procurement Officer, Chevron Corporation

"From strategy to early supplier involvement and cost modeling . . . offers a detailed playbook on how to drive bottom-line profitability."
—Jack Futcher, Senior Vice President and Manager, Worldwide Procurement, Bechtel Group, Inc.

"Transform the supply chain into a strategic moneymaking machine by applying the best practices outlined in this book."
—Thomas J. Piersa, Vice President, Global Procurement, Maytag Corporation

"My prescribed antidote for years of bad practices and management neglect of this strategic process."
—Ken Stork, President, Ken Stork & Associates, Inc.

"A virtual gold mine of best practices from top firms with exemplary supply chain reputations. . . . Read this to discover best practices across the gamut of supply chain dimensions."
—Bradley J. Holcomb, Vice President & Chief Procurement Officer, Waste Management, Inc.

"A gourmet's delight of recipes for success. . . . Pick the recipes that look interesting for your company . . . then adapt them to fit your system."
—Jeffrey Liker, Professor of Industrial and Operations Engincering, University of Michigan

"For any leader who has a passion to transform traditional purchasing into an inspired force of professionals intent on deeply impacting financial results."
—John R. Oakland, Staff Vice President, Sourcing Operations, 3M Procurement Operations

*f*P

Other Books by Patricia E. Moody

The Perfect Engine,
Anand Sharma and Patricia E. Moody (fall 2001)

*The Technology Machine: How Manufacturing Will Work
in the Year 2020,*
Patricia E. Moody and Richard E. Morley

*The Kaizen Blitz: Accelerating Breakthroughs in
Productivity and Performance,*
Anthony C. Laraia, Patricia E. Moody, and Robert W. Hall

Powered by Honda: Developing Excellence in the Global Enterprise,
Dave Nelson, Rick Mayo, and Patricia E. Moody

*Leading Manufacturing Excellence:
A Guide to State-of-the-Art Manufacturing,*
Patricia E. Moody, Editor

Breakthrough Partnering: Creating a Collective Enterprise Advantage,
Patricia E. Moody, Author

Strategic Manufacturing: Dynamic New Directions for the 1990s,
Patricia E. Moody, Editor

THE PURCHASING MACHINE

HOW THE TOP TEN COMPANIES
USE BEST PRACTICES
TO MANAGE THEIR SUPPLY CHAINS

Dave Nelson
Patricia E. Moody
and
Jonathan Stegner

THE FREE PRESS

NEW YORK   LONDON   TORONTO   SYDNEY   SINGAPORE

*f*P

THE FREE PRESS
A Division of Simon & Schuster, Inc.
1230 Avenue of the Americas
New York, NY 10020

THE FREE PRESS and colophon are trademarks
of Simon & Schuster, Inc.

Designed by Brady McNamara

Manufactured in the United States of America

10   9   8   7   6   5   4

The authors gratefully acknowledge permission from the following source to reprint
material in its control:
Harcourt, Inc., for excerpt from *Pilgrimage on a Steel Ride: A Memoir about Men and
Motorcycles,* copyright © 1997 by Gary Paulsen (reprinted in 1999 as *Zero to Sixty: The
Motorcycle Journey of a Lifetime*).

Library of Congress Cataloging-in-Publication Data
Nelson, Dave.
    The purchasing machine: how the top ten companies use best practices to manage
their supply chains / Dave Nelson, Patricia E. Moody, and Jonathan Stegner.
        p.   cm.
    Includes index.
    1. Business logistics—Case studies. I. Moody, Patricia E. II. Stegner, Jonathan.
III. Title

HD38.5b. N45 2001
658.7'2—dc21

00-050324

ISBN 0-684-85776-6

When we think of Larry, we can see him leading a group of suppliers to Honda in the first conference to showcase the very powerful improvement methodology called BP. Larry stood at the front of the auditorium looking tanned and gloriously successful. After many years of struggle with outdated quality improvement drives, Larry's organization at Parker Hannifin, where he was a group president, raised their hands and volunteered to try a different approach. The results were stunning, and we all thrilled to watch the videotape of the first employees' reaction, down in Batesville, Mississippi.

Larry was, as we learned much later, unbelievably successful in his personal life as well. His wife, Polly, was credited by some with helping him make big choices that took him down a different path; together they "adopted" a foster child in Florida and helped maintain a broken family while the mother found a new path. Together, they embarked on other quietly charitable gifts. And sadly, flying together for the first time in their marriage—too soon—they left our earth off the coast of Nova Scotia. We gratefully dedicate this book to their memory, to their courage and beneficence, and to the honor of lives well lived. Blessings.

CONTENTS

Contents

IBM's Transformation Leads an Industry Movement

The mantra for corporate America in the 90s was "outsource everything you can and focus on your core competencies." In this new decade, the emphasis has to be on leveraging and managing these outsourced activities to maximize the effectiveness of the corporation's new vital partners—the suppliers of these outsourced products, components, and services.

As early as 1988, IBM spent less than 28 percent of annual revenue with outside suppliers. By 1999, almost 54 percent of annual revenue was entrusted for the first time to non-IBMers, i.e. suppliers. What suddenly became essential was having a procurement function that could sort out the followers, a group that could find the few very best leaders in the world and actually help those suppliers improve their performance. Then, it became the role of purchasing to manage these core suppliers within a supply chain that balanced price, quality, delivery, and technology.

The new IBM suppliers had to be convinced that procurement people would take the long view. We knew that solid, long-term relationships built on pragmatic trust would foster the financial confidence necessary to support supplier investment in new plant, equipment, technologies, and people. But without the suppliers pushing the technology envelope, as IBM supplying plants had in the past, IBM's new products and services would not be competitive in the demanding B2B marketplace.

The new type of team that was needed had to be more than multifunctional. A multi-company supply chain had to be created and made to work, real-time, everyday, under every potential business and market condition.

My Role

Lead by CFO Jerry York, IBM brought together the best procurement leaders to be found from inside and outside IBM to centralize procurement, to improve supplier relationships, and to ensure that IBM's billions of dollars were being spent with only the world's best suppliers. I was fortunate enough to be at the head of this procurement team. The total spend was $40 billion in 1994; by August of 1999 the total spend had grown to $45 billion.

I had learned the procurement craft at Ford Motor Company over twenty-three Job #1's (Job #1 is the industry's name for new model start-ups). Ford's procurement operations, in the last few of those twenty-three years, were learning fast from the Japanese—and particularly from their partner Mazda. A greater emphasis was being placed on quality and long-term supplier agreements that would support supplier investment in new technologies and equipment.

The lure to head up a procurement operation took me from Ford to Black & Decker, with a spend of $4 billion, and then on to Hewlett-Packard—spend $10 billion—and the fast-moving, very global, high tech industry. All these experiences were great preparation for the challenge of bringing together the decentralized, somewhat demoralized procurement people of IBM. The company's willingness to let me recruit inside and outside IBM for key leaders made the assignment fun and doable.

Over the next six years, the IBM procurement team racked up an impressive list of accomplishments, including:

- Savings of $9 billion, over 5 percent per year of the total spend.
- Improved satisfaction rating by their internal clients from 43 percent to 89 percent.
- Greater responsiveness to suppliers' expectations. Improved effectiveness assessment by suppliers rose from rating IBM almost last among suppliers' major customers, to rating IBM first. IBM developed its effectiveness survey jointly with Michigan State University's Bob Monzka; Michigan State conducted the survey as a third-party facilitator. The survey questions were designed to rank IBM relative to its competitors. Supplier feedback the first year was a shock—in 1995, IBM placed number five or six out of seven or eight competitors. By round two in 1997, we rose to number 3, and in 1999 IBM captured first place.
- Audit readiness rose from 66 percent to 100 percent. Audit readiness is a measure of business control; IBM's internal auditors spend a week or two with various procurement people to assess business controls, the manner in which the company spends its money. They review operations procedures around quotes, and ask questions like "did you get three quotes?" or "did you document the reason why you did not get three quotes?" or "what was the reason why supplier A was chosen?" to evaluate the goodness of our procurement procedures. The first-year audit results showed procurement to be horribly out of control. By my last 24 months in office, however, we did not fail a single audit.
- Purchases over the Internet from zero to $13 billion in two years.
- Contracts reduced from 40+ pages to 6 pages.
- Winning Mr. Gerstner's Chairman's Award for e-procurement excellence. At the annual meeting of the senior management group, the four hundred most senior managers in IBM, Chairman Gerstner presents two Chairman's awards. For IBMers, this is an enormous honor and recognition among the best. Winning team members from all over the world receive a standing ovation, shake hands with Mr. Gerstner, and take away a crystal star and certificate.

For years I sat in the audience wishing that procurement would win an award. Although we were nominated every year, it wasn't until 1999 that we left the ranks of the also-rans and joined the winners on stage.

Lou Gerstner is a very customer-oriented guy, and one of the many brilliant things he has brought to IBM is customer focus, apart from internal IBM measures. Gerster put an end to the inevitable and legendary result of assembling a "couple hundred top ten percent of their class college grads, and turning them loose with no focus on the customer-intertribal wars." But Gerstner had come to IBM as a customer, and he viscerally understood the power of a shift in focus to the customer's point of view.

Procurement does not appear at first glance to be a customer-focused activity, so we thought our chances of winning were slim. Every year teams of marketing and sales people, like the other 1999 winner who pulled together a multibillion-dollar global sales breakthrough, walked off with the award. It was hard—we were outwardly focused too, but toward the supplier.

But in my area, our e-procurement team had moved $13 billion onto the Internet. Twelve multifunctional pros who assembled the systems to accomplish that remarkable breakthrough stepped on stage to receive a Chairman's Award that was actually inscribed with the names of some forty team members. We knew that winning was testimony to the critical role purchasing played in IBM's newest transformation and recovery.

• Winning *Purchasing Magazine's* Medal of Excellence 1999.

However, the most important accomplishment of IBM procurement and of all ten of the outstanding procurement groups described in this book is to have become a vital, critical factor in making their companies successful.

No longer is procurement viewed as a necessary evil, a back office function that doesn't play a key role in determining success or failure in the competitive world marketplace.

What must follow the intense focus by corporations on only their core competencies? Without a doubt, the next step is to make procurement their most critical core competency—or else these corporations won't win in the marketplace. Read on and find out how ten procurement organizations achieved the excellence their companies had to have. The future is now.

R. Gene Richter
Retired Chief Procurement Officer and VP
Global Procurement, IBM Corporation

PREFACE

WHEN IT WAS TIME for me to get serious about a mortgage and car payment, I turned to manufacturing, specifically the slice called purchasing, for relief. I had grown up in manufacturing and "knew" that materials management—the energy, coercion, and negotiation highs one could obtain only from the thrill of the hunt—was where the action was. Manufacturing was a black box, but purchasing was about money, and the rules were clear. We never set foot on the factory floor, we never chatted up suppliers, and we never, ever shut the machines down. Our measure of success was the twenty-pound purchased price variance report—Christmas bonuses and vacations ran hot or cold on this document. It was a severely limiting environment for someone headed for a career writing business books and columns, and although I was unaware of the exact path things would take, it did not take too long for the hardening boundaries to press my "restless" nerve.

From an entry-level position grounded by a two-ton Frieden calculator, the electronics industry looked exciting for all the reasons that short life cycles and market swings the size of rogue waves attract creative types. And I was not disappointed. All the excitement of making *things*—first cables, then memory boards, and disk drives, and finally entire systems destined for real customers like newspapers and scientific labs—caught me in their adrenalin rush. The first week of every new quarter was a dazed lull as we struggled to recover from the previous two weeks' marathon push to make shipments; the second week of the month established a rhythm that by week three paralleled the push and pulls sparking the production area; by week four we were fully engaged—both purchasing and manufacturing personnel moving in parallel to push, push, push those machines. Marketing and finance people had no appreciation for the eighteen-hour rush to completion that every one of us shop floor types lived.

For most supply management professionals, the changes from what we now self-consciously label traditional purchasing, to partnering and the extended enterprise, has been overlaid with changes on the other side of the wall, in the manufacturing area. Now, at the turn of the millennium, most supply management professionals can safely look back on their beginnings—fortunately most of us reach a limit of our memories at twenty-five to thirty years max!—and see how clearly we were headed to an acceleration of process that would have made no sense in the era of punch cards and expedite orders when it all began. But we were right all along—manufacturing, and specifically materials management, was exactly the right place to be.

Supply management—purchasing, money and material flows, ownership of acquisition and sourcing strategies, and even intellectual property movement and control—is absolutely the most exciting spot to be in today for a manufacturing professional. For the next ten to twenty years the decisions and structures we put in place to run our operations will determine whether our companies and our teams—call them the extended enterprise—will be among the winners, losers, or hangers-on. It has become very clear that the winners have already mapped their strategy and secured a few of the necessary resources for their journey. And it is equally clear that the losers, the arthritic companies in whom no creative heart beats, and who are unable to build or draw on sheer power, will occupy sad spots in the depths of a networked hierarchy *of their own making*, a seventh ring of hell populated by low margins, missed bids, failed deliveries, questionable quality, and management clinging by the raw tips of their fingers to a perceived home advantage.

For those emboldened professionals who want to be on the right side of the field when the scores are posted, we offer the best path to success—learn from the leaders who have continuously practiced creative excellence, take the lessons, and apply them to your own organization. You must create real change and leapfrog the competition with out-of-the-box ideas. It's not enough to simply improve on winning performance. The histories of companies like IBM, Chrysler (now Daimler/Chrysler), Honda, and Toyota are long enough to prove their turnaround muscle and lasting hearts.

The downside of benchmarking and adopting Best Practices is that you are only as good as the process benchmarked at a particular time, and for many companies, this in itself may be a huge leveling up. For others, it may be only a fraction of what is possible with out-of-the-box thinking and process transformation. Use Best Practices as the launching pad, not the destination.

Hire the very best supply management and manufacturing professionals, pay them well, and expect that they will inevitably be tempted to move. Build your company's team with an eye to building your enterprise—your competition even now is one enterprise against another—and you must assemble the best suppliers, the best planners, the best engineers, and the best systems if you are to maintain your customer base and grow.

We believe that right now, a few simple changes in traditional practice can have enormous impact on markets, customers, and suppliers, and we urge you to implement them immediately. Intelligent cost systems, new product innovation teams, and web-based communications will take your group very far into the competitive arena. By the year 2020, when the game will change again, if your enterprise has been structured to move fast and accurately against new performance targets, your successors should enjoy equally satisfying successes. We urge you, *now*, however, to move quickly and to keep your eyes moving to the horizon; learning to see is your first and most valuable survival skill. Everything that follows is athletics—

toned, flexible, and persistent; the best enterprise—customers and suppliers both—will cross and recross the finish line together. The next twenty years for the winners will be a time of group successes, group work, some individual brilliance, and for some stragglers, group survival. Good luck to you all!

Patricia E. Moody

THE
PURCHASING
MACHINE

INTRODUCTION

WHENEVER INSTITUTIONS begin to crack and crumble, people feel the tremors and wonder, "Is this the end?" Churches, schools, companies, countries, even families seem to pass through stages of development and decline that cannot be easily graphed or plotted. But we know something is changing because we can feel and sometimes see the movement.

Manufacturing and purchasing as important contributors to the creation of wealth and real growth are being reexamined because technology pushes forward so fast that we humans feel as if we are losing our direction. And the reality is, no Global Positioning System, no cell phone network or satellite linkage can tell us precisely where we are going, when we will arrive, and if anyone will be there to greet us.

Some organizations live on the eternal edge of chaos and transformation. Others seek a more predictable route. This book is written for professionals who understand and truly expect that the next ten to twenty years will carry them into a changed organization. They are the change leaders and adopters who believe that groups of enlightened workers and thinkers can prepare for change and meet its challenge.

We believe that training, education, and persistence—and occasionally luck—are the talents that will make the difference. And we especially believe in the power of education and training, because each of us has lived a personal success story that could have happened only with many different types of learning experiences—some happily transparent successes but others well-deserved "failures."

Well-Deserved "Learnings"

Co-author Nelson was raised in Indiana in a farm family, where responsibility and hard work were taught and expected, even of five-year-old boys. One spring Dave's mother handed each of the four boys a small bag of pinto beans, with instructions that they were to go out to the field and drop three beans into each of the furrows. She carefully explained that each planting should be spaced two feet from the next one. The older boys rushed out to finish their task, patting down each fresh mound and dousing the hill with the watering can. But ole Dave, the sunny dispositioned child whose mind tended to wander, thought he would take a shortcut. He carefully planted the first two rows of beans, but by row four, the seeds were falling heavier in the holes—first three, then a half-dozen, and finally entire handfuls of beans found themselves covered with dirt and patted down, firmly. Not a trace.

With good water and the warm spring sun staying longer in the sky, beans sprout fast, and their shoots push up through the soil to announce the new crop's upcoming harvest. Beans have been known to grow over six inches a day in Pike County, Indiana, and unfortunately for Dave, his sowing produced visible evidence of good intentions diverted by springtime idylls—a few large, tangled clumps of fresh sprouts crowded higher and higher, next to his older brothers' ordered plantings of exactly three young shoots spaced exactly two feet in all directions.

As a schoolteacher, Mamma Nelson had seen it all: the forgotten homework, the missing notebooks, and a few unfed chickens. And as Dave learned just before supper that night, there is no easy way—

nowhere to hide—and there are not too many shortcuts to getting the job done right that won't eventually show themselves, even at considerable distance. Next morning before school he was out in the field, separating and replanting the bean sprouts, . . . one at a time. Getting it right.

We could say life is like that. There are lessons in the garden, lessons in nature, and lessons in the marketplace. Sometimes the job teaches us persistence and cleverness, and sometimes that's what we bring to the work. Every part of manufacturing, including procurement and the supply chain, is being redesigned for better, more predictable performance, the kind of performance that can be achieved only by doing the work very well, every time. The Best Practices companies we have chosen to highlight are not perfect in all areas; for some, success is enough to be exceptionally skilled in new product introductions, or to be brainiacs with systems innovation; a few others rank highest in supplier development. But what they have learned is to do some things extremely well, and we would bet that as they rewrite the rules, they will do the next job equally well because of their very demanding leaders.

In the process of talking with these Top Ten companies, and a few of the leading runner-up contenders, we discovered that while we started the Best Practices project thinking that we would be looking at mechanics, we very quickly were drawn to leaders. Because each of the Top Ten is distinguished, by one—seldom more—gloriously positive, smart, and sometimes procurement-aggressive leader. During the study our focus moved somewhat to listen to what the leaders had to say, because we came to the conclusion that *they made all the difference.*

We were interested in where they came from, and how they managed to take a path that led them into supply chain, the heart of manufacturing. Nelson, for his part, found his way from manufacturing into purchasing as a natural transition, part of a career rotation that led out of production into a white-collar job. Moody, however, found herself in purchasing as a way of moving into manufacturing, out of the white-collar world onto the shop floor, where she truly loves to be. Stegner, trained in Economics, first learned manufacturing systems as he sold and implemented computer systems in the late 1970s. He decided to change from the sales to the purchasing side of the desk because he believed he could affect greater organization and process change in that role.

We found that the best purchasing executives have strong credentials from other areas. They may or may not be engineers, but each one of them is an outstanding communicator. Each of the Top Ten leaders is charismatic. Willie Deese of SmithKline Beecham listens well and can place very high demands on his people without losing them; Garry Berryman from Harley speaks and the crowd listens; his credibility smoothes the way for many difficult changes, especially among supplier groups. Roy Armes of Whirlpool has command of very "heavy" numbers, and he uses them well and strategically to drive what was a low-margin business to globally competitive levels. Mike Doyle of NISCI (National Institute for Supply Chain Integration), a former Army Intelligence officer, is as smart as the old McNamara Kids were at Ford, his former corporate employer. The list continues, through the Top Ten, leading us to the thought that what we were profiling was not just the best practices of the world's leading supply chain organizations, but we were really drawn to the ten best leaders, the guys most likely to be winners in a future filled with a few winners, a few more losers, and many lost corporate souls.

We came to the conclusion—but we'll leave it to you to see if we were right—that for this difficult growth and transition phase of supply chain transformation, especially in its linkage to lean manufacturing—charismatic, tough, brilliant leaders have made all the difference.

Learning to See

Our second insight reflects a bias that the three co-authors share. Each of us has great respect for the power of education, whether it is delivered as classroom training or degrees, internships or apprenticeships, mentoring, books, or occasional forays into after-hours classes. Although we don't subscribe to the credo that a guaranteed fifty-two hours of required training per year will produce the perfect work-force, we believe that rigorous exercise builds muscles, whether they are on the legs or in the brain.

Learning to read and becoming completely comfortable with the basics is so terribly important. And we happen to think that laying a solid foundation in manufacturing and supply chain is equally important, because only good solid skills will carry us through this transition.

1

THE SEARCH FOR THE BEST

Unseen Gains, Lost Profits

EVERY DAY, thousands of companies leave billions of dollars on the table, hard-earned dollars that could have appeared in lower consumer prices, exciting products or fatter shareholder returns. The losses are not leveraged cuts demanded by Lopez-type leaders, but invisible, unrealized savings that could put their organizations in the top tier of healthy, resilient supply management leaders. And every day, those same millions—lost opportunities—slip into someone else's pocket as the silver certificates flutter and drift farther away from their original owners. Profitable majors like Daimler/Chrysler, Honda of America, Harley-Davidson, IBM, and John Deere all recognize the power of profits realized when supply management professionals focus their attention on best practices in all areas of their operations, and these winners continue to reap the benefits of their intense cost focus. In these unique and powerful supply management leaders, the discipline of acquiring and moving material has become a key strategic advantage that enables lean manufacturing and responsive customer focus.

Unfortunately, although most industries cannot afford to let their profits blow away, many of them don't even notice the constant slipping away of cash. Sure, they have studied and struggled with MRP systems, ERP, outsourcing, and supplier development, and some of these techniques have produced temporary, noticeable gains. But their central focus is tuned to tracking everyday purchasing challenges of delivery and quality, and their peripheral vision is not engaged. Some of them may be too preoccupied with manufacturing to see the areas at other ends of the supply chain.

Opportunities for enormous savings in time and money lie at the far ends of the supply chain, most notably in procurement and design and development. In the middle, where manufacturing occupies a thin slice that converts an idea through the delivery process to consumable cash, processing operations account for an increasingly smaller slice of the continuum, because most world-class organizations have for the past fifteen years or so addressed and conquered manufacturing weak points. The problems of excess inventory, waste in the process, bad quality, inflexibility in scheduling, and a better and more professional workforce are well on their way to extinction. The expected result—truly flexible, lean manufacturing—will have been achieved among the winners in most manufacturing sectors within the next ten to twenty years or so.

What remains, therefore, is the challenge of bringing procurement in an extended enterprise into an equally powerful and responsive strategic position.

Manufacturing's Transformation

The past two hundred years have seen a long series of process and human innovations in the area of manufacturing, starting with Francis Cabot Lowell and Paul Moody's reintegration of the disparate textile processing functions in a single mill on the banks of the Charles River. These entrepreneurs, and a few other members of an enterprising elite called the Boston Manufacturing Company, realized 200 percent and more profits through use of simple economies of scale and expansion: bigger brick mills; longer days; faster machines; more

The Manufacturing Continuum

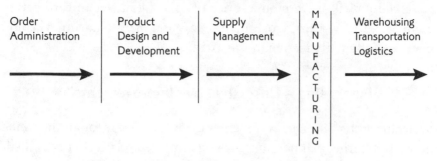

Order Administration

Product Design and Development

Supply Management

MANUFACTURING

Warehousing Transportation Logistics

Opportunities = time, quality, cost, flexibility

Copyright 1998 Patricia E. Moody, Inc.
PEMoody@aol.com

Figure 1.1 The Manufacturing Continuum*

*From Patricia E. Moody and Richard E. Morley, *The Technology Machine: How Manufacturing Will Work in the Year 2020* (New York: The Free Press, 1999).

workers; taking raw material—cotton—and carding, dying, weaving, rolling, and shipping finished goods from a single location. Issues around purchasing and logistics—where and when to acquire the next raw material shipment, where to store the in-process goods, and how to ship out to a market screaming for North American goods—were smaller questions than issues involving direct labor and the machinery that drove the looms. Innovation, therefore, centered on improving, which usually meant going faster, basic production operations. Workforce policies around productivity focused on speed rather than intelligence, perhaps even more than quality.

Limitations of Bigger, Faster Growth

This profit model preceded what we have come to call Taylorism, the perfected system of standards and incentives that further controlled and "improved" how human hands worked. Finally, as competitive threats shifted profits out of the Western world to Eastern production centers like Japan, North American manufacturing leaders adopted in quick succession a series of episodic moves toward better quality, MRP systems, workforce teams and profit sharing, reengineering, and finally lean manufacturing.

Purchasing—Unscathed by "Improvements"

Still, although the huge improvement waves rolled through the ranks of manufacturing planners, purchasing remained relatively untouched. As late as the early 1990s, many organizations could point to no integrated systems assist that completely eliminated paperwork transactions, for example, or that linked purchasing to other production operations. Purchasing systems were an afterthought, frequently too complex to manage quickly or too awkward to change directions. Headlines about procurement tended to focus on cost-cutting drives and limited efforts to roll procurement into the picture.

The Manufacturing Continuum

To some degree, purchasing professionals have enjoyed a pleasant separation from other siloed functions (see Fig. 1.1); twenty years ago few buyers, for example, set foot in their shops or at their suppliers' sites. It was even possible to plan and manage entire commodities in the computer industry without ever having touched a motherboard or heard the hum of a disk drive. The typical buyer/planner's day centered on acquisition and tracking of materials at what was considered competitive prices. Strategically, few purchasing professionals participated in business planning decisions; tactically, purchasing planners, buyers, and expediters could not be overlooked because they frequently compensated for system and supplier failures—missed performance in deliveries or quality—a conflicted position from which no human could easily find resolution or progress.

Where manufacturing pioneers evidenced a dedication to bricks and mortar, and more and bigger machinery, purchasing studied and practiced the art of negotiation, business travel, gifting, and locating back-up supply strategies. For a few years, this approach worked, but as operations professionals redrew *their* landscape, procurement was challenged to get involved. Technology advances—the CNC machine, the PLC, the personal computer, and the Toyota Production System—took large chunks of direct and indirect labor dollars out of product processing and shifted the mix of labor to materials.

Further, as some companies examined their dedication to vertical integration, they migrated toward perfecting a few single competencies. They chose to "offload" certain processing steps, for example, "to the experts." Where companies like St. James Paper owned forests, shipped and stripped logs, and transported finished product on their own trucks, other commodity producers began to disinvest, freeing up cash to be more carefully applied among competing suppliers.

Shifting a percentage of in-house produced components and assemblies grew the second tier producers, which raised purchasing's strategic importance within large organizations. It is not unusual for final assembly producers to purchase over 50 percent of the components, making them the assembly and procurement experts and a world of specific commodity competitors. So as manufacturing trimmed down and tried to speed its own processes, procurement found itself with more of the dollar responsibilities for sourcing into final assembly plants, a task most purchasing professionals were unprepared for, and surprisingly, were somewhat blind to. The shift happened almost overnight.

Life Cycles—From Seasons to Months, from Days to Hours . . .

The electronics world grew and adopted new technologies the way farmers used to plan and harvest crops. Computers, for example, during the seventies and eighties were built to a lurchy, spastic rhythm dictated by huge market swings and technology challenges. Pioneers struggled with the movement from core to semiconductor memories, proprietary software and extremely specialized equipment supported massive in-house production of everything from motherboards, to displays, to simple cable assemblies. Completely vertically integrated companies had essentially created a deadly mutual dependence between manufacturing and purchasing; manufacturing pros felt they were all-powerful and decisive, as did purchasing, but all were ruled by marketing and accounting gurus.

But when, in the mid-seventies, the twin stars of predictable, consistent quality aligned with leakage of technology to smaller company experts, the big computer makers—Digital, Data General, Computervision, IBM—found good reason to "get out of town," to outsource bigger and bigger pieces of their products. Who wanted to be in the business of forecasting, stocking, sourcing, building, storing, shipping, and redesigning thousands of varieties of cable assemblies, for example? Why not shift the burden to the folks who really wanted to be in that high-volume, custom business? That shift to outsourcing—from 10 or 20 percent outsourced material to 50, 60, even 70 percent—marked the rise of professional purchasing and supply management, the birth of the extended enterprise, and the need for this and the next generation's purchasing executives to rise to the challenge of becoming strategic enterprise leaders. Quite a challenge.

The Vision—Supply Management Twenty Years Out

When Fujitsu joined with EMS (electronic manufacturing services) provider EFTC, of Denver, Colorado, the result was a movement in the electronics industry's restructuring—the next stage—that will take supply management professionals out of the world of purchasing into strategic sourcing that will direct sourcing and allocation of *ideas*, as well as materials. If what we see for the next twenty years happens as quickly as the demassification of vertically integrated electronics giants in manufacturing of the 1980s, we believe that purchasing is not ready for a shift of such amplitude.

The EFTC/Fujitsu alliance proves the point. Like another success story, EMC, the Massachusetts Miracle producers of high-end mass storage devices, EFTC started its corporate life in a less glamorous, dirtier career, making boards for big customers. The company discovered and enlarged on its repair and logistics talent to transform a piece of its business into an original equipment provider. In other words, EFTC made history in the computer world by taking on the assembly and order administration of Fujitsu computer orders through a third-party provider remote to Japan—a Tennessee plant site. This restructuring of the building blocks of a typical computer introduced yet more demands on sourcing that sought to manage not only material being purchased, used, and shipped but also designs. Completing manufacturing in an area remote to headquarters is distributed, intelligent manufacturing; purchasing and supply management professionals must be able to support this new production method in other industry sectors all over the world. It is the biggest challenge procurement professionals have faced in over twenty years, and most of them are not ready. The shift for purchasing, therefore, over the past 150 years is historic:

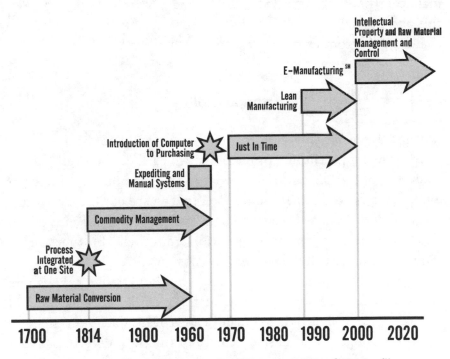

Figure 1.2 The Procurement Continuum to E-Manufacturing ℠

E-Manufacturing (E-Man),^{SM} Intelligent Manufacturing Distributed Globally

The progression of the procurement continuum visibly demonstrates several key challenges facing overwhelmed purchasing professionals today:

First, they must broaden their vision to understand and possibly direct the quick and perfect completion of many high-technology tasks.

Second, they must understand and broaden their vision, in preparation for leading their enterprise team in both material and intellectual property acquisition and use.

Third, they must continue to "mind the store" by working to chisel out better costs from more perfect process management—they become technology as well as costing and communications experts, another seemingly impossible and gigantic challenge for a profession in transition.

An Impossibility?

With such seismic shifts under their feet, it would not be unreasonable for many purchasing professionals to pack up their cell phones and head out to the parking lot. Given the technological forces in their paths, however, they would soon find escape blocked by a number of barriers: the market, customers, systems developments, global competition, and internal competition from their "brother" functions—manufacturing, engineering, design and development, and customer administration. Dazed and stumbling supply managers must come to understand that the earth is moving for *everyone,* and the safest survival tactic is not to duck and cover under your desk—it is to run, dodge, and find the security of the right enterprise from which you can make forays into foreign territory.

The Extension of Excellence, the *Next* Procurement Challenge

Any process contracted for by a provider and intended to make customers happy belongs under the eye of procurement—from the front end of the system, design and procurement, logistics, packaging, to customer service. Any processing of input—ideas or material—belongs in manufacturing unless that process is in itself outsourced, when it also falls into the management domain of supply managers guided by technology experts back home.

In Plain Sight

In clear view of such bottom line results as experienced every day by companies in our Top Ten list, winners like Honda, Daimler/ Chrysler, Flextronics, IBM, and others, why do so many supply managers still struggle with the basics? Why do they appear to be so shortsighted and tactically driven by pieces and parts? Having wrung all the gains out of manufacturing facilities by perfecting efficiencies of flexibility and flow, quality and workforce improvements, too few are proficient in target costing, value engineering, and supplier development—the "new basics of supply management."

These practices, as well as extension of excellence throughout the supply chain—laterally, and downward into the second, third, and even fourth tiers—remain the biggest challenge for supply management professionals of this decade.

It is time to throw out the college textbooks that detail how to market before the arrival of the Internet, or how to measure the value of labor via cost accounting, or even how to develop a forecast that takes its shaky place at the top level of a complex, push-driven MRP system. Fortunately, or perhaps unfortunately, because fewer academic programs have been created to train purchasing professionals, we are faced with a smaller stack of books to burn. A few dedicated innovators are changing the way markets function, and the way goods flow in and out of processing operations, and the way cash is farmed at the point of electronic capture. And they are effectively rewriting the supply management rules for a new group of process professionals.

Companies like Dell and Solectron are benchmarked innovators within their fields of final assembly and customer administration. Indeed, they are not far from achieving an integrated vision of manufacturing and supply in the year 2020. Their competition—Compaq, Gateway, and smaller EMS suppliers—have lost competitive advantage and must run twice as fast simply to stay in the race.

The 2020 Vision—Intelligent Systems, Distributed Manufacturing, E-Man℠, and the Chinese Box

For those procurement executives drawn to adventure, let us paint a picture of the production function twenty years out. We call it the Island of Excellence, and it is a world torn by interenterprise rivalries, an area of prosperity bordered by a chasm marking the line between the excellent enterprise and The Others. There will be simply these two classes of enterprise, and the choices will be clear.

The Island of Excellence organization will do many things extremely well—processing, idea movement, realtime customer design of product, and simultaneous production. The workforce and other resources required to fulfill customer needs will be technologically better prepared and trained than even the best facilities today, the ones typically found in Ph.D.-staffed Intel plants, for example. In the winners' circle, enterprise workers will appear as an elite corps united by their complete commitment to lifelong enterprise alignment. Their language, culture, clothing, training, hobbies, and families will all blend in a way not ever dreamed of in the post–World War II conformist 1950s.

The Island will present a picture of balance and harmony among well-trained corps of engineers and technology experts. People will live where they work and work where they live, much as they did in eighteenth-century factory villages.

The Chinese Box

Another earthshaking redesign of the manufacturing process should reinforce our new vision of the procurement professional. Picture a complex molded resin product, a twenty-one-foot speedboat, for example. Traditional manufacturing and procurement require weeks of advance planning, slotting, layup, grinding, polishing, and trip work before the unit can be completed. Further, the process is fraught with possible quality issues, and rework and repair take additional time. Boat making, even in the fiberglass sport arena, is an art enveloped by science.

Remote, Distributed Manufacturing

Enter the Chinese Box, an automated, portable, perfectly consistent trailer-sized production unit that produces boats or bathtubs, custom colored, to customer orders, in hours rather than weeks or months. The possibilities for new designs and varying applications loom on a horizon that twenty years from now will be populated by manufacturing on wheels and electronic sourcing. Who will be the keepers of the design instructions and the processing formulas? What unit in the advanced manufacturing group will control the acquisition of raw materials and resources? Quite probably the superhero of our story, the fully prepared and highly leveraged supply management professional.

For other living examples of the Chinese Box that extend the possibilities into small appliance production—VCRs, TVs, communication boxes, textiles, and other customer-designed apparel—all that will be required will be smaller active replication centers, like the sport boat example, drawn from Pyramid Molding in Greenville, Pennsylvania. Replication units enjoy the benefit of movement; boxes can be helicoptered to Third World countries that have limited internal manufacturing resources, or they can be set up on Antarctic bases, or even in space.

Remote, *Intelligent* Manufacturing

Earthbound, family-centered operations with a power source and wheels will be capable of downloaded licensed product design and process data from the Internet, for immediate located production.

And supply management professionals will be in charge of maintaining ownership of localized manufacturing intelligence.

At Long Last . . .

For purchasing professionals, the picture of long-anticipated levels of professionalism will be welcome. Their strategic positions within the enterprise will signal finally the accomplishment of long overdue dreams. And for those fortunate and extremely well-directed associates on the Island, this enterprise will indeed be a dream come true.

And for the Others . . .

But for the sad inhabitants of groups on the other side of the chasm, the daily struggle to make things—marginally useful kitchen appliances, hastily assembled three-wheeled motor vehicles, plastic dolls, and entertainment chips—will bring out all the worst qualities of a struggling, underpowered lower-class paradise. Health, safety, education, food, entertainment will all be marked with a scratched plastic veneer of second-class cheapness, and workers will appear to have a jumpy, unrestrained muscle movement suggestive of pharmaceutical deprivation and lack of exercise. The contrast between life on the Island and across the chasm with The Others is so clear that choices will hopefully be made at birth, choices and paths guaranteeing lifetime affiliation with the Island. Because with no border zone and little hope for undereducated and undercontrolled workers to bludgeon their way to the top tier, the remaining inhabitants of Mad Max's world will enjoy short, unpleasant lives marked by chaos and a never-ending struggle, a kind of twenty-first-century 7th ring of Hell. For purchasing and manufacturing professionals, we urge, make your choice, prepare well, and don't look back.

Beyond World Class

One of the most overused phrases from the 1980s is "world-class"—a nonspecific, overly defined view toward enterprise excellence coined in reaction to global competition's wake-up call. Over time, we have developed our own understanding of what constitutes world-class supply management. World-class organizations share the following traits:

1. Top leadership understands purchasing's importance and provides needed resources.
2. Benchmarking is used to assess performance and set tough goals.
3. A culture of shared knowledge prevails—collaboration flourishes internally and with suppliers.
4. The view of supply management includes the entire supply chain.
5. *Best practices are institutionalized.*

Clearly, commitment from top leadership is vital to sustain world-class supply management. But world-class organizations don't wait for the CEO to get on board. They make sure that supply management's agenda becomes part of the CEO's plan.

World-class supply management organizations use internal and external benchmarking to gain perspective about overall performance. But they don't stop there. They use that information to establish tough supply chain objectives and metrics. They reward, rather than punish, the risk-taking necessary to meet these goals.

Best Practice organizations recognize that no individual—and no single partner in a business relationship—has all the answers. They share knowledge tapped from the supply chain and their own companies to understand and meet customer needs.

They do not view supply management as a functional silo. They understand that the dynamics of organizations and different groups must work together as an extended enterprise.

Finally, world-class supply management organizations use Best Practices to continually improve. A short survey asking fifty purchasing execs to name the practices that in their opinion were the most important yielded these responses:

1. Cost management
2. Supplier development

3. Value analysis/engineering
4. Maintenance, repair, and operating supplies (MRO)
5. Supplier quality circles

Exponential Excellence

The real power of Best Practices derives from applying them at more than one level of the supply chain. World-class procurement professionals not only seek out the best today—the best suppliers, the best improvement aids, the best metrics—but also seek to understand and see what is coming tomorrow, no matter how challenging and surprising the vision may be. [*]

The Performance Gap

Clearly, there is a big gap between the reality of what most supply management organizations are now doing and their great potential to contribute enormous growth and savings that fall immediately to their bottom line.

But leading supply management organizations, companies like Honda, Harley-Davidson, and Flextronics that understand and focus on Best Practices understand the power and energy trapped in their supply management organizations. They work hard to unleash the terrific financial potential in every one of their supply management centers. These companies want to be smart *and* rich, and we call them the Top Ten.

Two other young organizations attracted our attention—Intellimet, a start-up in Arizona, and a nonprofit think tank, NISCI (National Initiative for Supply Chain Integration). Each of these groups has created innovation much needed by supply chain management, and each of them continues to tackle bigger challenges that can only benefit industry.

---

[*]R. David Nelson, "The World-Class Organization," *Purchasing Today,* August 1999, page 2.

TOP TEN

American Express
SmithKline Beecham
Daimler/Chrysler
Harley-Davidson
Honda of America
IBM
John Deere
Whirlpool
Flextronics
Sun Microsystems

Top Ten, Excellence in Supply Chain Management

Each of the Top Ten companies can point to at least one area of outstanding excellence, the kind of performance that breaks records in innovation and causes competitors to scramble for a quick win.

- American Express shines in breakthrough computer systems and creative new product ideas.
- SmithKline Beecham's procurement organization is structured to run aggressively after commodity market goals and metrics.
- Daimler/Chrysler enjoys a well-deserved reputation among its supply base partners for trusting relationships, especially in the area of platform teams and savings shared under the program called SCORE.
- Harley-Davidson/Buell is an exciting story of an American company living its fourth new life, as is
- IBM, a continuously amazing source of innovation and purchasing power in a complex organization.
- Honda of America, of course, set the benchmark for supplier development and training, which has been met and bettered by John Deere (indeed, quite a few Honda veterans have found their way out of transplant territory in Ohio up to Iowa's all-American soil).

- John Deere, in our opinion, has now passed Honda of America in supplier development strength. Testimony from seven supplier companies who have experienced the Deere development method, among other customer programs, support the validity of the process and its results.
- Whirlpool, in an incredibly tough global market, continues to aggressively leverage purchasing and cost management skills that positioned them as the number one.
- Flextronics, a California start-up run by CEO and grand visionary Michael Marks, moved quickly and quietly to invent systems for procurement that locked in superior partnerships with companies like Cisco, 3Com, Hewlett-Packard, and others.
- Sun Microsystems, a matured start-up that won the 1996 Purchasing Medal of Excellence, continues to innovate in its partnerships with suppliers, its new applications and creativity around systems, and its continued focus on networking issues.

Finally, the nonprofit supply chain think tank NISCI and Arizona start-up Intellimet are included as honorable mentions because of the innovation they continue to bring to supply chain management. To NISCI's dedicated members—companies like IBM, Trane, Daimler/Chrysler, and Harley-Davidson—NISCI represents an absolutely necessary coming together of the highest-level executives in North America's most influential procurement positions to change the world of supply base management.

NISCI

NISCI CEO Mike Doyle, as well as members of the group, recognize that the company is taking a high-risk approach to reformation of their profession. Since the beginning, when founding members like Honda coughed up $60,000 for membership, everyone felt that this coming together, although overdue, would be a management challenge. And members have not been disappointed as each took on a critical supply chain challenge. Harley-Davidson, for example, worked through an entire chain on a trust model. Next on the list of tasks facing NISC is a more complex challenge—understanding and measuring the entire economics flow of a complete supply chain, including efficiencies, money flows, blockages, and hidden problems—supplier development at the macro level.

Co-author Dave Nelson believes early NISCI experience with its trust building across the chain software had an unexpected benefit: participants learned that in some areas, "You may never have trust, but you damn well will have a system"—simulation and realtime control systems, for example.

Chrysler, for instance, has credited its SCORE program with cutting thousands of dollars in costs on a single new vehicle, while Honda of America points to its 1998 Accord, a totally redesigned vehicle, as a brilliant example of the power of strategic sourcing; this one vehicle cashed in on over 26 percent in purchased cost savings. John Deere's Best Practices initiative, a program similar to Honda's, recaptured millions of "lost" savings opportunities within months of its start-up.

Purchasers Speak

We surveyed 247 heads of purchasing and supply management at companies—OEs (original equipment producers) and suppliers—headquartered or operating in North America, and we found amazing similarities in their responses to questions about Best Practices. We wanted to understand what makes their procurement groups so effective and what areas of their operation are the most important to procurement and supply chain success. We started by reviewing our respondents' priority ranking on about thirty Best Practices. Gradually, the Best Practice list trimmed down to approximately twenty key areas of competence.

Next, co-authors Nelson, Moody, and Stegner followed up responses to our survey questionnaire with over one thousand hours of interviews and site visits; not surprisingly, the interviews and visits pretty much confirmed company leadership's perspective on their relative performance. Although respondents were not made aware of their comparative ranking, most executives "knew" where their groups were on the excellence journey, what they did well, and where they had considerable challenges.

Manufacturing Precedes Procurement in Best Practice

We visited all the top contenders for the Top Ten, and we can say that the "performance gap"—the gap between what companies and their suppliers are capable of achieving and what they currently demonstrate through their cost controls, quality performance, and customer responsiveness—is real.

Unfortunately, most North American purchasing groups have trailed the progress made in manufacturing as the movement into Best Practice—away from a purely tactical focus—has taken longer to catch on. We are not clear on all the exact causes of this gap between manufacturing and procurement, but we think that the answer may be quite simple: as manufacturing groups have learned and moved ahead with innovative, better methods—like Six Sigma quality, kaizen, or lean manufacturing—they have hit the operations side of manufacturing first, shop floor followed by white-collar areas such as engineering, new product design, and order administration.

Drivers for improvement have rippled out laterally to what may at the time have been considered the second targets for improvement—"collateral" groups like purchasing, logistics, and order administration. We think that this priority for change is flawed, given the uneven distribution of money and other resources in manufacturing, compared with order administration, for example, but as a rule this is the pattern that most companies have followed.

Visual Excellence

Further, we noted as we visited organizations throughout a range of industries—aircraft, automotive, pharmaceuticals, electronics, foods—as well as first, second, and third tier suppliers, that high performance is somewhat predictable from a good look at the surroundings. In other words, if the data and the survey indicated that an organization was a possible Best Practice procurement leader, it was usually true that a visit to the plant with some time spent in purchasing and out on the shop floor would also reflect a predictably high performance level. Excellence tends to shine throughout an organization, even though there may be some unevenness among pockets of high performance in purchasing or operations, for example.

Benchmarking the Best

Toyota and its suppliers, for example, tend to model all their processing on the Toyota Production System guidelines; one would naturally expect to see excellent housekeeping, ergonomic improvements, and perfectly designed lines and work cells. Even at the first and second tier levels, usually that is what we see. And within procurement, among the planners and suppliers for the material that flows down these lines and through the work cells, we tend to find the same attention to detail, the same quality and performance measurements that guarantee consistently good practices.

Struggling for Profits

Companies at the other end of the performance gap, unnamed organizations struggling with overwhelming performance challenges, primarily in quality and delivery, can't seem to get control of their own processes. We visited a big, very profitable producer of high-end cabinetry. This southeastern producer offers unlimited variety in a strong consumer market that will hopefully carry them well into the next millennium; they enjoy the advantage of relatively cheap and available raw material and a semi-educated workforce. But operations like production and purchasing clearly occupy lower priorities than marketing and sales.

The performance gap assaults the senses the moment a visitor steps foot in this plant. The air is filled with sawdust; health and safety violations abound that in an earlier era would have seen OSHA on their doorstep daily; expediters on foot and in a fleet of fork trucks keep lines flowing from final assembly, an erratically unpredictable flow, all the way to raw material cutting operations. Moreover, inventories at all levels of processing fill every square foot of racks and side aisle storage, as tractor trailers line up in the parking lot to disgorge days' worth of raw material input. This supply management nightmare will continue as long as the market holds up. Because although this company is leaving hundreds of thousands of dollars of waste—lost material, unnecessary movement and processing, bad quality, and missed delivery dates—on the floor, as long as customers are willing to wait two, three, or even four months for their complete orders, nothing is driving management to make any major "disruptive changes," and all this is clear to the trained visitor within fifteen minutes of arrival.

Manufacturing Is Hardwired to Procurement

Bad processes breed bad quality, missed deliveries, painful new product introductions, and missed profit opportunities. There is a direct connection between excellence in manufacturing operations—single-minded dedication to quality such as we see every day at Honda, for example—and quality metrics in the supply base that are rewarded with increased business and supplier recognition conference awards.

There is a direct connection between making the delivery schedule with no "just-in-case" excess days, as most automotive assemblers and their suppliers know, and their ability to manage high-performance logistics suppliers. In North America particularly, the location and travel requirements for managing suppliers located twenty-four hours or more away is challenging. It takes the very best purchasing and logistics people and systems to bring in seats from Michigan, carburetor assemblies from Tennessee, and radios from Mexico, to keep lines moving at the rate of one perfect vehicle every minute.

Bad Practices Cost Millions

Bad performance at any one of the many stages of production—at the final assembly line, at the first tier carburetor assembly plant, even at the machine parts level—is expensive. At one Midwest transplant the cost of stopping the assembly line for just one minute is $26,000. With six lines running, the price tag for output down time is well over $150,000 per minute. Every day that suppliers produce bad parts that must be recycled for repair or discarded, every minute that operators must stop their work and consult with materials and purchasing buyers about in-transit missing pieces, and every day that trucks continue to transport significant excess materials carried on the books as "in-transit inventory" reinforces the cost of the performance gap between what purchasing is for many North American organizations and what it could be.

Last year, visiting an engine supplier to a major OEM, we walked into an atmosphere of anger and denial. It seems that the president felt that they could not earn their 5 percent after-tax profit. The supplier felt they were being squeezed by their biggest customer for big cost cuts; their relationship was at rock bottom, and even the customer's purchasing vice president acknowledged that this supplier was only barely making the grade.

With such negative findings, we knew that this customer could be hard-pressed to find a way to reach their own desired quality, delivery, and price performance goals. This was an unhappy conclusion to a fifteen-year partnership, and it was caused by a customer that demanded price cuts—in blood—and ignored all the other valued performance benefits that this supplier had been producing. In the end, the customer won their price cuts but also lost cooperation, design input, and above-average delivery performance.

The supplier was unwilling to go the extra mile for this customer, because they felt they had been violated. The bottom line is that companies will gain tremendous savings, not 5 or 6 percent cost cuts, when they attack the seven wastes, reduce manpower and inventory, and practice continuous improvement. They will achieve better yield on raw materials as specifications improve. The gains from all these changes add up to at least 25 percent of total purchasing costs, a huge amount of unrealized profit potential for even the smallest supplier.

The postscript to this story is that the new vice president of purchasing understood where the relationship with his engine supplier had gone wrong, and he worked quickly to reverse the damage. He traveled the following day to the supplier's plant and offered them a "price up"—unheard of among this level of suppliers—he would meet their demands of a 5 percent price increase to satisfy the lost 5 percent after-tax profit, in exchange for a new commitment to work with him, shoulder to shoulder, to wring the real excess costs out of the process. The VP knew that no matter what the level of improvements, they would realize 10 to 15 percent gains with reasonable attention to the task, totaling tens of millions of dollars of improvements in quality and delivery, as well as development speed. Further, the development speed that the customer and supplier generate together would move both businesses along, well out of the marginal operations into the first tier of excellent performers. What a reversal!

Excellence *Can* Be Replicated

We believe that if companies address purchasing Best Practices the way the high performers have for the past ten or fifteen years, they will experience the same remarkable results that adopters of JIT, lean principles, the Toyota Production System, and Six Sigma quality have experienced. We *know* that when companies put procurement and development of a high-performance supply base in the center of the universe, at the heart of their list of change initiatives, they will attract and retain better purchasing leaders and more responsive suppliers. And as the Top Ten organizations are proving every day, when companies deliberately, with speed and thoroughness, bring performance excellence into their purchasing organizations, the millions of unclaimed dollars left lying on the table every year by unaware producers will find good homes in the bottom line of reenergized supply management leaders.

What we call "leveling up" is a great challenge for most organizations, but as Honda, Toyota, and their suppliers are proving every day, it is not an impossible one. Let's look at the change in performance metrics among procurement leaders as we rounded the fifteen-year mark in quality and delivery systems:

Metrics	Leaders	1993	1996
Quality (ppm)	under 300	5426	2339
Delivery Performance	over 95%	76%	85%
Total Inventory in Days	under 25	40	31
% Sourced Preferred	over 85%	75%	80%
Training hours/person	over 80	46	32

Quality measured in parts per million rejected among the leaders continues to improve exponentially; a Six Sigma goal of 99.996 percent perfection translates to 3.4 defects per million. Delivery performance, an on-time measurement that typically looks at days before and after the committed delivery date, is a direct reflection of cost of expediting and cost of lost customer orders; here the performance gap, the difference between 90 percent performance to promise or better and only three-quarters of orders delivered to promise, becomes painfully obvious in the wasted profits spent on premium tracking, expediters, and overtime at the bad performance level. *You cannot run a very profitable facility when three quarters of incoming material isn't there, or when over a month of twelve months' potential profits sits untouched in inventory.*

The last metric, training hours per person, at first glance seems to indicate enormous differences from one company to another. Companies with a long history of well-structured and well-funded in-house universities, like Motorola University and the Nypro Institute, believe that to retain a professional workforce, serious training initiatives are an absolute requirement. They would not agree, however, on how much funding is required to deliver the training. This is one area that should encourage small and medium-sized suppliers, because with careful, piggybacked initiatives, like Web-based training, and curriculum shared with established colleges and universities, they have found ways to deliver high-quality and cheaper training to more workers without establishing a bricks-and-mortar, dedicated in-house operation.

When organizations compare the performance of the Top Ten to their own demonstrated current performance and to the unrealized potential of their own people, they will undoubtedly be surprised, not just by the range of improvement possible with a small amount of attention focused on the right places, but with the excitement and positive energies unleashed when people are encouraged to do better. But we understand that moving a single organization, and then an entire supply chain, along an aggressive improvement journey that started about 150 years ago in manufacturing, can be a blinding challenge for a single dedicated individual. We don't recommend that anyone attempt this alone. It will take a small team of focused, multi-skilled professionals to attempt any of our Twenty Best Practices.

Be forewarned: some of the Twenty Best Practices will show results immediately, and others will reveal great potential only after first-pass efforts. Certainly improving quality and delivery is easier when performance is in the low 50 or 60 percent range—any improvement is bound to realize big results—but once organizations move into the high 90 percent range, close to Six Sigma and zero defects, they must completely understand their process and their supplier's process. They will need to carefully evaluate new technologies for performance potential, and they will demand superior systems to extend the limitations of the human hand, eye, and mind.

A Superhuman Challenge?

This is an enormous challenge, not an impossible one. In the next chapter, we take you through the Twenty Best Practices and the companies that have closed their performance gaps by perfecting them. Not all Top Ten Practice companies excel in all Twenty Best Practices; Honda of America has enjoyed a superior reputation in quality training and quality performance, but its computerized systems have always lagged behind other large-vehicle producers' systems.

American Express, however, is brilliant at data management, but its business tends not to involve actual conversion of raw material through processing into shippable products. And among our long list of possible Best Practice groups, we surprised ourselves by uncovering Wild Cards like Buell Motorcycles, now joined with Harley-Davidson, and Auburn Industries, the seat of great systems innovation in the John Deere supply base—smaller organizations whose innovation and energy gained them recognition in certain outstanding performance characteristics, but whose overall operating performance still does not match the smooth and consistent superior performance that marks their more established colleagues and competitors.

2

THE TWENTY BEST PRACTICES, LEVELING UP

Leveling Up

Each of us works with different cultures, different size companies, companies at different points in their life cycles, and different tools and languages. But we all face one common challenge: sweeping change marked by a performance gap, a chasm between performance that the market demands and our limited progress toward the ideal, consistently superior performance.

Even the best of the best, companies like Honda and Toyota, are continually challenged by change. The global automotive shakeout and market restructuring tests their organizations' ability to respond; their flexibility and human strengths may be more resilient or more energetic than that of many others, but they are still working within the basic limits of human enterprise, and a challenge to even their expert performance is still a challenge.

The Center for Advanced Purchasing Studies

A research arm of the National Association of Purchasing Management, CAPS (Center for Advanced Purchasing Studies), headed by Dr. Phil Carter, conducted a study with AT Kearney, several universities, and an independent consultant to better understand the big and small changes the purchasing profession will face over the next decade. The studies look at supply management's future and what we can expect over the next five to ten years. The predictions, which include changing expectations from senior management, delineate a performance gap between current critical factors performance and market demands even as few as five years out. The gap between current performance and near-term future requirements is big; it is clear that supply management needs to level up.

Raising the Bar

The image of leveling up suggests stretch performance, raising the bar, leapfrog technology gains, and other big jumps in performance. But leaders in the profession need to understand that leveling up means raising the professional level of the way supply management organizations do business—procedures, policies, training, systems, and learning new skills for new-found visibility.

For some companies leveling up represents not one single big change but a series of many small, very important improvements that add up to a quite different "look" for the organization and its suppliers. Sourcing all materials with line-side, certified deliveries will not change all the supply chain's performance problems, for example, but as part of a complete improvement program that also includes better timing of deliveries and improved new product design times, the changes begin to add up.

Purchasing Becomes Strategic

The challenge extends to management styles, policies, and procedures. The CAPS study reiterates one of our themes in *The Purchasing Machine*: supply chain professionals must begin to think as management thinks, to speak as management speaks—a different language— and prepare to handle more complicated strategic business issues.

The CAPS study projects four broad changes over the next ten years:

1. More global, regional, and local customer-oriented focus to meet unique customer needs. Globalization will affect all functions, from product and service design to supply management.
2. Selective globalization to achieve competitive advantage, focusing on interfaces among business units and geographical and functional activities.
3. More executive rotation and other flexible management strategies to leverage companywide capabilities.
4. Cross-boundary and cross-functional management practices will become the rule, rather than the exception; and, of course, the predictions include more and different types of strategic alliances between customers and suppliers.

These changes have immediate and pervasive implications for purchasing and supply management professionals. An increasingly global economy will make regional and global sourcing strategies a critically important source of competitive advantage.

Shift from Tactical to Strategic Supply Management

Furthermore, individual companies will continue to reduce the number of key suppliers with whom they do business. Reductions in the supply base from thousands to hundreds of excellent suppliers will continue as intra-enterprise alliances focus on only the proven, strong performers, for whom finding new customers will be no problem, leaving marginal producers to scratch for a range of customers. The contrast will be even sharper than it is today as the best suppliers will pick the customers that bring them the most money, the best technology fit, and the most manageable schedules, all with the preferred lowest "paperwork" or service costs. We don't expect the best suppliers to shift frequently from one customer to another once the customers have made their selections; good suppliers will find a winning enterprise team and try to stay there.

Executive expectations for supply management will increase because of growing cross-function and cross-boundary emphasis on new alliances. Purchasing professionals, typically buyer/planners, who spend little time on the shop floor—either locally or in the supply base—will find themselves challenged to initiate supplier searches, identify technology experts, and participate in supplier development initiatives, while they tend to business back home.

Purchasing and supply management will become increasingly integrated with the strategic plans for the company to maximize companywide leverage and responsiveness. Business and strategic planning programs, for example, typically contain factors that cover:

Revenues or marketing objectives

Product mix percentages

Production demonstrated capacities

Headcounts

Targets: inventory, backorder, profits, etc.

Although most business planning spreadsheets do not include supply management objectives or measurable results, every business strategy meeting's successful performance to the plan depends on purchasing performance to supplier selection, quality, and delivery goals. No business plan or marketing program can be successful without complete purchasing performance, and we believe that the key to improved profits for most North American companies—without huge jumps in revenues or deep cost cuts—lies in the wide domain of supply chain management.

Supply Chain Moves to the Boardroom

Purchasing, however, which for many years has resided in the arena of materials management, under the control of operations management, must take a parallel position at the highest levels of executive management, because any company whose spend is dependent for 50 to 70 percent of purchased buys needs to pay close attention to the implied profit potential of that huge opportunity area.

CAPS sees four other shifts happening in the coming decade:

1. Purchasing and supply management performance measures will become further aligned with companywide measurements. For example, quality production (manufacturing) parallels metrics that track customer order satisfaction (order administration and shipping), which parallels supplier quality performance (purchasing). Other common language parallels within the organization will become clearer, particularly around timing and flexibility of inbound raw material acquisition, and total company performance to new product introduction goals, an enterprisewide exercise. Purchasing will not be able to continue with its own special set of niche performance criteria and metrics—purchased price variance, for example, or volume discount histories. Purchasing will by necessity, because top management and management systems will in essence dictate it, share common metrics and performance objectives with the rest of the organization, including, most importantly, engineering, manufacturing, research and development, and logistics.

2. Information systems and technology will become instrumental in sourcing enterprisewide strategies. Where e-commerce has meant sharing production schedules and forecasting data via fax, systems one generation beyond offerings like SAP a.●l Baan will fully integrate procurement with all other processing functions.

3. New, more complex skills and focus will be required in supply management to operate in a globally complex world.

4. More flexibility and external customer focus will be required in purchasing and supply activities to maximize supplier contributions.

Outsourcing Shifts Power to Suppliers, and Responsibility to Buyers

Inasmuch as suppliers become experts in their commodities and in certain technologies, they create dependencies among large end producers who have chosen to become less vertically integrated, and more dependent on outside suppliers for critical and noncritical commodities. With this outsourcing shift, companies typically acquire cost benefits, speed, and better technologies, because it is difficult for a company like Daimler/Chrysler, for example, to be number one in plastics, stamping, vehicle design, fabric, and air-bag technologies, in essence to compete with supplier experts.

This does not mean, however, that when purchasing decides to outsource a component or a commodity, the process issues and technology issues go away forever. Purchasing instead becomes a kind of corporate air traffic controller, eyes to the horizon, watching for bleeps and weather changes, as headphones continue minute-to-minute updates on specific vehicles' position and flight path. Indeed, supply management workers become multisensed professionals, rather than agents who move at only one speed, in one place, with a single focus. This is possibly the biggest shift that individual professionals face as they jump from tactical to strategic management in their day-to-day activities.

The Deepening Performance Gap

At most companies, even among the stars, a huge gap separates the thinking of supply management professionals from that of their senior management. Our experience is that senior management wants to support supply management operations at a strategically higher level. Certainly supply management leadership is eager for their operations to gain a higher profile—greater visibility and better rewards, as well as becoming part of the corporate leadership ranks. On National Association of Management surveys the eagerness to move up continues to rank as the number one issue on every professional's mind.

What then, could be standing in the way of thousands of well-trained, energized, and motivated professionals from achieving such perfectly reasonable goals? Or from taking leadership positions in our best corporations?

At most companies, the performance gap separating the thinking of supply management professionals from that of their senior management stands in the way. Supply management professionals, unfortunately, have failed to level up to what is most important to company leaders at the highest ranks, and they are not being heard. They have failed to translate their procurement initiatives into meaningful metrics well recognized among leaders; their approach to strategic profitability and market growth discussions, therefore, is limited to simple tactical achievement of someone else's objectives. Naturally, rewards, recognition, and advancement are limited by this very narrow approach to their careers.

Most well-meaning supply management professionals still fail to recognize and communicate how the superior performance of supply chain work can catapult a company ahead of the pack. They fail to remember the procurement success stories that so powerfully leveraged the successes of companies like Toyota, Solectron, IBM, Chrysler, Johnson Controls, and other purchasing groups now competing at world-class levels.

Purchasing executives have only about three to five years to remedy this shortcoming, to bring their objectives and communications into closer alignment with executive expectations. A 1997 AT Kearney CEO Global Business Study asked CEOs at 463 of the world's biggest companies what they felt were the most critically important concerns for their businesses. In this ranking, they were:

1. Customer relationships
2. Cost competitiveness
3. Effective use of information technology
4. Change management
5. Shareholder value
6. Revenue growth
7. Industry restructuring
8. Globalization
9. Value-added relationships with suppliers

If your procurement group cannot identify these nine top issues on your radar screen, it will be barred from working at the highest senior management leadership levels in your company. Moreover, are your priorities in sync with those of senior management? If not, then your group is in a performance gap; to move ahead, you must level up.

Understand and Prepare to Meet Top Management Priorities

Here are four guidelines to align your operations more clearly with management objectives:

- Senior management is results-oriented. Purchasing and supply management professionals need to become proactive at all levels of the enterprise. They need to manage for results, not reactions. Leaders focus on "I can" thinking, and so purchasing must focus on presenting workable solutions to big challenges, and reinforce daily achievement of good work and Best Practices that continually move organizations in the right direction.
- Senior management understands and looks to organize behind competitive strategies, clearly recognizable themes like "number one in the market" or "guaranteed fastest delivery." Purchasing pros must understand and seize clear competitive advantage that will level up their organization around these corporate banners.
- Executive officers speak the language of

    Metrics and measures
    Financial performance
    ROI, ROA
    Customer satisfaction
    Competitive advantage
    Shareholder value

At John Deere, co-author Nelson reports supply management metrics to senior management monthly, by factory and division, worldwide. The information is used to identify gaps, resource needs, and opportunities for internal leveraging. The reporting elements include:

1. Quality measured in parts per million (ppm), delivery performance, technical support, and wavelength

2. Financial measures, including cost increases and decreases for direct and indirect labor and supplier cost reduction idea sharing performance stats
3. People-resource allocation by process; tactical vs. strategic measures; direct and indirect; training hours, and education levels
4. Suppliers—number of direct and indirect
5. Achieving Excellence category (Deere's internal supply management strategic plan)
6. Inventory levels and process cycle times
7. Supplier lead times

Money Talks

As a supplement to these seven performance measures, Deere reinforces its supplier relationship building with reports that document customer/supplier success stories. These anecdotal histories record the projects, team activities, challenges, and methods used to address problems, and, most important, the hard *dollar savings* that were realized, because money is the language of management. In fact, purchasing executives at Deere continue to capture every success story because nothing illustrates better the power of supply management for the bottom line than real, demonstrable, part-based cost savings. This approach highlights what we call the "incredible payback" of supply management.

The Cost of the Incredible Payback

Racheting up supply base performance through adoption of Best Practices and more dedicated professional focus does not come without some up-front costs. John Deere has added 175 new strategic supply management positions, 100 for supplier development, 50 cost management specialists, and 25 Best Practice specialists. At Honda of America, purchasing amounts to over 400 professionals, many of whom are dedicated to supplier development initiatives alone; at one point there was one purchasing professional, either a buyer or a purchasing engineer, for each of Honda's three hundred plus suppliers.

Supplier Development Paybacks

Savings realized from these up-front expenditures are considerable, however, an incredible payback. The potential, in management terms, is clear—cost-downs typically amount to three to five times the salary of supplier development engineers. For an initial investment of $100,000 per year, savings, therefore, are projected to reach a minimum of at least $300,000 per year. This is the heart of the incredible payback.

Other management measures relate to the customer base, and these metrics must also be tracked by supply management professionals, because purchasing's field of vision must expand to include end and internal customers. Customer satisfaction metrics include loyalty and repurchase percentages, warranty results and costs of processing, and manufacturing cycle times—demand flows, estimate-to-cash conversions time, and project stats.

These metrics will expand purchasing's field of vision and improvement visibility to management. Better alignment between management objectives and purchasing Best Practice objectives is also bound to strengthen the entire enterprise's performance to strategic goals.

When reasonable alignment appears to be taking hold, confirmation and continuous, disciplined attention to Best Practice performance will bridge the performance gap and elevate purchasing professionalism.

Unseen Profit Potential

When millions of dollars of unrealized profits are left forgotten on the table, chances are this cash is slipping away through neglect of simple Best Practices in procurement. The unseen leakage of profits continues when employees fail to focus their attention on Best Practices in all areas of their operations, not just manufacturing.

For small and medium-sized suppliers, the unrealized and unseen profits usually represent the difference between healthy growth through new capital investment and products, and simply making payroll. Companies that operate in the 5 to 6 percent profit margin arena need to see and capture every single savings opportunity. Where financial goals translate into corporate policy, Best Practices are the best, and first, opportunity to look inward to find long-term, consistent gains. Alternative profit solutions—new product development, new market development, and severe cost cutting—tend to take longer; the first opportunity—gains from instituting Best Practices—should be addressed before or in parallel to other, more strategic and more difficult approaches.

Figure 2.1 illuminates the bottom-line potential of three approaches to costs:

1. Keeping up with purchasing price index (inflation)
2. Adopting some Best Practices, without a sharp, focused cost approach (Company M)
3. A cost focus that draws on all opportunities for Best Practice internally in the supply base (Transplant Companies)

Proven results from transplant companies and the better North American purchasing organizations show that their focused cost approach consistently yields savings of one-quarter of their total spend. If your company procures $1 million per year in materials (the spend), Best Practices will yield 25 percent savings, or $250,000. If your spend totals $1 billion, expect to realize over $250 million per year.

What Is the Cost of Improvement?

Given this bottom-line potential, all arguments over partnering with suppliers, early supplier involvement, supplier training and development, and strategic purchasing lose their strength. Paybacks for sup-

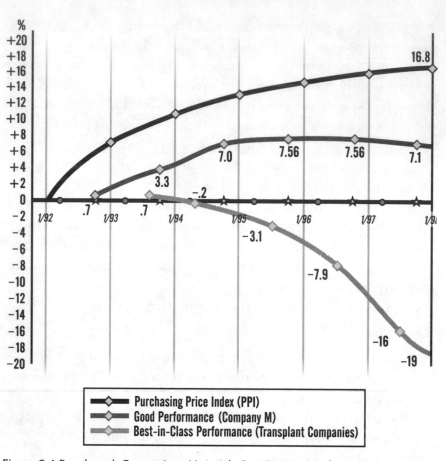

Figure 2.1 Benchmark Comparison Materials Cost Between Industry Average (PPI), Good Performances, and Best in Class Performance.

plier development professionals in purchasing are three times their annual cost; typically, the total cost for a seasoned supplier development pro skilled in kaizen techniques and good communications is three to five times his annual $100,000 salary package, or from $300,000–$500,000 in annual realized cost reductions.

Twenty Best Practice points will change the purchasing profession. We do not recommend that companies work on all twenty simultaneously. Instead, we emphasize that among our list of Top Ten companies, none of them did equally well on all twenty points; each of them excels at one or two performance points.

BEST PRACTICE #1, COST MANAGEMENT—WHAT IS THE TRUE VALUE OF BEST PRACTICE?

Best Practice Leaders: Honda of America, Whirlpool, Toyota, Allied Signal

In Chapter 1 we told the story of a Japanese transplant engine supplier located in the Midwest, a well-publicized manufacturing pioneer, that angrily reported to a visiting customer manager how for some time they had not been able to earn 5 percent after-tax profit. "Why," he asked, "after fifteen years of working together, would anyone not ask what had happened?" Challenged to be constructively critical, a principle of continuous improvement well practiced by Japanese management, Mr. Iwo's upper lip twitched as he fought to contain his anger.

"All you did was take, take, take—you never gave. We trusted you, and we have lost money for fifteen years." And indeed, that company had been "taken," as American purchasing managers continued to play a different game with different rules, the old bait-and-switch game. Misplaced trust led to minimum performance as over time the customer "won" on price but lost cooperation, received no valuable design input, and saw delivery performance fade. Iwo's company became, in the words of his customer, "just a supplier, no longer a partner."

The meeting ran on for two hours, as the transplant supplier and the American customer cautiously explored continuous improvement points. On the shop floor, as the group walked down the main assembly line, an area praised for its immaculate housekeeping and perfect layout, the American spotted a steel bolt on the floor. Managers untrained in the philosophy of continuous improvement would have ignored it and moved on with the tour group. Instead, to demonstrate his belief in continuous improvement, the American executive bent down and quickly retrieved the bolt. His Japanese host rushed to take the bolt, murmured "thank you," made a small bow, and deposited the bolt in a small bin.

Next, the customer spotted a wrinkled piece of shipping paper. He again stooped to pick up this very visible evidence of flawed plant housekeeping. Again, his Japanese host bowed and uttered his thanks. The pattern was clear. Later, as visitors viewed mounds of shipping cardboard and stockpiles of pistons and engine casings, the American's observations were carefully heard by Iwo—"is there not too much cardboard coming into the plant?"—and "obviously inventories have exceeded targets." His answers were cautiously direct: "Yes, we do understand the problem of recycling and shipping materials disposal, and we have launched a project that reuses all cardboard at least three times," and "Of course, it may seem that we are building excess inventory, but please understand that we must cover seasonality in our engine business."

Meeting Supplier Needs for Mutual Advantage *Before* Cutting Costs

First steps to recovering this relationship included rebuilding trust eroded by fifteen years of hammerhead tactics. Next, the customer extended an unusual offer that could return the supplier to a potentially profitable position by giving him a "price-up," a 4 to 5 percent price increase that would meet his survival needs and more clearly indicate customer willingness to rebuild the relationship, the first of twenty Best Practices—cost management. The supplier's commitment in return—to work shoulder-to-shoulder with his customer to wring costs out of the process—however, remains the more visible, powerful change in their agreement. Expected improvements in quality and delivery, as well as development speed and new product design input, would more than recover initial cost increases as customer expectations in the 10 to 15 percent improvement range, representing tens of millions of dollars, will flow into their operations.

Nontransplant purchasing organizations in North America can still enjoy huge savings in the area of cost management as they continue to improve supply base organizations' visibility and professionalism. But they must focus the same top management attention and zeal in the supply management area that they mustered over twenty years ago for production.

Included in Best Practices Cost Management techniques are:

Target pricing—tracking price components, from new product concept, through the new product introduction cycle to develop the total target price to a level equal to or below market cost;

Cost tables—detailed management data developed on each component that specifies a supplier's material, labor, tooling costs;

Jikon—customer/supplier financial metrics review meeting in which open-book cost and margin data are compared to competitive market goals.

Kaizen productivity improvement techniques, like Honda BP, Kaizen Blitzes, and Gemba Kaizen events. These shop floor kaizen events or projects typically, in about five days' intensive work, take inventories in process down by about 23 to 33 percent; cycle time improves by approximately the same percentages, and floor space usually drops about 7 to 10 percent.

Best Practice models Honda and Toyota, both of whom have enjoyed 30 percent cost-down savings, lead the way. Indeed, the tally of benchmarking visits per year to each of these giants numbers over one-hundred visits, including Detroit competitors eager to observe the transplant version of continuous improvement and Best Practice. Their focus and rigorous attention to cost details have positioned Honda and Toyota in the top three of profit per car producers.

BEST PRACTICE #2, SUPPLIER DEVELOPMENT

Best Practice Leaders: Honda, Deere
The market measures the effectiveness of various supplier development initiatives several ways:

1. Localization, or the ability of producers to land product directly in a local market
2. PPM Quality
3. On-time delivery
4. Supplier involvement in new product and other technical issues
5. Training time

Localization, or the development of a self-reliant supplier network, is the end objective of most lean manufacturing efforts, including Honda's when the plant complex was first built in the late 1970s, and now John Deere's new extended enterprise. Not just because of regulatory formulas do transplant companies work to improve their percent of locally sourced components. Compaq Computer has also worked hard to locate prime suppliers close to assembly plants, as has Hewlett-Packard, and Nypro (custom plastic injection molding), and Abbott Laboratories. While other producers may continue to source some key components far from their assembly point, transportation, local currency, and other risks underline the usefulness of local suppliers. Supplier development is key to making world-class suppliers from companies struggling with unrealized potential, even though logistically they may be closest to their assembly plant partners.

PPM (parts per million) quality and on-time deliveries were early targets for improvement in all the transplant producers; without predictably improving PPM and superior delivery performance, they were frequently forced to rely on offshore mother plant sourcing, a logistical challenge that inevitably cost premium transportation rates. Honda BP (Best Position, Best Productivity, Best Partner), the supplier development methodology created by guru Teruyuki Maruo, for example, in its Phase I ("soft side" improvements) and Phase II (capital equipment) hits hard the issues of waste, process analysis, and associate involvement in expert solutions for its supply base.

Other early Honda supplier development practices, including Quality Teams, Quality Training, Supplier Study Groups, and Monthly Supplier Seminars, are credited, especially the Quality Teams, with moving ppm for Honda suppliers *from approximately 1,500 in 1987 to just over 100 in 1996.* Further, on-time deliveries of components improved even beyond their high level in *1970 of 97 percent (97 percent of all parts delivered on time—not early and not late), to 99.9 percent on time,* the absolute minimum for JIT (Just-in-time) systems.

Quality leaders source all parts as certified, requiring no receiving point inspection.

Supplier involvement in new product and other technical issues is realized by initiating Honda BP and other supplier suggestion systems. TRW and Parker Hannifin also point to their own strong supplier development programs; Parker's "Targets" program has been extended to dozens of second and third tier suppliers, all with big waste reductions and improved quality and production efficiency.

Training time, the first step in spreading a wide range of Best Practices quickly across an entire company or industry segment, is in fact a measurement included in the Baldrige Award. Motorola recommends fifty-two hours per year training for all employees; smaller suppliers, however, have needs that are not mirrored in the big customer training model, and customers need to be responsive and flexible to understand and meet these needs. Language skills and other basics are more frequently a requirement for small and medium-sized suppliers than the elaborate and somewhat complex Design of Experiments or QFD, for example. Training offered through community colleges located near John Deere factories has delivered many hours of useful improvement methods at relatively low cost to suppliers.

Other Supplier Development Best Practice techniques include:

1. Tooling and technical assistance centers
2. Supplier support centers
3. Loaned executives, including guest engineer programs.
4. Supplier seminars—suppliers select and voluntarily meet to thoroughly explore particular improvement subjects, such as government health and safety regulations, or human factors engineering.

For one or two days, a subject expert is made available to study groups for formal presentations and on-site Q & A. At a cost of $7,000—$10,000 per day covered by groups of 100–200 suppliers, the expense is minimal. Harley-Davidson is also a strong believer in supplier and dealer councils.

John Deere Supplier Development

For many years John Deere supplier management and supplier development efforts were as uneven as their decentralized manufacturing network. However, since 1998 there has been significant restructuring of the supply base, as well as intensified supplier development programs to cut costs and raise the quality, delivery, and levels of all suppliers, and results have paid off. Deere has joined the ranks of Top Ten companies because of its aggressive supplier development program and powerful systems tools, some based on genetic algorithms.

In the supplier development area, starting with seventeen engineers who reported to local factories, the group is being grown to one hundred professionals responsible for strategic improvement projects. The results were immediately noticeable; with a 1999 goal of savings of $100 million net of price increases, the final tally reached $120 million. PPM and delivery goals are receiving similar very focused attention, with equally significant results in a short time.

John Deere purchasing engineers have racked up hundreds of improvement projects worldwide, across a wide range of industry and technology bases, worth millions of dollars. A new cost management system promises to provide ongoing problem-identification and metrics support.

Bill Butterfield, Deere's supplier development process owner, believes that in the world of supplier development, "Things don't change unless you want them to." He points to an example among dozens of similar efforts, a single project conducted at R & B Grinding, a family-owned manufacturer of machined parts and assemblies supplying approximately $9 million of parts to many Deere units. Like many supplier development target companies, R & B started as a small job shop and continued to operate in that mode, despite substantial growth. Eventually, bad practices caught up with them. A multifunctional project planning and implementation team identified a Deere bearing assembly for its project focus, a good candidate, with high production volumes and leverage potential.

R & B Grinding Results

Process mapping revealed a ninety-six-hour manufacturing cycle time, over dedicated equipment in functionally organized departments. Deere engineers proposed reorganizing the already dedicated equipment into a manufacturing cell. Smoother parts flow reduced the manufacturing cycle time by approximately 70 percent; the new layout allowed daily production requirements review and flexible staffing based on demand. Work in process dropped about 60 percent, as did non–value added material handling by 80 percent; lot sizes dropped to match Deere's Horicon works' daily production pull. On the bearing assembly quote, the project realized a 4 percent cost savings.

Results were, as they typically are, so encouraging to R & B personnel that they took the improvement process to other areas in the plant. In one cell, the power takeoff (PTO) shafts, whose parts represented $322,000 annual dollar volumes, process mapping revealed enormous opportunities—production required fifteen steps and resulted in manufacturing cycle time over forty-two days, during which period the parts exited and reentered the plant twice for outsourced operations.

Rearrangement of equipment, along with standardization of tooling and fixtures, produced an 88 percent setup time reduction and smaller lot sizes, and eliminated travel to outside operations. Total cycle time for manufacturing dropped to fewer than two weeks, from 1.5 months, including two outsourced operations. Work in process inventory dropped 68 percent.

Auburn Consolidated Industries

Another Deere supplier, Auburn Consolidated Industries, Auburn, Nebraska, holds the record for savings on a single part number, the big frame for the planter. A series of improvements that included changes in trucking, work on welding, inventory reductions, better prices on the steel buy, moves to cell manufacturing from functional areas, and quality improvements added up to annual savings of $1,625,000. Cycle time dropped from 120 hours to 24 hours, and quality improved from 35,730 ppm to 8,000 and dropping.

Part of the work of Deere's new supplier development focus, says Butterfield, is to pick the right projects that will produce the best and quickest results. Deere engineers use a spreadsheet called Decision Focus, a kind of policy deployment tool, to set project priorities. By simply concentrating on suppliers that represent 80 percent of the spend, it is clear that any improvements will have significant dollar impact. Any dollar improvements inevitably improve quality and lead time, and so prioritization became most important as Deere purchasing engineers evaluated the improvement project possibilities. "They want to work on systemic problems," says Butterfeld, rather than "heroics that will keep the lines running."

Deere's solution to avoiding heroics among supplier development personnel is to maintain separate groups, an important lesson for all companies facing this two-headed monster of a challenge.

Deere Breakthrough Systems Innovation

Founder John Deere, a Vermont blacksmith who emigrated to the Mississippi valley over 150 years ago, was an innovator. His work in the heavy dark soil of Illinois convinced him that the plow he used was a problem because it caused farmers to stop frequently and scrape off soil and plants as they clung to the metal. Deere, a metals expert, tried a few other varieties of metal and settled on steel that could be imported at that time only from Great Britain, but his persistance paid off, and over the years his company grew from that first self-scouring blade to become the world's leader in agricultural equipment and lawn products, as well as contruction and other heavy equipment. And it all sprang from restless innovation in the heart of the Midwest that inevitably seeks a better, faster way.

Two John Deere projects are making history in the move from lean manufacturing to e-manufacturing. An off-the-shelf genetic algorithm package from Palisades Software called Evolver, layered over Microsoft Excel, is being used to solve multivariate production problems and to produce optimization solutions that would be nearly impossible for the best human minds to calculate because of our limited ability to handle variation. Thousands of part numbers passing over thousands of possible routings through various pieces of equipment are impossible to schedule under traditional push methodology. Indeed, lean manufacturing is inadequate to maximize scheduling of these parts using simple pull, kaizen methods. It takes computer power to process the thousands of possibilities, and to select the best schedule to sequence huge variety. And that's what Evolver's genetic algorithm offers scheduling personnel.

The application runs on a laptop, so that, unlike earlier behemoth packages, it can be carried to the supplier's site for in-plant approval and implementation. At a cost of under $1,000, it's a software miracle whose roots extend to Darwin's theory of evolution and advanced thinking about how to structure high-variety manufacturing operations. And it is bridging the gap between traditional pull methods typically found in the spaghetti-like flows of job shops, through kaizen and other simplification efforts, on to twenty-first-century smart manufacturing using integrated software products, or e-manufacturing.

BEST PRACTICE #3, VALUE ANALYSIS

Best Practice Leaders: Daimler/Chrysler, Whirlpool
Value Analysis, also called Value Engineering, is the careful analysis of design early in the new product cycle, to determine best materials, best tooling, and best manufacturing processes. Traditional purchasing practice "silos" purchasing expertise from supplier input and manufacturing process know-how, so that commitment to specifics of a design is made too late to affect total cost and manufacturability. Pioneers of value analysis, or value engineering, include IBM, Lexmark, Hewlett-Packard, Motorola, and some custom plastics suppliers. Value Analysis and Value Engineering are proven techniques to decrease significant costs, but the key is to do the work. In most companies, it is a great opportunity waiting to happen.

BEST PRACTICE #4, MRO (MAINTENANCE AND REPAIR, INDIRECT MATERIALS AND SERVICES, NONTRADITIONAL PURCHASING)

Best Practice Leader: IBM, Harley-Davidson
MRO (Maintenance and repair operations) are an unexplored gold mine, typically handled off-line from production components. MRO operations, a second cousin to the more glamorous commodities,

continue to present opportunities for billions of dollars in savings. Many companies have redistributed costs for these materials to outsourcing experts. Varian, for example, in some operations has outsourced complete commodity groups to expert distributors who bring in volume price reductions, combined with more efficient procurement operations. Jack Barry, a partner of Pegasus Consulting of Boston, estimates that Better Practice around MRO procurement is one of the quickest routes to millions of dollars of savings with minimum initial investment—"low-hanging fruit"—that should be tackled before more difficult challenges.

John Deere and TRW have both developed MRO commodity programs, each with different approaches. Recognizing that leaving MRO products to be managed along with other assembly components inevitably works to their disadvantage, TRW had pioneered innovative MRO management practices, including outsourcing, group buying, competitive order pricing, and central purchasing.

BEST PRACTICE #5, SUPPLIER QUALITY CIRCLES

Best Practice Leaders: Honda, Toyota, Nippondenso, Parker Hannifin
In the auto industry, transplants Honda, Toyota, and Nippondenso lead in supplier quality circles, or quality teams initiatives. Team competitions, which for many participants represent their first public speech, as well as the groups' first team-building experience, shine a spotlight on the strengths of production workers as they tackle tough production problems with a range of classic techniques, including Ishikawa Fish Diagrams (Cause and Effect), Deming Circle Activity (PlanDoCheckAct), and Root Cause Analysis. Nippondenso's consistent quality and continually improving performance is a credit to its dedication to the teams; shop floor quality teams tackle tough technical problems, with input from engineering and procurement experts, and their repeated wins of customer performance awards demonstrates the effectiveness of their involvement approach.

Unfortunately, too few companies in the United States help their supply base implement the power of teamwork, involvement, and participatory management. Yet the payback in loyalty and eagerness for suppliers to do their best results when suppliers are approached with a well-planned assistance program.

BEST PRACTICE #6, TRAINING

Best Practice Leaders: John Deere, Honda, Motorola, SmithKline Beecham

In the purchasing area, competition for excellent procurement specialists has heated up among automotive producers. In the electronics industry, Hewlett-Packard, in comparison to other, smaller growth companies, for example, continues to demonstrate its dedication to employee training and development.

Best Practices in supplier training and development include study groups, technical courses, some sharing of training costs by customers, and benchmarking visits.

Internally, training for purchasing professionals includes a variety of courses; basics, however, include quality methods (Deming, Root Cause Analysis, kaizen), and "human factors" training in communications, running meetings, and even languages. Many companies have superb training for their own employees. Best-in-class companies make this same training available to their suppliers for little additional cost.

BEST PRACTICE #7, SUPPLIER INFORMATION SHARING: SUPPLIER STUDY GROUPS, SUPPLIER SEMINARS, TOP MANAGEMENT MEETINGS

Best Practice Leaders: Honda, Harley-Davidson, Daimler/Chrysler

Organizations like Honda and Toyota that are trying to bring suppliers up to a certain level of consistency around procurement and manufacturing methods, and who want to encourage top management discussions about new methods, find that supplier study groups work. A type of informal learning, many supplier groups include top managers from groups of suppliers looking at one particular subject, like Ishikawa's quality principles. Managers who learn these approaches are then able to train their own associates. Also, suppliers find contacts in their own groups breed a kind of inter-enterprise cooperation as the executives see where they are performing relative to our companies, and where opportunities to improve lie. Supplier study groups are a powerful and underused tool in the United States, especially because they can be used to thoroughly improve capabilities along narrow themes such as improved accounting, health and safety, or environmental practices. These particular subjects can involve government regulations and practices that may require expensive experts to teach, and supplier study groups are a much more economical approach.

A unique Honda practice is to hold monthly seminars for the entire supply base. Suppliers select which seminars to attend from a large selection of world-class experts on many subjects. Again, the cost of monthly seminars may initially appear high, but the price drops when we consider how much suppliers learn and can pass on in value to the customer.

There is no substitute for providing opportunities for a customer's top management team and a supplier's top management team to discuss common needs and issues. The result is enhancement of the customer-supplier relationship at a high level.

BEST PRACTICE #8, SUPPLIER CONFERENCE

Best Practice Leaders: Honda, Harley-Davidson, John Deere
Recognition is a powerful tool that builds loyalty and cooperation from suppliers, and we believe that all companies should hold annual supplier conferences to provide positive, upbeat recognition of the highest quality—best delivery and best cost performance by suppliers. Honda's Annual Supplier Conference is a celebration of good results. Once per year all suppliers meet at one of the plant sites, hear presentations about upcoming strategy from the president of the company, and review quality and delivery performance against goals. About thirty suppliers are recognized each year for supplier performance in quality, delivery, and "extraordinary management efforts."

The conference is designed to be a memorable party in which the suppliers are the stars—food, decorations, live music, videos, gifts, and photo ops underline one of Honda's key management principles in continuous improvement, "Celebrate the Results."

Harley-Davidson conducts similar celebrations. Best Practice organizations understand that the thanks and recognition must be passed on from a typical supplier's sales force or executive to the associates who did the work and generated the good ideas and energy to win the prizes. Honda's unique supplier visitation program, "Two-in-Twelve," in which the head of purchasing and all other manufacturing vice presidents hit the road immediately after the supplier conference, taking the message to individual plants, underscores the company's commitment to its associates. Most supplier employees are astounded to hear the president of the assembly plant thank them personally, but the strategy works as they begin to understand the company's historic commitment to its workforce.

BEST PRACTICE #9, SUPPLIER PERFORMANCE REPORTING

Best Practice Leaders: Honda, John Deere, Sun Microsystems, Solectron
Continuous communication that provides a supplier with technical subjective measurements of quality, delivery, and cost performance is essential. But supplier performance reporting unfortunately covers a range of systems, from manually developed reports showing quality basics, to full-blown computer systems tied to warehouses and other receiving points, with instant feedback to suppliers and customers alike. A third element of successful supplier reporting is the personalization of feedback; purchasing vice presidents at Honda each month send handwritten notes to suppliers commenting on their improvement or extra effort.*

BEST PRACTICE #10, SUPPLIER SURVEYS

Best Practice Leaders: Honda, Motorola
Motorola pioneered the development of supplier surveys that ask how the customer is communicating and working with the supplier. Supplier

*See *Target* features on "Two-in-Twelve" visits, and *Breakthrough Partnering*, Moody, Wiley 1993.

surveys are an excellent way for suppliers to report to the customer the obstacles they face getting the job done. By using information gathered from the surveys, customers can improve internal practices that impede their supplier's performance. Suppliers recognize that they need specific information from their customers on products, schedules, and strategies to do a good job. Supplier surveys are the first step toward bringing suppliers into the product development and improvement process.

Implementation or response steps arising from supplier feedback are as important as the survey itself, and several large customers have fallen into the trust-destroying habit of survey without follow-up action.

Motorola's innovative supplier surveys have been followed up by similar ones at Sun Microsystems, Solectron, Honda, and Williams Technologies.

BEST PRACTICE #11, DELIVERY IMPROVEMENT

Best Practice Leaders: Harley-Davidson, Honda, Johnson Controls
Delivery Performance actually falls into the category of quality performance because parts received either too late or too early count among the Best Practice leaders as no parts at all. However, the complexities of transportation, sequencing of assembly parts, and shortcomings of many computer systems designed to handle JIT delivery requirements make this one of the biggest challenges for North American companies. Johnson Controls has developed superb delivery capabilities and systems links to the Big Three and various transplants. A delivery improvement program is a focused, continuous program to work with suppliers who make the highest negative impact on the customer's delivery results.

BEST PRACTICE #12, TOOL AND TECHNICAL ASSISTANCE CENTERS

Best Practice Leaders: Honda, Toyota
The Honda WEK fire story and Toyota's brake supplier fire each point to the value of suppliers' participation in tooling design, maintenance, and recapture. Further, a few very innovative, high-quality,

premium tool designers like Minco in Dayton are setting new standards for fast, innovative tool design.

Not all suppliers specialize in rapid, custom tool design, and to compensate for this and to avoid offshore tooling suppliers, Best Practice leaders maintain tooling and technical support centers solely to assist suppliers with expertise they might not have in all component areas.

Moreover, including these technical assists in purchasing, or purchasing engineering, emphasizes their strategic value.

Imagine purchasing professionals who have no idea of the actual cost of the tooling they buy. Often, a buyer's lack of knowledge about tooling costs leads to uncontrolled costs in this "magical" area; an investment in a tooling cost expert pays back many, many times. According to co-author Nelson, cultivating tooling experts on actual tooling costs "is the easiest money you will ever make because the customer expert can cause suppliers of tooling to look hard at their real costs. Tooling groups generally bring tooling costs down by about 15 percent."

BEST PRACTICE #13, SUPPLIER SUPPORT (SWAT) TEAM

Best Practice Leader: Honda
The supplier support (SWAT) teams are groups of dedicated experts who assist suppliers in various ways by arranging meetings, study groups, and seminars, for example, but in particular, they advise suppliers on labor issues. At Honda, supplier support services also offers some legal assistance and plant location studies. But the most important activity they conduct is working on well-perfected procedures to help suppliers defeat unionization campaigns, in one day.

BEST PRACTICE #14, LOANED EXECUTIVES

Best Practice Leader: Honda
When a small supplier loses a key manager or technical employee, finding and locating a replacement can take up to a year. Because most JIT customers cannot tolerate that type of delivery risk, the best ones make available key experts to suppliers should the need arise. Honda, for example, in the early stages of its Marysville production

complex development, had fifteen professionals loaned out at any one time. If the customer has created loyalty and trust with its suppliers, such emergencies will be well known, and a customer's generous response will create further loyalty and trust.

BEST PRACTICE #15, EARLY SUPPLIER INVOLVEMENT

Best Practice Leaders: Daimler/Chrysler, Honda, Harley-Davidson/ Buell, Toyota, Lexmark

Early supplier involvement practices count in the new product introduction cycle as well as ongoing product lifetimes. However, the auto and electronics industries have discovered the power of suppliers to change, or even take over new product design and specification to the point that they either live on site with their customers or maintain virtual systems, separate from other information systems, that allow this kind of critical collaboration. Lexmark, for example, has cut introduction times in half simply by involving three key suppliers.

Specific practices that facilitate collaboration include Design-In Guest Engineer programs (from concept through development), the Factory Guest Engineer program (from development to mass production), and a New Model Group located in purchasing, tied to R & D and Design Centers.

Chrysler's Platform Teams are a breakthrough approach to early supplier involvement, although in the five years since they were instituted, the car producer has recognized a need for more involvement throughout its supply base, a challenge for all first tier producers. All companies recognize the benefits of development engineers working together during the concept stage of new products, where most of the process and materials costs are set, but not all of them have used this organizational tool to bring suppliers in earlier.

BEST PRACTICE #16, NEW MODEL DEVELOPMENT GROUP

Best Practice Leaders: Harley-Davidson/Buell, Honda, Daimler/Chrysler, Toyota, Nissan

New model development groups located in purchasing manage issues that extend purchasing's traditional role into the areas of cost and time (schedule) management. They are an investment by the customer that brings supply management and engineering together with suppliers to work during the earliest stages of new product development. In new technology areas like aluminum castings or new plastics applications, their role is essential to the success of the project.

BEST PRACTICE #17, WRITTEN STRATEGY FOR EVERY SUPPLIER AND EVERY PART/COMMODITY

Best Practice Leaders: Honda, Toyota
Purchasing commodity experts, especially in high-tech companies like EMC[2] and Sun, dedicate specific individuals to watching market trends and developing reaction scenarios. Early Honda efforts to increase the rate of localization was facilitated by part and commodity strategy experts as they dug into local available resources and located potentially excellent sources. Without a written supplier and part/commodity strategy, traditional purchasing organizations usually revert to chasing low-cost offshore producers (Digital in Puerto Rico) or leveraging local suppliers for price cuts (GM and Volkswagen).

BEST PRACTICE #18, STRATEGIC PLANNING AND ADMINISTRATION

Best Practice Leaders: Harley-Davidson, Honda, John Deere, SmithKline Beecham

> *When your strategy is weak and shallow, what you gain by your calculations is little, so you lose before you do battle.*
>
> —Sun Tsu, *The Art of War*, translated by Thomas Cleary, (Boston: Shambhala, 1991)*

Traditional purchasing departments are not involved in strategy, a problem that typically results in cost overruns or technology problems. However, Best Practice leaders like Toyota and Honda increase purchas-

---

*We thank Garry Berryman, vice president of purchasing and supply management at Harley-Davidson, for this quote.

ing's role in strategic planning by developing a strategy for each supplier and for each part, sometimes for each commodity as well. This
means that not only are purchasers looking one to two years down-
stream to understand timing of new product launches, they are gathering information on commodity markets and technology capabilities, as
well as technology leaders, three to five years in advance of their need.

Further, in an industry like automobiles, electronics contract manufacturing, and electronics capital equipment, in which overcapaci-
ties will defeat the weaker players, this group is in the lead for
determining where and when to open new production facilities.
Honda's South American plant strategy, as part of the Strategy for
the Americas, Toyota's expansion into France, and Varian's struggles
with market ups and downs all highlight the importance of strategic
planning embedded in purchasing.

BEST PRACTICE #19, CAREER PATH PLANNING AND ACADEMIC OUTREACH PROGRAMS

Best Practice Leaders: John Deere, Honda, Harley-Davidson, Motorola

Michigan State and Arizona State Universities offer graduate and
undergraduate purchasing degree programs. Other organizations like
NAPM, partnered with APICS, and the Council of Logistics Management, supply industry with certification and professional training.
But few traditional purchasing departments maintain a rotation program like Honda's that brings in engineers and rotates them through
two weeks working on the assembly line, followed by experience in
other key departments. Consequently, many purchasing departments
are caught in the practice of maintaining professional roles limited to
paperwork processing. We recommend that companies seeking Best
Practice performance throughout their supply organization work at
developing deeper and richer technology expertise with all their people; career path planning and hiring is the only way to guarantee
predictable results in that area. John Deere's new program—a
distance-learning program that leads to a supply management master's degree—is the first of its kind, just started in the spring of 2000.

BEST PRACTICE #20, PURCHASING SYSTEMS

Best Practice Leaders: IBM, American Express
Purchasing systems traditionally were not included in the first MRP systems developed. As later add-ons, they became, unfortunately, as Gene Richter noted when he headed up Hewlett-Packard Procurement, stand-alones; scheduling, cost, bill of material, and other data had to be imported and compared to purchasing transactions and databases. Although software vendors eventually discovered this problem, their solutions often concentrated on improving a limited number of purchasing functions. Not until the early 1990s have major software suppliers like SAP come to understand their true role in mass-produced procurement packages. Until commercial packages are perfected, Best Practice leaders will continue to rely on a mix of homegrown systems solutions. John Deere, long a leader in adopting new, powerful systems, continues to be a leader in purchasing and manufacturing systems, as does IBM. Interestingly, Honda of America's weakest performance area lies in purchasing systems. As few as ten years ago, bill of material structures were still manually maintained and exploded!

Conclusion

The top ten purchasing organizations consistently meet most if not all of these twenty criteria, but each of them excels at one or more of the twenty. We have focused on how the best of the best developed superior performance in that single strength, and in the chapters that follow, we more closely examine the challenges and the results. As judged by a 1992 AT Kearney survey and a 1997 Booz Allen Hamilton survey the top organizations consistently score in the seven to ten range in all categories, closely followed by a cluster of excellent companies who demonstrate strengths in some of the Best Practice categories. Studies by the CAPS Research program of the National Association of Purchasing Management show strong performance by Lockheed, Nortel, Coca-Cola, Bayer, General Mills, Pacific Bell,

Kodak, Dial Corporation, Lucent, Johnson and Johnson, AT&T, Boeing, Teledyne, Bell South, Federal Express, and Cyprus. Another group of well-managed companies offers potential for purchasing innovation, including Pepsico, Fritolay, Compaq, Steelcase, Herman Miller, Southwestern Bell, Disney, and Mellon Financial.

Drawing on the Best Practices Survey conducted in 1998–99, we have grouped our findings into roughly three segments—the Twenty Best Practices, illustrations and specific company examples of best and worst practice at work, and our recommendations on how companies can achieve Best Practice performance levels in the areas that are the most important to their competitive environment. In our next chapter, The Strategic Power of Supply Management, we underscore the potential that Daimler/Chrysler, for example, a company now headed by its former purchasing chief Thomas Stallkamp, can discover when they make excellent supply management practices their focus.

3

THE STRATEGIC POWER OF
SUPPLY MANAGEMENT

Three of our Top Ten companies have come back from the dead to again become industry leaders:

1. IBM Corporation
2. Chrysler Corporation, now Daimler/Chrysler
3. Harley-Davidson

All three dropped into moribund positions from which they worked and thought their way back up. Although they are producers for worldwide markets of technologically advanced and aesthetically impressive vehicles, they live with very different supply bases and somewhat different organizational "faces." IBM carries the reputation and size of Big Blue; Harley-Davidson carries the mystique of an underdog, its image supported by owners' devotion to their products and "the club." Daimler/Chrysler, however beautifully designed and received their product may be, has less of the obsessive cult following associated with Harley-Davidson.

Yet each organization has struggled not just with bringing innovation into their enterprise, much of it from suppliers, without disrupting their own organization structure; but also, each of these giants has struggled to harness innovation in ways that make new ideas commercially successful. Chrysler's reputation for engineered designs has from time to time in the company's history gone too far; the Swept Wing Dodge, for example, epitomized an exaggerated styling that took the company too far to the edge. Harley has also grown in model and accessory variety, a combination that Harley has learned to manage and move quickly along the new product continuum. Both iconoclasts have arrived at strategies and tactics that they believe will bring them the best of both worlds—the power and economy of a large company, linked to the flexibility and creativity of an aligned supply base. And now, with Chrysler's merger with giant Mercedes, expectations are that the German company's advanced technology breakthroughs can be popularized and brought to bigger markets through Chrysler mass-marketing strength.

IBM, Daimler/Chrysler, and Harley have come to realize the vital contributions their suppliers make every day to their vehicles' success. Harley's market is more competitive than ever; although would-be Harley riders may be willing to deposit thousands of dollars and then wait, even years, for the bike of their dreams, there is new competition, and old nameplates have resurfaced—Indian, Norton, and Triumph—cruising for Harley customers. Consumers worldwide have more choices in class of bike—road vs. sportster vs. dirt bike or racing bike—as well as price range, colors, and accessories. Likewise, Chrysler's merger with technology giant Daimler raises the ante as the company becomes the number three car company in the world; consumers will see a broader, deeper product mix as assemblers can access more excellent suppliers to mass-produce leading engineering technologies. It's a combination that should also work to bring down prices per vehicle for the consumer, but these companies know that significant reductions cannot come without thoroughly engaged and high-level supply base performance. Strategically, these organizations must work every day to win the market, and they know it.

IBM

Bill Schaefer, IBM vice president of procurement services within IBM's Global Services, believes that IBM has firmly transitioned into a powerful business based on what he calls a "three-legged stool—hardware, software, and services." Growth over the past six or seven years, going back to 1991, has averaged 20 percent per year. Strategically, Schaefer's division occupies an important sector in IBM's total business strategy. Global Services represents one-third of IBM's revenue, 40 percent of the people—130,000 out of 290,000.

A Strategic Transformation to Services

IBM was traditionally known as a hardware company selling PCs and other equipment, but because services and software became so clearly a large part of the value customers were looking for, it made sense strategically for IBM to shift. "It's a wonderful success story," says Schaefer. "We've become the leading service business in the industry, and we are beginning to look like a little Internet!"

Services have become a key growth area and a keystone of IBM's business plan. "If you think back to why we are in the procurement services business," says Schaefer, "it goes all the way back to the early 90's, the dark days for IBM." The company had lost $8.8 billion. Pundits predicted the demise of IBM, and predictions ran rampant about the breakup of Big Blue.

When Lou Gerstner became chairman, however, he, along with Jerry York, CFO at that time, reversed the downhill slide, and instead of breaking the company apart, Gerstner took a surprising strategic position—*Big Is not Bad*—if you do it right, and he began looking at ways to leverage size effectively, and to provide value to customers. Several areas needed overhaul at that time, one of them being procurement, which had been organized to ship hardware; procurement reported to the vice president of manufacturing, and Schaefer reflects, "procurement was buried within the manufacturing organization—a second-class citizen."

It gets worse. Because procurement was so decentralized, each division, each location, and each plant had its own business structure. Purchasing became very much an administrative function, not a high-skill job. "In fact," says Schaefer, "if you had asked me at that time if I wanted to be associated with procurement [in 1993 Schaefer had worked in manufacturing with procurement under him] I would have refused."

A Strategic Transformation

The hiring of Gene Richter, chief procurement officer, out of Hewlett-Packard (and previously Black and Decker, and Ford), changed all that. Richter launched procurement's strategic transformation, starting with a few key steps.

One Common System

A common system was needed to run procurement across the entire business. "We selected SAP as the engine to run our enterprise; we needed a common system," recalls Schaefer, "otherwise it was hopeless—we could not operate against all our lines and across all our lines." With SAP for the back end, procurement systems experts wrote a requisitions catalog as a front end for the employees. "We found that although SAP is wonderfully huge, it is not the world's most user-friendly tool for access and simple ordering."

The front end IBM attached was Lotus Notes; sitting on the employee's desktop, it's a simple point-and-click system that allows associates to select from catalogs, enter descriptions, or use a contract that allows repeated reuse and reordering. The front-end tool classifies the buy and translates a nonprocurement request to buy into procurement terms, and the system automatically routes the transaction to various managers for approval. All of this desktop process is connected to the ledger and the financial systems. Deployment started in 1996 in the United States, then spread to Europe and Asia.

Strategic Consolidation

"So the first step," remembers Schaefer, "was to get control of the information—what we were spending with whom, at what prices, so that we could direct purchases to the strategic suppliers." That done, management was able to consolidate the buy, squeezing thousands and thousands of possible sources down to a considerably smaller number.

Procurement was split into two types—production and nonproduction. Production is defined as all the parts that go into building a product, and nonproduction is "everything else—temporary personnel, office supplies, facilities, travel, advertising, telecommunications." The buy as of 1998 amounted to $41 billion in total purchases, of which $21 billion was nonproduction and $20 billion production. Schaefer points out, "If you look at our revenue, that represents 50 to 51 percent of our revenues, but in the early 90's we were vertically integrated, producing more ourselves, with less reliance on suppliers. And during those years, we learned that the spend was going up as we shifted reliance to our suppliers, and that's when we saw purchasing become more important to the bottom line. We knew we had to change our strategic purchasing process."

Next Step, Mending the Organization

The next step, moving from a completely decentralized organization—"everyone was doing his own thing"—took a lot of doing. Purchasing had a population of procurement personnel who were largely administrative. "We did some studies in the early 90s, and found that our people were mainly generalists, just trying to support the purchasing transactions, not strong in the area of strategic sourcing, or in-depth knowledge of industry segments." Employees were spending about five hours per day answering phone calls on administrative issues, "and that is symptomatic," says Schaefer, "of not having a well-developed end-to-end system."

By putting the system in place IBM facilitated the process of changing people—hiring critical skills and changing the procurement organization into a much more professional group that could put in the right deals with the right suppliers.

Step two, changing skills and creating expertise, took several years. "We had to hire people from advertising to do it, and engineers for capital equipment; we brought in subject matter experts, and elevated the systems our new people used."

Step three formalized strategic sourcing by putting in written strategies, what IBM calls commodity strategies. The group created commodity councils in which global responsibility was assigned to a group of top experts in a particular area. Everything from office suppliers to advertising was targeted, and purchasing pros developed written strategies for each one. Strategies in hand, planners were able to implement them, consolidate the supply base, and put contracts in place that would leverage the best value for the spend and improve service too.

Step four was to make the process as automated and efficient as possible; purchasing used integrated business processes based on technology tools that enhanced how planners handled day-to-day transactions. The nonproduction procurement side is very transaction-intensive; planners buy office supplies and many other smaller items, a higher transaction ratio than buying parts for production.

Buyerless Purchasing

"This particular area of the business," says Schaefer, "is very vulnerable to using buyers to do processing, more paperwork, and so we implemented the end-to-end system around SAP and the Requisitions Catalog, with a bolted-on programming extension to SAP." The resulting enhancements produced purchasing efficiency, while automatic transactions allowed planners to shift focus to a different way of buying. Buys could be processed without stopping at the buyers' desk. "We called it Buyerless Purchasing," says Schaefer; "the requester goes into the Requisitions Catalog to order an item, he classifies the buy, which is routed directly to the supplier, and the system then leverages our spend in a very efficient—'Buyerless'—manner. It's faster—no stopping for approvals—because the request moves directly to the supplier, electronically either through EDI, or over the Web. Further confirmation comes back electronically—it's a complete e-business process. Buyers that had been spending five hours per day answering phone calls have been relieved to perform more strategic work because now the system routes approvals, giving feedback each step of the way. The system provides feedback and updates as requests are received by the supplier, all the way through shipment."

Step Five—Centralized Management

Richter made some organization changes that helped rationalize the reporting structure and began the move to centralization. All non-production people now report into corporate (versus unit managers); production procurement personnel report 50/50 into corporate; 50 percent of their evaluation is done by Gene Richter, and 50 percent by the local team. The new structure creates dual loyalty, which, in Schaefer's words, "makes sense—we need loyalty to get the product out, but we operate in the greater confines of the IBM business." The new structure answers the question of how to efficiently operate as a single IBM business unit. "The end game," says Schaefer, "is to get high compliance, to use the purchasing process to make buys. You can have the best deals in the world, but if they go around it, you will never see the benefits. In the old days we had 30 to 40 percent non-compliance—and many companies were in the same boat. Although we all had a purchasing function, people ordered the way they wanted to, and there was no way to control and challenge the spend. It was impossible to achieve our compliance target of under 2 percent noncompliance, or 98 to 99 percent compliance."

IBM has found that this is a most important strategic measurement of the effectiveness of a procurement system. If the spend is really going through procurement—not around it—the possibility for leverage exists.

"However," Schaefer emphasizes, "it cannot be done without a good system and strategic sourcing, and of course the right deals with the right suppliers." For example, when Schaefer was running IBM North American procurement, he noted a lack of internal satisfaction directly tied to the degree of noncompliance, and he recommended that if planners continued to be unhappy with what they saw, they might want to redirect all the creative energy it took to "go around" into focus on what really mattered. As management learned, high compliance had huge benefits for the company. In fact, over a four-year time frame, through 1998, planners reaped over $6.5 billion in savings (not including market pricing) on consolidated spending.

High compliance resulted in other dramatic changes beyond savings; purchasing order processing time dropped from an average of thirty days to one day; buyerless purchasing takes two hours, from approval of requisitions and confirmation from the supplier; planners expect that time to improve as flows move out of a batch mode. One general business objective, to drive over 80 percent through the buyerless electronic method, shifting the remaining, more complex 20 percent off-line for more traditional handling, could in fact not even have begun without the technology and the process to support it. "You can't have one without the other," says Schaefer.

Supply Base Technology Linkages

Although IBM procurement started electronic transactions with EDI, the company recognizes the importance of the Web, the possibilities of creating an e-business transformation among the supply base. As a result, IBM gave its suppliers the capability of doing business over the Web starting in 1998, a win-win that allows them to transact business electronically between the companies. In December 1998, planners completed $600,000 transactions on the Web with suppliers; the goal for 1999 was $12 billion—a huge number that is completely dependant on how efficiently the e-business operates from a procurement perspective.

An interesting side benefit that Schaefer notes began to appear as the organization was improved. "You would think that as we became more disciplined in procurement, internal customer satisfaction would drop. But we went from a low 40% in satisfaction with procurement, to over 85 percent in the years 1994 through 1998. We scratched our heads, and thought maybe we really are providing value, saving money, and providing systems that directed the spend. We think the system is easier to use, and it's the combination of all these steps that has resulted in our higher satisfaction rate. It turns out that the satisfaction rate is an important indicator—if people are not satisfied, they will find a way around."

Next Stop, Proliferation!

It's hard to hide a good thing. IBM management discovered after benchmarking other companies' processes, and sharing Best Practices, that there was a need for their approach to procurement management. Kent Brittan, vice president at United Technologies, visited IBM purchasing in late 1997 and asked for help fulfilling his chairman's $750 million savings goal. Britton's request led to another service offering from IBM.

An installation of Requistions Catalog and SAP at one UTC division, Carrier, in late January 1998 was followed by an agreement in June to do a companywide outsourcing of nonproduction procurement to IBM. Planners encountered the usual evils—more suppliers, a very decentralized group of employees, and completely decentralized business units operating without the information they really needed. The front-end tool, the Requisitions Catalog, was made Web-based; planners now access a Carrier home page, then point and click their way to IBM buyers who handle the transactions and the invoices, all the way to the end of the process. A reconciliation file is sent from IBM to Carrier with up-to-date payables lists, and payment is handled electronically by the bank.

Although some customization takes place, "nine times out of ten," says Schaefer, "what we developed for IBM works for them. In effect we are providing them all our investment and expertise—they can get there faster. We have a game plan, the end-to-end system. It's a strategic decision for companies who want to offload a non-strategic activity. They could do it themselves, but that takes time, and the question is, is this core to my business, something that I want to invest in?" Nonproduction, buying office supplies, travel, is generally viewed as noncore. Ask yourself, "if I am really not good at this, and we are leaving lots of dollars on the table, do I want to build that capability in a non-core area, or do I want to look to somebody who has the solution? Which will get us there faster?"

Innovation Rewarded with the Crystal Star

It's a very exciting concept, and one that many companies would like to address quickly. But for CEOs who know they must invest in a procurement system but are unsure which one to pick, and when, the wide variety of choices can be simplified. Schaefer's system works in twenty-eight different countries, over different currencies, and with new Internet capabilities, strategic outsourcing of procurement itself makes a lot of sense. In fact, in 1999 Chairman Gerstner recognized procurement's contributions by awarding the chairman's award, a Crystal Star, to the entire combined internal external e-procurement team that took IBM's new system to the customer base. Gerstner reinforced his message about innovation with this: "Procurement is something we don't normally focus on in these meetings, but I wanted you to know that this team has lived out and implemented my vision of e-businesses. What we have accomplished in this end-to-end system is what I have been preaching about. Congratulations and well done."

Daimler/Chrysler

Jeff Trimmer, director of operations and strategy, reports to Tom Sidlick, executive vice president of procurement and supply, President Thomas Stallkamp's successor. "You have to go back about ten to twelve years, maybe further, to the time when Chrysler was the smallest of the Big Three. Chrysler outsourced typically 65–70 percent of the parts, or more. That was a real disadvantage in those days; GM derived tremendous volume and profits from producing internally." GM, as the fully vertically integrated producer, kept dozens of GM-owned parts suppliers busy cranking out components and systems for their sister assembly plants.

"When [Thomas] Stallkamp came over, he worked with company executives who were desperate to find pockets of Chrysler advantage, largely in cost situations at the manufacturing level. 'Let's figure out what we have going for us,' he said, and "basically," says Trimmer, "they realized that by having the ability to select and work with the supplier, to tap the creativity of the supply base, to move more quickly, Chrysler could gain advantage over vertically integrated companies." The new strategy started to take form, a vision that was later dubbed, and registered as a Daimler/Chrysler trademark, The Extended Enterprise®. "This was not just about procurement," says Trimmer, "it was a corporate plan that depended on product development programs as well." The company was determined to streak ahead based on the added boost that could come only from a partnered, and positive, winning supply base. Of the Big Three, Chrysler most needed suppliers to *want* to work with them.

Suddenly, Chrysler brought new competitive energies to the race. The company discovered by leveraging the supply base that they could move more quickly, especially with new product introductions. "When we started this process, the typical product development cycle took five to six years. When we created platform teams focused on special products, like the mini van team, we found we reduce time typically about 2.5 years, depending on complexity—or 22 to 30 months—mostly by working with suppliers and bringing them in early in the program."

SCORE

The improvement program SCORE has received much attention in the past five years, but this continuous improvement approach focused on suppliers is just one of six elements of the Extended Enterprise strategy. "The overriding philosophy of the Extended Enterprise," says Trimmer, "is that we are not just going to work with suppliers—we will work with the chain to manage all the key elements from raw material to the customer." To reinforce that strategic objective, the company has developed powerful specific measurements for quality, cycle time, cost, and the number of innovations on new products brought in by suppliers; an example might be a new processing technique, a new way of fabricating aluminum castings, or it might be a new product design, like an integrated seat belt on a convertible seat. Whether the improvements are process- or product-oriented, the way they are treated reflects the philosophy of managing not just the suppliers but the entire chain. If procurement is working on a new seat system, planners would work with Johnson Controls as well as their leather supplier, for example, because the raw material cost represents a significant part of the vehicle and warrants working down through many levels in the supply chain.

To enable extending purchasing's work further into the supply chain, the Extended Enterprise is designed around six basic elements:

1. Supplier relations. It all starts with mutual respect and trust; without that, Chrysler cannot accomplish much; the objective is to build a long-term relationship based on good communications, what Trimmer calls "doing what you say."

2. Commodity strategies. Cross-functional teams research specific pieces of a vehicle, seats, for example. The teams research everything about seats—who the best and near-best manufacturers are, where the technology is going, costs, and so on. There may be thirty seat suppliers, and the teams will identify the best—the companies that have the technology, the management, and the processes—that will bring something incremental to Daimler/Chrysler products. The top suppliers are identified as part of the commodity strategy for that vehicle section; the idea is to identify the best suppliers and develop the commodity strategy for that system well in advance of the start of the design to production cycle.

   For example, if the commodity strategy for seats identifies Johnson Controls or Lear as the leading potential suppliers, when the new product has been put into concept, planners already know who the suppliers are, and the decisions and selections have already been made. That means that time wasted on bidding, and other preliminary qualification exer-

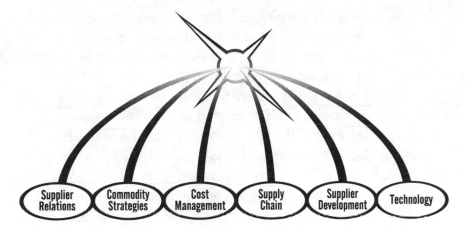

Figure 3.1 The Extended Enterprise

cises, is eliminated; the approach becomes "it's their [the suppliers'] business to lose."

3. Cost management. Because of the commodity strategy selections that have already been made, cost management extends beyond simple attention to price; instead, Chrysler planners focus on total systems cost, including parts (manufacturing) cost, logistics, warranty, and packaging. "This," says Trimmer, "allows us to not concentrate on knocking down the price of the component—if we can reduce assembly labor in plant, that's an advantage, but we want to look at total systems cost." Planners manage costs three ways:

   a. Target cost. The target cost is set on new products based on a determination of a share of the total that buyers afford to spend. Essentially, the formula starts with what the vehicle end customer would be willing to pay, broken down into material cost "chunks," for tires, seats, instrument panel, and so on. The data are run through some comparison analyses, and the supplier contained in the commodity strategy is selected, without negotiation or deal making; it becomes the supplier's job to design his system to meet the cost target.

What happens if the unit fails to hit target? Chrysler experts work with them, reviewing the design, or running kaizen and other improvement workshops, to be sure the target can be met. "Fundamentally we don't place a purchase order until we have met the cost target or found an offset in another part of the auto," says Trimmer, "so that the total target cost remains in budget."

b. Material economics. Because a vehicle may be in production for three to five years, Chrysler doesn't want to be locked into a hard-and-fast agreement if the price of certain raw materials fluctuates. This customer wants to be able to adjust to commodity price swings.

c. Continuous cost improvement. This is where SCORE comes in as just one element of the total cost management program. The idea is to work with small and medium-sized suppliers because to successfully manage costs, planners have learned that there must be continuous improvement, especially in the area of waste reduction. Notes Trimmer, "We drive out waste, and we ask suppliers to come in with reduction suggestions worth at least 5 percent per year of their total business with Chrysler."

The principle is simple—suppliers make suggestions, and they keep half of the gains. "The point is," says Trimmer, "that if you work with us, your margins will improve, and our margins will improve, current as well as future. There is a future advantage as well, because we prevent costs from entering our cost structure. Suppliers receive SCORE credit for example, if they come in below target cost."

4. The supply chain concept. Supply management is an integrated procurement and supply organization. "We don't just buy—we schedule and order material and deliver to operators on the line," adds Trimmer. It is an unusual idea of extended responsibility for the extended enterprise that is unique even among the Top Ten. Materials management, which is part of

procurement, develops the production schedules based on orders received from marketing, issues schedules to suppliers, and plans inbound logistics. Even the high-lift drivers in the plants are procurement and supply employees. This allows manufacturing to concentrate only on process: "We don't just buy stuff—we deliver material and finished goods to dealers even. We believe this creates accountability because it is too easy to say, 'I bought it, I'm not responsible for expediting.' No more 'he missed the date,' and no more throwing problems 'over the wall.'"

5. Supplier development. Chrysler is not unique in this fifth element of their Extended Enterprise strategy; Japanese transplants Honda and Toyota continue to dedicate significant resources—personnel, training centers, supplier conferences, study groups, and development/improvement engineers—to bringing their local supply base to the same performance levels that would be available in Japan. For Daimler/Chrysler, the starting point is a rating that identifies weaknesses for which the producer provides training and other assistance, some internal, some from outside industry sources. Chrysler can provide specialists to work with suppliers on process or design, in a wide variety of functional areas. There are value engineers, value analysis, and continuous improvement, five-day kaizen workshops for targeted suppliers. Gurus are available for as long as suppliers need them, even as long as a year.

6. Technology. One of the principles of the Extended Enterprise is that Chrysler does not want to expend engineering resources when suppliers themselves have the technology expertise. If a supplier is the expert in seat design, for example, the end producer will not work on seat design itself—that would be redundant. Instead, the supplier will concentrate on how the seat system fits in the vehicle and how it works with other systems. The approach apparently is working, because by limiting Chrysler's design activity and leveraging supplier creativity, the company has been able to reduce R & D costs, says Trim-

mer, to only 3 percent of sales of total revenue. "But," says Trimmer, "we still have technologically very competitive vehicles. Suppliers have to trust us to share their technology—without that trust won't happen."

Since the Daimler merger, the approach has shifted somewhat, because Daimler strategy is to drive technology, and be first to market, by identifying high-tech suppliers and working with them to invest to develop new technology. Now, the combined companies have new opportunities to leverage Daimler's advanced technologies that were previously applied to lower volumes, with Chrysler's mass markets. High-tech improvements—new fuel systems, for example, or safety devices—might start with Mercedes and migrate to Chrysler. The combination is good for suppliers too, because their markets have automatically expanded; active suspension, electronic stabilization systems designs, for example, that were available on the S Class Mercedes, and in the near future, fuel cell design packages, will be migrated to the popular product range.

Mercedes is bringing its own supplier management program to the merger; a Mercedes supplier relationship program called Tandem will be integrated into the Extended Enterprise to preserve the best of both worlds, including Mercedes's R & D on new technologies and their supplier communications programs, a well-developed network of meetings at all levels, journals, and so forth. The best feature of the Chrysler program, not just to a first tier supplier, is the way it manages the entire supply chain and shares the benefits. The benefits extend for suppliers to multimarket, multibrand opportunities because a Mercedes supplier can become a supplier to Chrysler, and vice versa. The expanded opportunities for bigger markets, e-based communications, and virtual engineering programs are exponential.

The Strategic Systems Challenge

Trimmer believes that the newly merged company still faces systems challenges because, as many other industries have learned, particularly in procurement, "systems have lagged." The merger offers an opportunity to abandon legacy systems in favor of newer, more comprehensive common systems. But first, a system capable of handling the volume and complexity of the entire global network, not just specific functions, must be found. Discussions with the big software houses have not produced the right solution. Although e-based auction package providers have offered their assistance as well, Trimmer feels that these are not the right approaches for an organization committed to its commodity strategy, its technology management style, and partnering with suppliers: "We don't want to do bidding, we are not out there trying to find the cheapest price." Maybe these auctions work with certain commodities—pencils for example; but for other critical commodities—steel, for instance—where the customer is working with suppliers to obtain the quality and grades they need, Chrysler cannot, says Trimmer, "afford to bid on a wide open flea market."

How Are We Doing? The Heart of Supplier Communications and Surveys

Every two years procurement conducts a survey of suppliers to see how they are performing as a customer, a realtime evaluation of their extended enterprise communications strategy and commitment to follow up. And the results have been encouraging as Daimler/Chrysler is ranked in the top three with Toyota and Honda; next comes Nissan, followed by Ford, whose position has dropped, with GM perpetually holding down the bottom rung. The survey looks at twenty-six benchmarking core questions; each year the survey takes on an additional focus—the first year emphasized platform, with year two focusing on the Extended Enterprise, followed in year three by globalization, as the survey is enlarged to include global Mercedes suppliers.

Trimmer sees the strategic goal of achieving perfect quality with no shortages across the supply chain as a continuous improvement challenge that will require many good tools, as well as many good suppliers. "We give them tools—like a supply chain mapping tool we developed internally makes it easier to map the supplier chain, to understand where the control points and the flows are." Mapping forces discipline, "but makes it easy." They started by developing a version of Viseg, and the plan is to make it available to suppliers. The goal—to identify the waste, and look at material movement, blockages and disconnects, financial flows, and informational flows—is multidimensional. "We believe that if you can understand the structure of the supply chain, you can start to manage it. It gets very complex—Chrysler had 900 production suppliers from 2,000 total sites around the world, just in Tier One; if you add fifty or sixty thousand Tier Two suppliers, you are then into big interlinks. We need to simplify. This is a typical control systems problem, and if we try to manage all the components, we won't be successful—we need to recognize that there are only a few key control points."

Where Does This Lead?

The next phase, says Trimmer, the whole process of trying to understand the supply chain, is "fascinating. I think when I was at school [MIT for engineering, and Harvard for his MBA], we were all taking functional courses—finance, marketing, operations, etc., optimizing the individual functions. The eighties reengineering push got companies working together—that was the reason for platform teams. Now we are into the third step. It's not good enough to optimize the firm—we have to optimize the supply chain. *But no one is king of the supply chain.*"

So the challenge becomes the structure, the discipline, the rewards, sharing the benefits over an extended enterprise, even between companies in different industries. "It won't be easy, but it will surely be a fascinating challenge," concludes Trimmer.

Harley-Davidson/Buell

The second strategic transformation that was enabled by a completely redesigned procurement and the supply base is Harley-Davidson's. Harley's manufacturing and supply chain initiatives have been addressed with such complete company commitment that they reflect the owners' parallel desires to belong to the movement, to ride in parallel with other "members of the club." There is a strong gravitational pull among Harley and its owners and suppliers that tends to align stakeholders around common themes, a dislike of Japanese bikes, for example, and a respect for "big styling"—chrome, the sound of the pipes, the tank design, as well as the "look" of the rider.

Harley-Davidson

As I drove into Mankato, there was a Harley dealer, and that dealer saved me as sure as if it had been a spider or garlic. . . . I watched the bikes and let myself go. Away. . . . Gone. In and out of myself, away from what I was in danger of becoming . . . I . . . let it talk to me. . . . Start the bike, the thought said. Start the bike and let it run. Just go. Leave the Chevette, leave it all. Ride. For a second. Clean thought. Clear thought. Start it and go. Never look back. . . . Ride. . . . I felt strange but in some way whole. It was like an extension of my body, and I cradled down in blue steel and leather and chrome and sat that way for a time, perhaps a full minute, and let the bike become part of me.

–Gary Paulsen*

Harley-Davidson is a cat that has enjoyed three lives: Harley's beginnings, in the golden era of cycling, when it was not certain that autos would become the preferred method of motorized transportation; to its tumultuous, brief life as a trailer to the AMF conglomerate; to its buyback and re-creation as an American icon, skilled in manufacturing and supply management, as well as heart-throbbing marketing and design.

It was Vaughn Beals, a former president, and Tom Gelb, who headed up manufacturing, who are credited, among others, with changing Harley's approach to production. According to AME founder Doc Hall, legend has it that Gelb stood at his mirror shaving one morning in the early eighties, feeling his throat constrict and his stomach tighten as

*Zero to Sixty, The Motorcycle Journey of a Lifetime, Gary Paulsen, a Harvest Book, Harcourt Brace & Company, New York, 1999, pp. 19, 20, 34.

the reality of their end approached—nearly one hundred years of machinists, and assembly guys, company parties and good-byes, first-, second-, and third-generation workers from the heartland shut out forever. Eighteen months had gone by as they "kicked the tires" and thought about survival, and talked about getting better, but the cash had run out. The Japanese bikes were capturing new markets and all the media attention; Dick Schonberger and other upcoming manufacturing gurus were making the pilgrimage to Kawasaki in Nebraska, bringing back tales of lean manufacturing in an era when most North American giants were running to MRP-driven batch and queue push methods. The prospect of a bigger Japanese invasion was frightening, and no one knew how long the market for big Harleys—a market capable of tsunami-sized swings—would hold up.

Looking into the mirror, Gelb realized there was no time left. "The biggest SOB in the place is me," he thought, so he drove down to the engine plant, and for the first time in years, shut all the machines down, pulled everyone out to the floor, and offered them up a choice. Take the company back and make it work—or walk away now. Their blood-stirring response—"Let's do it!"—foreshadowed nearly a decade of struggling with suppliers, new manufacturing methods, and taking back lost market share, a struggle to keep the faith. Along the way, the market fell out from under their feet, and technologies changed, but Harley persevered.

HARLEY-DAVIDSON'S STRATEGIC MOMENT:

Raising the bar for twice the quality, in half the time, with a double digit cost improvement challenge.

Now Harley-Davidson has slipped into its fourth life, and another set of challenges. This time, from a position of strength and profitability, as well as the revival of competitors like Excelsior Henderson, and others, the company is innovating not just the look of its bike lines but also the way it builds bikes—its design, procurement, assembly, and supply management processes, all the way down through multiple tiers to raw material suppliers. Harley is asking its suppliers to tackle quality, delivery, and costs in a way they many not have experienced before. In an April 1999 supplier conference, Harley-David-son Vice President of Purchasing, Honda veteran Garry S. Berryman, raised the bar—"twice the quality, in half the time, with a double digit cost improvement challenge."

Creativity from Buell Acquisition

With the addition of the Buell Motorcycle Company, Harley's posi-tion at both ends of the market—the smaller, light racing bikes and the larger, heavy cruiser market—is hopefully secured against the onset of competitors attacking from all sides. Management is opti-mistic that with continued profitability and a wider range of exciting new products, they will capture and retain the youth market as they continue to cater to more traditional buyers of bikes and very prof-itable accessories and after-market add-ons. It's a big global challenge for an organization that has already experienced so many years of struggle and transformation.

At this point, purchasing and the supply base have stepped to the forefront, taking the same commanding position that manufacturing held back in the anxiety-filled days of the early eighties, because Harley-Davidson executives realize that this next phase of healthy growth can be achieved only with the full participation of a proactive, enlightened supply base. This phase has moved beyond partners and cooperation, to the hard-nosed numbers that will carve out more competitive pricing and product introductions.

Doug Hevner, the director of purchasing/operations, whose office is in the York, Pennsylvania, plant that formerly housed the main assembly plant and now produces 65 percent of all Harleys, believes that the company does a number of things extremely well. The first is to really understand the stakeholders' interest in purchasing: "we are very close to the floor—our people don't reside in cubicles." York purchasing pros work on a mezzanine directly above the assembly line, and there are purchasing resources located in every other manu-facturing area as well.

Assembly, for example, is considered a functional area; likewise, where form and fab machines are located, so is purchasing, as is paint and chroming. The York plant is a JIT facility running lean at forty-two turns per year, on some items holding six to seven days of material; high-ticket items like on-site raw material—plate stock, bar stock, sheet stock—have daily delivery.

Running Lean

Manufacturing is cellular, running to one-piece flow. A three-container system—a container on-line being consumed, a container waiting to go on-line, and an empty container back at the cell waiting to be filled—keeps the material flowing kanban style—maximum parts count is two days' worth—but on average, materials like to run at less than a day. In 1984 York had over 40,000 feet of material storage, compared to a current "leaned down" total of 5,000 feet. Further proof of living lean is that 88 percent of all incoming material goes directly to the production area, to the line or to racks where some staging of certain components or assemblies is performed line side. Lines receive 1,000 parts per day, out of a bike's total part count of 2,300–3,200 pieces.

Suppliers are moving closer to final assembly operations as Harley-Davidson welcomes the help of five "in-plants," supplier purchasing pros who reside at Harley as "virtual" Harley employees, having desks, computers, and Harley systems access, and attend ongoing production meetings. This pioneering in-plant concept, which received much notice when the Bose Corporation was doing manufacturing using supplier in-plants, cuts planning and reaction time as it smooths forward and new product planning.

"Twice the Quality"—The Harley-Davidson Quality Strategy

Strategic initiatives around cost, quality, and time continue to dominate supplier meetings and forward planning of resources. Hevner believes the big challenge will be making sure that everything is paperless, and that quality levels continue to improve—across all suppliers. The goal of approximately 48 ppm, communicated to suppliers in stages starting in 1996 when the ppm stood at about 10,000, is steadily improving.

The road to perfect quality is mapped out using a plan that absolutely challenges supplier capabilities, as it provides direction for the journey. Suggested tactics to support the strategy include ISO certification and the Production Part Approval Process (PPAP), which has been incorporated into the product and process methodology. PPAP is important to the conceptual and development stages of new product launches, when suppliers can affect parts dimensionally and when they can review their own process capabilities.

The other key supportive role any original equipment manufacturer (OE) can offer small and medium-sized suppliers is of course supplier development, or continuous improvement. Harley-Davidson locates continuous improvement engineers at each facility, specifically dedicated to the supply base, not internal operations. Seventy suppliers make up approximately 80 percent of the buy, so even though the supply base numbers approximately three hundred suppliers, there is about one continuous improvement professional for every ten suppliers. Supply chain analysts are trained in continuous improvement industrial engineering methods; indeed, 20 percent of supply chain analysts, a new position for the company, are engineers.

Hevner feels that this strategy is moving performance to a new level, and suppliers need to evaluate how they want to position themselves in the enterprise, a different perspective from what their other customers may be doing; Harley-Davidson is "challenging them to go where we want to go, not specifically telling them the way, but our expectations are clear that they need to be thinking in more of a strategic context." The dialogues about stretch objectives are carefully cascaded through a number of strategic supplier communications lines, the Top 70 meetings, for example, in which purchasing leadership meets to review progress, along with one executive from Harley, and one platform level purchasing or materials pro, with a plant purchasing rep. The idea is to bring all interested parties into the discussion early, develop a strategy that moves in both directions, understand how suppliers fit in the strategy, decide what portion of the business they represent, and offer HD support where it is occasionally required.

What will be the result of all Harley-Davidson's carefully planned communications and strategizing with suppliers? Hevner believes, "It's all about relationships. Back in '97 we had a theme at the supplier conference—"Growing the Business"—we knew volumes were rising, and we talked about taking an inward look—we were challenging the supply base to do the same thing." In 1998 they added the phrase "Through Relationships We Count On"; finally, the enterprise came into the picture, and the theme became "Growing the Business Through Relationships We Count On Across the Enterprise." The approach included talking with suppliers about how they can improve their business relationships with suppliers. Another session covered human resources issues, including specific training programs from the Pacific Institute to help facilitate the change process—change starts within.

The company knows there are suppliers committed to moving forward, and some who may be unwilling—it's a balancing act, and the first time the company has proceeded this way. Rather than telling suppliers through specific goals exactly what they will accomplish, they are hoping that given the corporation's three strategic objectives, suppliers will individually exercise their creativity and tell their customers what is possible. It may be the first time suppliers have been challenged to create a strategic plan for growing their partnership with Harley-Davidson along with their process and product capabilities, but it will continue as an iterative process that can only continue to show good results.

"The Double-Digit Cost Improvement Challenge"

Albert Keal, a veteran of Cummins Engine and Digital Equipment, is a manager of materials procurement and logistics for large engine power train production in Milwaukee. Keal is positioned to bring some significant, early savings to the cost challenge facing Harley-Davidson, and he has achieved stellar results just by working smarter with his supply base. Keal's hard work in the area of indirect materials' spend of $86 million represents about 17 percent of the company's total purchased budget; by forming an alliance among key suppliers, Keal has consolidated a typical MRO supplier list—3,500 in total—down to 3 or 4 majors. Eighteen commodities are represented, including $1 million of abrasives, $5.6 million chemicals, $6.6 million office products, and $12M of perishable tooling.

A Simple Strategy for Big Savings

Keal's area has a five-year goal for cost improvement with suppliers, starting with the deal that for every dollar Harley-Davidson spends with these suppliers, the OE asks for $1, a one-to-one savings ratio. Suppliers met that goal, dropping the spend from $86 million to $57 million in one year. How did Harley-Davidson and its suppliers cut such a big slice out of costs? By essentially concentrating the supply base into three groups—chemical represented by Henkel Chemical Management, tooling under Engman-Taylor Inc., and general purpose Unisource Worldwide—who work together, company planners can dedicate more attention to strategic issues, and suppliers can deliver what they do best.

After only six months into the process the group had saved $1.7 million, with additional business benefits. For suppliers, it's the end of "selling, selling, selling" into a customer, as the focus shifts to the customer's process improvement goals. The question becomes not "how much can I sell" but "how can I improve the operating integrity of Harley-Davidson and thereby generate savings." The goal becomes in a manufacturing environment, for example, looking at the machinery run cycles and discovering what the supplier can do to keep 100 percent up-time and improve efficiency of cells with the process.

Supplier on-sites, also called in-plants, are key to this process, as they carry Harley-Davidson badges, have access to internal systems,

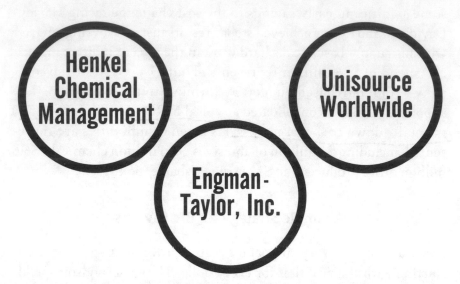

Figure 3.2 Harley-Davidson Indirect Materials Alliance

THE ALLIANCE

Henkel Chemical Management: chemical and gasses, facilities, raw materials used in maintenance, welding equipment, outside services

Engman-Taylor Inc., Germantown, Wisconsin: perishable tooling, abrasives, electrical, gauging, hardware for material handling equipment, plumbing, and power transmission

Unisource Worldwide: janitorial, office equipment and suppliers, packaging, safety items, gloves, and the like

---

and by becoming part of the Harley-Davidson organization, can study and improve processes as no "outside supplier" can.

Here's a typical example among hundreds of supplier-generated improvements. Harley-Davidson used to buy a particular cutting tool at $1.25 each. The supplier suggested substituting one that cost $1.50. A traditional purchasing response would have killed this apparently more expensive suggestion at the start, but the supplier noticed that the cheaper tool broke down every two hours and the engine component cell had been unable to meet production goals with too much downtime. By moving up to $1.50, the life of the tool—and machine up-time—tripled. Keal points to this simple shift as a change to "total life cycle costing versus individual piece price. If I had measured individual piece price alone, I would not have made the switch."

"With Half the Time"—Launch Strategy in the Supply Chain, New Blood Brings More New Ideas

Cost, quality, and manufacturing process issues are typically set in the product design stage. From concept through launch, development purchasing, headed by Greg J. Smith, one of three MIT grads hired by Tom Gelb during Harley's third transformation, is the functional part of purchasing linked directly to the product development process. Development purchasing resides within product development, in a new facility dedicated to new products. Smith has been with Harley-Davidson since 1996. Within two months of moving into the company he acquired his Road King Classic, black boots, and a leather jacket: "This is why you don't go into consulting, you can't have this kind of fun!" Smith started in a role called purchasing lead, an integral member of the platform management team. That experience, bringing a new Softail model from design to the market, made Harley-Davidson history.

A Multifunctional Strategy

Management needed to change the traditional engineering-run product development process used for years in most automotive and other vehicle producers, to something that was conducive to including other functions—engineering, manufacturing, purchasing, and marketing. And on each platform there is a sponsor from the functional leadership group, at the vice presidential level, to assure that the platform team would grow and learn organizationally, and understand the issues in the growth of the platform. Harley-Davidson's platform team concept is young, and it is achieving amazing results, especially in the area of the virtual build.

The Virtual Build

Designers have not totally abandoned older art to part methods, although given Boeing's experience in the 777 project, and software advances, it's not hard to imagine accelerated product design process reforms. Smith believes the physical mockup still represents a "good thing in our business," so the new development process still incorporates the physical mockup process, but Harley-Davidson is taking design and development to a new level. "We need early interaction to cut our product development time—we know the nature of our product is that it is stylized and cosmetic—and you can't throw 95 years of history out the window, so the company will strike a balance between virtual and physical mockup," says Smith. The product on the mockup floor is more advanced than clay, although it might start out in clay or other forms, but "styling is becoming more computer intense, using more computer based modeling."

It all started with a virtual build meeting held offsite in the summer of 1997. "We were studying the Softail, one of four platforms that we have today—this platform included half a dozen vehicles. Our designs were becoming more advanced, or more complex than the physical product—what we were modeling in there was a completely new vehicle—various systems and components, and how they interacted with each other." The modeling technology that Smith and his team were using was described as "still coming along," and the company was developing its competencies internally. "You can't fully assemble a vehicle yet," says Smith, "but you can take the model and add parts to the model as you go along. The CAD group also worked with assembly sequences, parts going together, something they learned, especially internally with suppliers, was important to understand."

Smith saw the virtual build as another opportunity to knit supplier relationships because today suppliers are invited to the physical builds where they work with the prototypes, and they also see how parts interact with the operator, as well as the packaging, and how the configuration fits into the vehicles. The Softail represented the first time this type of computer-driven method was used; other platforms have followed.

Organizationally, there have been big changes to support the new product development strategy. Smith's thirty-five development purchasing professionals, a group that includes a high percentage of engineers, is a balance of four technical areas: engineering, procurement, operations, and finance. The strategy for supply management had to include cross-pollination from people who understood product design and development, as well as commercial relationships with suppliers—"not three bids and cloud of dust." As the team works through development of new models, the idea is to understand the operations side of things, how parts are made—speed and feed and scrap and throughput. In the financial area, team members need to understand SG & A margins, the individual components of material and direct labor. Each team member has to excel in at least one of the four technical areas, and each must be able to "tread water in all four."

The department has grown since its beginnings in 1996, reflecting Harley's overall commitment to innovation and the speed, quality, and cost goals, from the beginning. The introduction of the model year 2000 bikes represented the first crop of models produced with this new organizational structure.

Virtual Commitment Made Real—Bricks and Mortar

The new product development center personifies the company's commitment to breakthrough design and technology advances that can be harnessed only through dynamic multifunctional interactions. The building housing the new product development center in Milwaukee is an open, airy, high-tech structure built to support col-

laborative product development. The site, which supports five manufacturing installations—two power train plants, the vehicle facility in
York, Pennsylvania, the vehicle assembly in Kansas City, and the
Tomahawk assembly—features lots of conference rooms and Pic-
turetel telecommunications systems. This building is also the source
of tooling designs, because even though it houses a product development center, with a road map for concurrent product and process
delivery methodology, speed requires simultaneous product and
tooling design.

One more layer of functional experts adds to the resources of the
development center—the category structure that purchasing engineers report up through—electrical and fuel systems, for example. In
other areas like castings and forgings, category engineers as well as
suppliers can be pulled into development projects happening on-site
as they are needed.

Harley-Davidson has taken an additional strategic giant step
toward innovating the way new products are designed and introduced, as well as fueling creativity in the products themselves. In the
fall of 1998 Harley linked up with the upstart motorcycle company
founded by forty-nine-year-old racer/entrepreneur Erik Buell.
Buell's bike company has become something of a laboratory for new
product and process excitement, as it drives to dominate markets previously held pretty much by prime European competitor Ducati.

The Buell Story, A Strategy of Growth and Speed, All Around

It was nice of Ducati to put on a race for us to win.

—Erik Buell, on receiving race results from a four-hour endurance
event in France in which fifty-two motorcycles competed, mostly
Ducati, from whom a Buell S1W stole the top position.

Erik Buell, the founder of Buell Motorcycle Company, now chairman
and chief technology officer, has a passion for racing and innovation
that has carried his young company—"Different in every sense"—
from a struggling upstart to a position as valued partner in the

Harley-Davidson transformation. Buell was integrated in February 1998, after producing their first hot bikes, and with the support of Harley-Davidson, and their eagerness to innovate, a new story is unfolding for this innovator in the sport performance bike market. Buell fits into Harley-Davidson's long-term growth strategy, particularly in the critical factor of attracting new, younger customers.

Buell's distinctive style and performance is what attracts them. Buells have been described in *Cycle World* as "a hot rod, the way it corners and goes into turns just puts a smile on your face." Chief Engineer John Oenick, the new owner of an X1, nicknamed "The hooligan bike" ("One of the top five bikes to be arrested on," said *Cycle World,* June 1999, somewhat tongue in cheek), uses what he learned from riding that machine to generate dramatic improvement in drivability. Shortly after joining Buell, John went to racing school on his Buell. "Our team is completely dedicated to understanding and living in the world of our customers," says Erik. Likewise, what engineers learned at the track was incorporated to improve the Cyclone M2, the bike that Buell describes as a light, potent American hot rod for the all-around rider. The Thunderbolt S3, a world-class sport tourer, is actually being raced on the track against Japanese superbikes in Europe—and wins. Buell employees love bikes, and their passion for these colorful, fast machines shines through, just as Soichiro Honda's early passion for racing carried him forward into founding an auto company, long after his racing days were over.

Innovation in Supply Chain and Manufacturing

The development purchasing strategy built around purchasing engineers is, in Buell's opinion, key to successfully growing his organization. "Since we buy everything—our suppliers are doing all the work—we need to know them well." Buell defines the absolute minimum in job skills to succeed in this very competitive market: "You need an engineering degree because you are like a designer, linking equipment back to the design, with the idea that development engineers must be capable of working with many different suppliers."

Choosing to Not "Do It All"

The only part of the manufacturing process that Buell has chosen to retain is body paint work and assembly; power trains are shipped in from Harley-Davidson thirty miles away. The transition out of some manufacturing processes grew as the company grew. "We used to make our own bodywork—fenders, tank, fairings—we used composites, engineered plastics, but as volumes grew, we could afford injection molding, we decided to phase that out and move people into other areas where the company is growing." But strategically, it made sense for Buell to retain one of the most difficult of manufacturing processes, paint.

At the beginning of each new project, a lead design engineer and a lead purchasing engineer come together, and they run the whole design from the original concept, starting after a request from marketing and styling, to conceptual designs. Their first task is, working with the bill of material breakdown, to put together preliminary data on various costs, on the cast tail section, for example. The union of these two technical experts is unique—one a "design guy" with good design and engineering skills, always thinking what is the optimum design for him, and the other, a purchasing pro advising on critical cost issues. They create the first B.O.M (bill of material) and cost of goods, start the overall timing to launch, start talking to subgroups, services, and so on, and pull the program into position for the start. From then on, it's a race against the clock.

The software they use to track and build product history is a simple desktop package. From there, they work the usual supplier project challenges.

Continuous Improvement Collaboration

Joining the new young bike company with Harley-Davidson's more established supply base and procurement organization produced some surprises. The continuous improvement program that Harley uses for working with suppliers, for example, was applied to Buell frames, three of which—the frame on the X1 Lighting, the M2 Cyclone, and the S3T—came out of the supplier's same manufacturing cell. Joe McDermond, an engineer and process lead for supplier continuous improvement in Harley-Davidson corporate purchasing, had been with Harley for five years and had spent six years at Honda of America's Anna engine plant in Ohio. There, Joe learned BP, the Honda continuous improvement approach, whose basic process elements are common to so many other classic quality management and quality control techniques derived from Shewhart, Deming, Juran, and Shainen.

The bike frame is a high-dollar (representing about 5–10 percent of total material value), high-quality subsystem that requires many different manufacturing processes—bending, welding, cutting, die changes, presses, and the like. A team composed of three employees from the supplier, Fleetguard Nelson in Wisconsin, three from Harley-Davidson, and three from Buell, came together to address a list of issues that one would expect from the traditional approach to parts processing of this type—schedules, quality, and cost savings.

Taking a Value Chain Approach

It was a good working opportunity to showcase strong, continuous improvement methods—mapping, waste analysis, batch vs. one-piece flow, kanban, floor space reduction—and to stay with a current supplier rather than begin alternative sourcing. Step one, mapping the process, took a month; step two, completing time studies and gathering critical shop floor data, preferably three months' history on various manufacturing indicators—downtime, rework, scrap, build quantities—produced a baseline against which the team could measure later process improvement proposals and actual changes, and allowed team members to better understand the flows.

Engineers wanted to understand and control material flow triggers and setup times. By running a calculation on batch and queue—almost every frame had previously gone through rework—the engineers learned how to change the process, to build the frame right, the first time, in a cell.

Team members spent extended periods in Wisconsin at the supplier plant, working side by side to eliminate rework and scrap along with in-process parts, to reduce the distance pieces traveled through the plant from up to two to three miles, down to a couple hundred yards. Team members continued to take a value chain perspective, as they pulled in Classic coatings, the supplier that paints the frame, and included them in the CI activity as well.

The results were stunning—the thirty-day lead time supply dropped to four days and the supplier delivery process was synchronized, à la Johnson Controls' elegant example of sequenced seat deliveries to auto assembly plants, to Buell's assembly line; cosmetic and inspected quality rose dramatically. Cost savings, what Buell's John Oenick had expected "would be a bonus," reduced the cost of frames by a whopping $70; savings in transfer cost were shared 50/50 between customer and supplier. "It was a big success for Buell," says Oenick, and a big factor in more closely knitting a new supply organization.

When a process improves, time, waste, delivery, and cost savings inevitably result. And when flawed processes are mapped, studied, and targeted, the inevitable result of focused continuous improvement efforts is a more robust process among very different partners in the enterprise.

Eighty Cubic Inches

Being there. You want to scream at the guy mowing his lawn to get a life, he has put a 1-inch cut in his wrist and he's bleeding his life away in the hot sun, hearing the hum of the wrong engine, housebound, cutting weeds and grass back to a brown, respectable stubble. You want to follow the Vietnam Vet down Route 128, his weathered American flag flapping in the prop wash, until the gas in the tanks goes to vapor. You want to coolly flick a glance at the next guy in the Nissan Sentra at the Route 97 traffic lights—"Hey, how're you doin?"—as all the Sunday drivers recoil from the noise. You want to find a formation and ride forever, up to the mountains and along the Gloucester Road that swings by Good Harbor Beach, back down by the quarries. You feel an urge to peel—at the intersection, to stand up in the stirrups, lift your clean white T-shirt, and flash your breasts at the mid-afternoon sun. Your thighs tingle as you chunk through all five gears—mouthing "Yeee-hah!," you swallow the road in big dry gulps. The heat index hits 90, a real July scorcher blasting waves of direct hit sunlight off the candy apple tank's chrome trim, as seven hundred pounds of iron slip into the turn, 1340 cc's away from heaven.

You wave to your neighbor, the orthopedic surgeon, as his eyes widen and he steps aside—your dog, newly chastened by the unbearable rumble, skitters down the steps, taking down four big flower pots in his rush to get to cover. What's Mom doing on that machine? Your husband's face lights up in an "I don't understand, but anything that makes you happy," smile as you try to speak the words that still don't convey the freedom, the escape of the road, the Harley experience.

Patricia E. Moody

Purchasing at Harley-Davidson is not about pieces and parts. It's about the passion to make a bike that deadens all previous motorcycle experience. My previous life scraping mud off my Parilla, my later years poking upright down the interstate on a BMW R-50—classy, no doubt, but boring—passes in the sheer blood rush of one-two-three acceleration—zero to sixty in seconds. It's a different approach to life, an American phenomenon that has not been duplicated by the competition.

Harley-Davidson is again under the gun to innovate and to flash multiple, diverse new products on a marketplace that cannot wait for the newest and hottest bike and accessory. It's a great position to be in, a complete reversal of the excess equipment position that the company found itself in during the eighties buyout. Innovation strategies for this American tradition, however, are emerging from different directions, and that makes this next transformation so exciting. From suppliers, Harley-Davidson expects fresh ideas and continuously improving quality. From Buell and its internal platform designers, the hope is that new processes, not just new product ideas, will drive new product introduction strategy to next generation concepts.

And Daimler/Chrysler, our first strategic reformation story, is also an American phenomenon, working on similar strategic issues. Coming from a highly engineered but trailing position into one of continued market innovation and speed, this company's strategy after the merger with Daimler can only become more powerful. Supply chain innovation, product and process design inroads, as well as continued cost initiatives will continue to make history for North American automotive operations.

Both companies, like most of the other Top Ten operations we have reviewed, continue to meet strategic challenges around their internal procurement systems. Strategically, most major steps forward have come from grit, determination, and raw intelligence, from new product introductions that create new markets, to manufacturing and supply chain innovation that lays out new paths. Unfortunately, procurement systems have not kept pace with other equally critical strategic initiatives, a failing that we hope either software companies or new idea generators will solve within the next three to five years.

4

LOOKING INWARD: WHAT'S WRONG WITH TRADITIONAL PURCHASING?

It's always about money.

WHAT'S WRONG with traditional purchasing? What organizational structures, or compensation schemes, or protocols is your organization still living with that prolong the hold that unresponsive practices have on your enterprise? Or worse, does your organization fail to recognize which practices fall into the category of traditional practices—habits, structures, and procedures that linger unseen and unquestioned from the era of all-powerful manufacturing housed in vertically integrated functional silos?

Bad practices will take your team nowhere. They will drain energy and responsiveness, leak hard-earned profits, and prevent you from capturing the gold from brilliant and well-intentioned new product development initiatives. Bad supply management practices will not lock in the winning suppliers that every enterprise aggressively competes for. Bad practices stunt growth and block evolution.

Even the Top Ten . . .

Each of our Top Ten companies has had to face repeated rounds of transformation, starting with manufacturing, then progressing to procurement and the entire extended enterprise. Honda's passion for engine design had to be supported with competitive manufacturing

"Bad Practices"

If your organization can answer yes to more than three of these ten traditional practices, your performance will be limited:

1. Highest level of purchasing executive is purchasing manager.

2. Buyer/planners earning less than one-third of highest purchasing pro.

3. Board of Directors includes VP Marketing, VP Finance, VP Manufacturing, and no representative of supply chain.

4. Strategic alliances guaranteed by written contracts.

5. New product development expertise centered in Engineering.

6. Planning systems in purchasing connected loosely to MRP/ERP and other manufacturing planning and execution software.

7. Supplier delivery schedules derived from faxed requirements.

8. Compensation of purchasing professionals based on cost data.

9. Point of consumption deliveries of certified materials represent 10 percent of receipts.

10. Product quality by commodity and part classification is the responsibility of manufacturing.

practices, globally, and the struggles to develop a supportive supply base, independent of the Japanese kieretsu, nearly exhausted the young company. IBM's transformation from a vertically integrated giant to an agile idea machine is well documented; along the way, the company shed noncore processes, including much of what had represented manufacturing. Harley-Davidson's acquisition by AMF, and its "last chance buy back" paved the way for two more lives—streamlining of manufacturing and excellence carried to the supply chain. Daimler/Chrysler has battled back from a "near-death" state, through multiple new product introductions and reemphasis on a healthy supply base, to become the lucky partner of auto giant Daimler; for Chrysler, the possibilities are unlimited.

Each of the Top Ten has perfected one or two glorious skills that carried them into high-performance areas. Their visionary leaders, executives like Iacocca, Gerstner, Richter, Tom Gelb and Vaughn Beals, Soichiro Honda and his partners, and Thomas Stallkamp, all understood and ran with a few very important corporate strengths. For each one of them, bad practices stood as potential barriers to realizing the force of those strengths. Within a plan and aggressive, proactive resources—supply teams, training, and systems money— their good intentions would have gone nowhere.

We believe that these charismatic leaders and their dedication to a few strategic strengths is what separates the Top Ten from companies mired in traditional or bad practices. The time required to create each of these reformation stories varies from fifty to twenty years, and even fewer; the plans, however, putting one step in front of another to tackle these huge challenges, called for immediate action. Chrysler, Harley, IBM, and even Honda were allowed little time to wander, discuss, and debate. We urge you to carefully review your own company and enterprise makeup, and start now to substitute intelligence and persistence for bad practices. It can only get better.

Ten Years Is *Now*

Within the next five to ten years your organization should have recognized, targeted, and transformed its genetic makeup so completely that your competition cannot recognize you. Software limitations, supply base challenges, personnel, systems, narrow focus—all these factors must change to smooth what for purchasing is its rite of passage.

But, as most North American challengers are learning, any change targeted for completion in five to ten years must have already been strategically developed and tactically deployed today for it to have impact in the very near future. Ten years is indeed the near future; what your organization is planning today must be achievable, understood, and resourced with energy, management focus, and the best professionals in the enterprise *now;* otherwise, your team is defeated before it has begun.

Learning to see in today's supply chain enterprise is about recognizing the tectonic shifts that have carried purchasing, an unwitting participant in its own rise, through periods of intense focus on outsourcing, computer systems, decentralization, cost cuts, and quality and new product challenges. Enlightened management will recognize the areas in which their enterprise needs to work.

Improve the Entire Supply Chain

Traditional organizations, for example, have only recently discovered the value of a strong and competitive supply base. Unfortunately, although they may have finally succeeded in mapping enterprisewide material flows, they fail to recognize the role customers must play in supplier development to raise the bar. Many traditional purchasing groups still do not believe in sharing training and other expert information resources with suppliers. When confronted with his impatient purchasing organization's budget for supplier development, one Midwest CEO denied their line item request with a "that's what we pay them for!" That may be true—suppliers are paid for more than delivery of materials—but suppliers still need help, and most of them cannot achieve very high performance levels by themselves.

Given that over twenty years of the Baldrige Award and many local and regional quality initiatives have still not established consistent results that guarantee an across-the-landscape, predictable Six Sigma performance standard, it is clear that the quality boost that small and medium-sized suppliers need can *only* come from one source, industry—not the government, not trade groups, not other suppliers, but original equipment producers, the only entity that is very close to true customer demands and trends. When industry managers finally understand the quality and delivery challenges they and their suppliers face from demanding customers and e-markets, the answer to the supplier development question becomes clear.

Management's goal in most companies remains, unfortunately, a contradiction in such a challenged environment. Managers are challenged to maintain the gains, to direct and decide, and to occupy a recognized spot in the orderly process of the design and delivery processes within the enterprise. In a bad practice environment, however, "making the month" is all that counts, or making payroll, or making up time. But truly, is that what the market demands of management now?

Juggling Today's Needs with Tomorrow's Vision

Every day, executives in Best Practice leaders like IBM, Flextronics, Whirlpool, and Honda must move their teams along strategic paths to tactical wins—they don't make it alone. These leaders are running to a plan that was set in motion years before the daily realities appeared, and they must meet market goals—like new product introductions, cost challenges, quality demands—as they continue to reach for bigger strategic objectives. It's a moment by moment juggling of corporate performance responsibilities with an eye to the future. How do the Best Practice winners live well in both worlds?

Learning to See

Recognition—learning to identify and communicate the value of a supply chain's contribution to the enterprise—is the biggest problem procurement professionals face today, their lack of understanding of their own strategic value. Most supply chain professionals are positioned too low in their companies. Understanding why they remain in the wrong place, with insufficient power and limited line of sight to impact enterprise performance, is key to making the changes that they must make *now* to succeed five or even ten years from now. Leadership must sharpen its vision to cover the width and depth of their supply base; they must see clearly where their weaknesses and strengths lie, and they must be clear about their strategic objectives.

Start with Mapping

Clarity comes from experience—looking around at benchmarks and looking inward to know your own enterprise. It also comes from simple mapping—sketching out, for example, where materials flow through the enterprise. Sometimes the managers closest to the challenge cannot see all the knots and loops in their own process, or they may not realize the extent of legacy problems—mostly timing delays—they have inherited from earlier procurement systems and procedures. That is why most continuous improvement techniques, from Honda BP, through Harley-Davidson's Continuous Improvement, and the Lean Enterprise Institute's Value Stream Mapping, start with a thorough mapping exercise. The process can take a few hours or many days, but the result of mapping flows is always a wealth of process detail, as well as eventual clarity around throughput.

Clarity—not simply being clear about objectives and tactics to deliver on goals but clarity of vision—will take purchasing executives from a chaotic landscape up to the clear, high winner's advantage. But it will be a steep and rocky climb, and many will not survive the trip.

Tectonic Shifts

During the sixties, three shifts shook North American manufacturing and started to move the institution, and some of its people, out of its mass-production mode. As manufacturing changed, so did the needs for traditional purchasing, but the buying function in most organizations missed the change and continued to structure and build systems to support a massive batch and queue production process.

The three shifts were:

1. Money: Big amounts of money started to flow through purchasing as the company structure shifted from vertical integration to outsourcing; manufacturing equipment and

expertise was replaced with outsourced, purchased processing and intelligence.

2. Power: Internal power shifted from 70 percent manufacturing power/30 percent purchasing to a ratio that reflected power—headcounts, for example—moving into areas outside manufacturing.

3. Intelligence: Skill sets shifted; process intelligence, for example, that would have resided inside a company's captive production organization became less useful as specific processes were subcontracted; these skills should have shifted out of manufacturing into procurement, where other sophisticated skills—contract management, for example—became even more valuable as companies struggled to became integration experts.

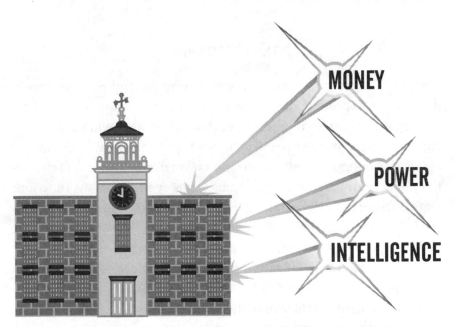

Figure 4.1 The Movement of Money, Power, and Intelligence from Inside the Brick Factory to a Galaxy of Big and Small Enterprises

The Remains of Vertical Integration

Fifty years ago the biggest and best producers were vertically integrated. US Steel owned transportation as well as processing and distribution centers, even the real estate the steel mills occupied. Paper mills owned not only pulp-producing and finishing plants but the forests and even the trucks and rail cars that delivered raw material to the pulpers. Whatever could be made and managed in-house was valued and guarded as a source of delivery and market advantage; organization structures and intelligence networks developed locally to support each individual facility. Decentralization was king; interplant rivalries fed class distinctions and win/lose competition that sometimes stimulated growth, and sometimes stunted innovation. Gradually, manufacturing began to assume power in organizations that had been dominated in the fifties by marketing or finance; the mysteries of the "black box" that was production were mainly curiosities among executives, few of whom passed through production on the way to higher positions.

The 70/30 Shift

It was a massive organization model that by the eighties had broken down; the footprint of the structure, however, remains, and purchasing organizations struggling to become enterprisewide masters of supply chain continue to be held by the traces of vertically integrated plants and decentralized organizations. Vertical integration left outlines of decentralized, stand-alone facilities even as various functions were outsourced or eliminated. Even in the sixties and seventies in the electronics industry, the trendsetting sector whose supply chain and new product development patterns leads other industries by at least ten years, decentralization clashed with a need to outsource for lower costs and specialized skills.

Manufacturing influence in decentralized organizations, in comparison with purchasing power and resources, typically ran in a 70/30 ratio. When purchasing held only 30 percent of a company's producing power, their primary skill was raw material acquisition to feed the machine; the most basic negotiation and planning skills prevailed. Paperwork drove a process that was much slower, and paced by transaction timing. In manufacturing, however, process and material expertise abounded. Companies like co-author Nelson's first employer, TRW, owned their own stamping facilities, their own press shops, machining departments, heat treatment, plating, forging, casting, and assembly plants. Procurement's 30 percent of the job was to make good purchases, yet for ten years there was no vice president of purchasing at TRW until the company lured one over from Ford, a slow transition. Still the company continued to struggle with information flows that were needed to change the process.

Outsourced Production, the "Killer Disconnect"

Twenty or thirty years into the shift to outsourcing, however, finds the amount of in-house manufactured material in most automotive and engine producers down to 10 percent or less, a demassification of the vertically integrated company into the supply base. Automotive producers have become kd (knock down) plants fed by three hundred to five hundred suppliers of raw materials, components, and complex assemblies. In the computer industry, we are approaching home assembly of custom components ordered over the Web, shipped directly from suppliers, with credit card payment to the OE (original equipment manufacturer) at the point of sale. It is puzzling, therefore, with such a clear shift of expertise to the supply base, why the 70/30 ratio continues to favor manufacturing expertise, power, and management attention all the way up to the boardroom. This is a killer disconnect.

Skill Set Shift

Purchasers not only control 70, 80, even 90 percent of the cost of a finished truck, for example, but they also manage a far more complicated and more sophisticated group of commodities than did their predecessors one generation back. On average, each new vehicle contains at least one dozen major electronic systems, that have either replaced mechanical assemblies, or augmented vehicle features.

The procurement skill sets required to manage this shift are not in place, and most traditional organizations are unclear on what skills they need to acquire. Yet as Thomas Stallkamp demonstrated when he moved from general management of parts divisions, over to purchasing, and then on to head up Chrysler, these horizontal shifts fuel new product and enterprise development.

Skill set gaps hurt more than individual purchasing professionals, however. Recently, a large engine producer in a highly decentralized company decided to optimize its steel purchases, looking to lock in best prices, at best quality levels, from a smaller list of the best suppliers. The company's in-house steel expert and her boss attended the kickoff meeting. The discussion uncovered a few shocking statistics; this producer's forty plants were buying from at least ten different mills and thirty-nine service centers, a list that the experts felt should be cut in half. Supplier consolidation would not only result in a flat-out 10 percent cost reduction, but inventory costs would also drop as in-transit, storage, and inspection stocks evaporated.

Further discussion revealed more material proliferation problems; not only were forty different plants ordering from thirty-nine different suppliers and distribution centers (D.Cs)—for a total steel buy of approximately $200 million—but supplier selections, quality, and technical specs varied enormously among customers. The obvious answer, consolidation, was a difficult challenge for this organization, which faces traditional purchasers every day.

Intelligence from Numbers

Let the data lead you.

> Dorian Shainen, Shewhart Award Winner quality guru

It is possible to miss the forest for the trees, as each consuming plant, and each distribution center, and even each supplier may at first glance appear to be performing to high levels of quality, delivery, and even cost. The aggregate picture, however, is much more the concern of strategic managers, and the total impact of the decentralization problem is tremendous.

Without solid data, even steel experts are helpless to find savings opportunities among such a proliferation of material flows. But this is indeed the way most purchasing is conducted today in North America, individually, hopefully aggressively, but in the dark, beyond the vision of even the most well-intentioned strategic manager. Although the Big Three have taken better control of this issue of consolidation and centralization of data, many other big producers are unaware of the size of their problem. Billions of dollars remain on the table, especially in global organizations with worldwide networks.

Data Analysis and Collection

Before purchasers can consolidate possible gains and rationalize separate data streams, they must adopt a disciplined and innovative approach to data collection and analysis. Supply managers in only a small percentage of North American companies have the kind of data and disciplined analysis they need to move forward. Once data has been found, it will tell you what must be done. An example from John Deere illustrates.

Deere buys thousands of different steel skus, each one of which is only slightly different in size or grade from others. Further, each small steel requirement, on its own, does not interest mills, which like to run to volumes and comfortable long runs. Commodity experts at Deere realized that if the data could be consolidated and optimized, purchasers could select sizes and grades, build them to the largest volumes possible, and become attractive to steel suppliers; sizable orders might even take the customer out of the distribution centers directly to the source. But what planners needed was data; their systems could not tell which steel mills throughout the world were current sources, which ones in Korea or Taiwan might come through, or what amounts and types of steel the company needed in Europe—decentralization left headquarters without the financials.

Clearly, the opportunities existed for consolidation—the same vehicles were being built worldwide, but without the numbers, no rational moves were open.

We believe this is not unusual; in fact, most global companies suffer from the same blind sight. In Deere's case, the savings potential was huge. Combined buys totaled over $1 billion—Deere's annual spend totals $200 million, plus the suppliers' $800 million. The possibility for even greater consolidation leverage existed, given good data, for Deere to follow in Honda's footsteps by buying raw steel for its suppliers.

But none of these intelligent solutions can be developed without good data. The answer is simple. Turn loose a few good people—the best are supply management graduates and/or engineers—with a laptop and airplane tickets, and they will follow the trail of usage and payables back to the numbers, and their data will lead to simple answers. Many sources provide pieces of the puzzle—receiving records, quality control data, production control usage. Analysts have been known to take a bill of material and blow it backward to find what system buys were being made, then to confirm amounts with buyers. Most times, the best information comes from suppliers, if they are willing to provide detailed missing numbers.

John Deere, one of our Top Ten supply chain organizations, has struggled to optimize a very decentralized organization in key areas like supplier development, sourcing, and logistics. Systems and data analysis have proven to be the most powerful aids to breaking down walls between localized networks of manufacturing and procurement, and Deere, a lover of innovation for over one hundred years, has been quick to draw on this strength.

The Glove Story

John Deere's fifteen North American plants purchased in one twelve-month period over 424 different skus of gloves, totaling $1.4 million of gloves; one estimate of the real sku requirement ranged from twenty to a maximum of twenty-five—for every different glove style, smaller volumes and unnecessary variety pumped up costs. It was a parts proliferation nightmare, although no one in production, or purchasing, knew the full extent of waste buried in this segment of the buy.

But a *student intern* logged out the answer by sleuthing what the competition was doing. Deere learned from one of its suppliers that the welding glove they sold to a competitor for $1.50 was cleaned after being used for welding, then sent out to the line for other uses—two applications for a $1.50 purchase price. But Deere's cheapest price for an all-leather, one-time-use glove cost $7.50 for a single use. Planners recognized that the custom solution glove at $7.50 was more than what the line actually needed, and its one-time use represented money thrown away every shift. By switching to a more sensible choice planners realized immediate savings of 35 percent out of the total $1.4 million spend for gloves alone! Three lessons arose from the glove story that allowed Deere to realize potential savings of $490,000—the value of data, the importance of analysis, the absolute necessity of consolidation of the buy, or rationalization of the purchasing spend, and standardization.

The same data and analysis problem existed in every other commodity—castings, forgings, plastics—but once the numbers were clear, the decisions became easy. Answers spring from the simplest analytical work. Taking 10 percent out of costs the first year is easy—it's the low-hanging fruit—but for years two, three, and four, after standardization and optimization of the supply chain, savings percentages typically drop to 3 to 6 percent, although the gains will continue to appear. In the glove story, a supplier provided key price data about a competitor that "opened the box," but most suppliers are not likely to help companies understand the issues unless a strategic alliance is in place guaranteeing the suppliers your business; most likely the data must be dug elsewhere.

Other savings opportunities abound in commodities like travel and entertainment, which were always neglected by traditional purchasers. When IBM wanted to understand and rationalize worldwide travel patterns and costs, they hired a vice president from United

Airlines who understood the air travel industry, and they also hired an operational vice president to cut the deals. Experts hired from Holiday Inn and Marriott further reduced travel costs. The gains were huge from digging data, analysis, and consolidation. Deere's analysis of comparative lodging expenditures over a three-year period led planners to negotiate cuts from $58 per night average to $38, simply from review and discussion of consolidated data.

Negotiating from clarity and strength, understanding where global expenditures lie, establishes a winning position in the enterprise. A smaller operation will also assume better network visibility if it can consolidate its requirements with a larger facility, an additional reason to knit small and medium-sized suppliers more tightly into the enterprise. It's a matter of thinking globally.

Toward a Stable and Competitive Supply Base

Not only do traditional purchasing groups fail to think and implement globally; they also miss the real value of supplier alliances. When we ask Fortune 500 supply managers what their number one goal is, most of them reply, "To buy the cheapest" or "To get the best quality"—almost none state that they are working first of all toward a stable and competitive supply base. Yet isn't this the absolute goal the markets demand?

"It's Theirs to Lose"

Traditional companies don't think strategically or globally, and they fail to develop good operating alliances with the best suppliers, the only route to implementation of those strategies. They seem to misunderstand the nature of the alliance and the supplier's investment in the process. The starting point is, of course, a relationship that tells the supplier that they "own" a piece of the business—"it's theirs to lose." As long as the supplier is doing the best job for the customer in R & D, cost, manufacturing process, and delivery, the total adds up to a stable and competitive supply base.

Daimler/Chrysler has turned around their reputation among suppliers; Chrysler worked hard to establish an exemplary reputation for reforming the way they dealt with their supply base. It has been a remarkable transition. Ten or fifteen years ago suppliers were scrambling to substitute other customers for Chrysler. Slowly, Chrysler purchasing, led by Thomas Stallkamp, established trust and reversed their leveraged power position—they needed suppliers to achieve innovation and quality goals. Chrysler purchasing redefined the entire customer/supplier relationship. Chrysler suppliers understand that the business is "theirs to lose"—their right of first refusal gives them the freedom to work at better processes, and more competitive pricing. If a competitor manages to outbid a Chrysler supplier for quality and cost, for example, and the original producer cannot meet the challenge, Chrysler has the right to move the business, even though the relationship is an alliance. Japanese producers may not run this type of agreement through a long legal document—in Japan there will be a purchase and sales agreement of only a few pages—but most North American companies use an actual contract that runs from six to sixty pages. The relationship challenge never goes away.

Human Assets

The second-biggest problem in traditional purchasing is people—unfortunately, we don't see the right caliber of professionals dedicated to areas that manage 70 percent of the spend. The organization chart of most decentralized companies shows a vice president of manufacturing at each plant, for example, but no equivalent vice president of purchasing or supply management. In fact, many of a plant's highest-level procurement managers are at lower levels than the suppliers with whom they work. Sometimes salesmen and buyers work at the same level; most business, therefore, is transactional, not very strategic, and even when the partners attempt to set a bigger course, they lack the clout to carry out their plans. This is a common North American problem that each of our Top Ten organizations has faced.

Allotment of executive positions proves this point. In one Southeast heavy equipment supplier we visited, finance, legal, sales, and marketing vice presidents were well represented, with 50 executives and 170 directors. Supply management or purchasing were not rep-resented in either ranking; they had no voice in the boardroom.

Systems, from Transactions to Realtime Flows

Gene Richter, former head of IBM procurement, also headed Hewlett-Packard purchasing. He knew, even though HP was the first to create a complete purchasing database called Promise, that the dis-connects caused by different "languages"—different standards, specs, sourcing processes—between procurement, particularly in new products and engineering, were hurting HP's ability to inno-vate. Back at Hewlett-Packard his dream became, therefore, "an engi-neer at every buyer's elbow." As simple as this database issue sounds, Richter's dream has taken many years to realize.

In the meantime, some companies use platform teams and new product groups to "bridge" noncommunicating systems, or to com-pensate for gaps between dis-integrated computers. And unfortu-nately, the systems environment is still a mix of legacy custom packages, innovative small solutions, and behemoths. The arguments over mainframe vs. mini's, laptops vs. networks, Unix vs. DOS, and McIntosh vs. IBM continue to plague impatient users. None of these hopeful combinations, however, will carry would-be winners into their next decade of enterprise growth.

Corporate purchasing systems should give planners more than tradi-tional transaction information—order quantities, shipping dates, sup-plier quality, and other operating data. Good systems will take users from the detail level up to strategic positions that improve their enter-prise visibility. But excellent systems summarize the right numbers from the right details that guide long-term planning and execution.

Data Rich/Information Poor

In decentralized organizations, the types of data that are scattered or missing will surprise even seasoned purchasing pros. At Deere, for example, planners needed more than six months of hard work to answer questions that had not been answered in many years: exactly how did the company purchase in one year, and what were total corporate headcounts, with a built-in variance of 10 percent either way. Gathering worldwide data to assimilate into simple answers was an exercise that had never before been attempted. Again, this data rich/information poor situation is typical for most North American corporations that think they are only in the game of building *things*. They misunderstand their mission.

Webspeed

Purchasing in any active market has to act like commodity trading on the Web. Transactions for information gathering, buys, tracking, and other supply base processes must be conducted with the multitasking speed that can only be offered by an integrated, closed-loop system as powerful as the ones gold and oil traders live with minute by minute. If your planners cannot operate with the same power and speed as brokers and traders, they are working blind. Market and customer requests in lean manufacturing can shift dramatically from minute to minute; purchasing's eye to the supply base must be as close to realtime as possible. Purchasing must shift its system from transactions to flows.

Manufacturers understand this well. For the past ten years they have "leaned down" their factories to expose the raw muscle they use to move raw material quickly through conversion processes. They have perfected lot sizes of one, cellular manufacturing, and quick changeovers to develop market-sensitive responsiveness. And they have introduced innovative logistics and order administration linkages, like those of Dell, LLBean, and EFTC, that put manufacturing if not physically at the foot of the consumer, at least continents closer. But the next step is for purchasing to assemble and manage the material flows so that manufacturing up-times are uninterrupted.

The best systems allow comparison among suppliers by plant, division, commodity, quality, and delivery. They offer interenterprise comparisons, along with at least three years' detailed and aggregated performance history. And most important, the best systems are *one* system. The buyer sitting at the engineer's elbow could just as well be looking over his shoulder at parallel data—there is no disconnect, no translation, and no conversion issue.

System Details Are Worth Examining

Many plants, particularly those in different countries, do not record price increases; others maintain careful records. But without a history, there is no starting point for comparisons or analysis of price increases, for example.

Ignorance Is Not Bliss

And factories that don't maintain this level of detail remain somewhat at the mercy of their supply base. One would expect a supplier who raised prices on aluminum castings, for instance, to raise prices equally all across their customer base. Not so! Many suppliers work multiple plants using a "divide and conquer" scheme, but your organization will never know when the systems don't provide timely exception reports by commodity or by supplier. Often, the smallest plants are the ones, like the one in the glove story earlier, that manage to control costs the best; suppliers frequently float just under bigger plants' radar. Comparisons require good data and analysis, both commodities that are not well sourced in traditional purchasing groups.

The Systems War

Who would have imagined that enterprise resource planning and its forerunner, manufacturing resource planning—the core of manufacturing information systems for the last three decades—would one day be viewed as the enemy of streamlined production?

—Doug Bartholomew*

*"Lean vs. ERP," *Industry Week*, July 19, 1999, p. 24.

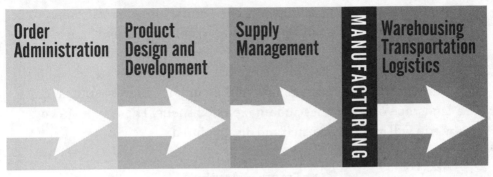

Figure 4.2 The Manufacturing Continuum

There is a war on, and supply management professionals cannot run from the battle because the borders that used to define so clearly the responsibility of manufacturing or information technology have blurred. Supply chain professionals are at the forefront of so many strategic decisions around new product development, pricing, and strategic sourcing that they cannot ignore the battle or wait to see who emerges as winner. Top Ten companies like John Deere, IBM, Harley-Davidson/Buell, and American Express have created breakthrough innovation in the midst of an ongoing systems war.

The Battlefield

The two contenders, along with various camp followers and cheerleaders, line up on opposite sides of a field littered with the remains of decades of misguided but ferocious forays into various crusades—operations research, quality, MRP, OPT, teams, concurrent engineering, ISO certification, partnering, more complex systems, and feel-good leadership. Manufacturing executives seem to be faced with only two seemingly opposed camps—the ERP systems forces and the lean, or flow, manufacturing contenders. Each side disputes the usefulness of the other, and each side will have had, by the time the war is over and they have moved on to the next one, a series of apparent successes. But where does this leave supply management?

The answer, even for Best Practice supply management, is on a dangerous and carefully planned passage through uncharted territory. Best Practice companies seem to "know" instinctively how to navigate the obstacles and gain an opportunistic position across the field. The bad practice groups, however, are less discriminating. They want to believe that their allegiance to one or the other cause will be rewarded with a safe passage, and so they unknowingly set out across a landscape of landmines and unexploded shells. Those that survive the trip will arrive exhausted and disappointed.

Fragrant Myths

Attack lean first, and then, once you've removed all the wasteful processes, you can standardize it with ERP.

–Stephen McMahon, Director of the Lean Manufacturing Business unit at Coleman Consulting

ERP is fast and powerful, and the natural successor to disconnected systems.
ERP will link your suppliers to your plant and improve delivery performance.

Excuse us—yes, eliminate the waste, but standardize good work processes with the well-known and endlessly documented discipline of standard work as practiced by Toyota, Honda, and dozens of other winners, including Maytag, Pella, Mercedes, Critikon, Wiremold, and Johnson and Johnson. Don't ever expect ERP to standardize anything, just as ISO 9000 and its cousins never produced Six Sigma quality.

Remember the geneology of ERP and the question becomes much clearer. ERP is the third-generation descendant of MRP, which was basically designed in the late 1960s at IBM by some group of brilliant computer systems pioneers. It was facilitated by the computer's newly created ability to take square roots, and it allowed the design of a cascading material structure protocol that created what we now call the heart of MRP and ERP: the bill of material. The bill of material module is simply a meat grinder, nothing more—it will chew up forecasts, customer orders, or projected capacity requirements and spit out bucketed requirements that can be used to order materials long-term or play with production requirements short-term.

The Answer Is Not ERP

ERP simply doesn't have the genetic makeup to solve simple factory flow problems such as those usually found at second, third, and fourth tier suppliers. It's not in the genes, and it was never designed to be a quick solution. Take out the waste, reveal the new, true process, and use the meat grinder to study long-term material and capacity requirements. Anything else is more complexity than most manufacturers want or need. Turn off the machine! Unplug the computers! Delete your passwords and hit the floor!

On the apparent conflict between ERP and lean manufacturing:

They can work together.

—Edward Frey, Vice President in Booz Allen Hamilton's
San Francisco office

Not so, not unless your company wants to sign up for another decade of high-pressure computer projects that like MRP end in mega-frustrations and huge consulting tabs, at the conclusion of which the exhausted and marginally successful project leaders are mercifully led out to the parking lot and shot. How much money do *you* have to spend on ERP and "integration" consulting at $5 thousand per day?

Don't get us wrong. We love consultants, and when co-author Moody did it for a living, it paid for her crystal, her condo, and her china. But Moody came from manufacturing, her whole family lived in manufacturing, and she loves the shop floor. And that's where the answers lie for the next five to ten years in everyone's supply base, not in the tightly knit pockets of code strung together as afterthoughts by the software houses and their handmaidens, big consulting.

Layer Good Systems on Perfect Process

Listen to masters of manufacturing like Tom Briatico at Maytag in Cleveland, Tennessee, who have survived the MRP wars and are now blazing new trails with innovation, energy, and intelligence in lean manufacturing initiatives that are beating the Toyotas at their own game. Then walk the floor, visit your suppliers, and map your own process, and the answer will be clear. It won't be ones and zeroes glowing on a blue screen of death; it will be clear even to the most inexperienced manufacturing consultant and would-be consultant—the only difference is a couple thousand dollars of billing rate. That simplicity beats the electronic solutions.

Terry Maruo, the father of Honda's BP kaizen methodology, told his acolytes, "Go to the floor. The answers won't be found in the boardroom. Go to the spot." And then, when you have visited every one of your suppliers and quietly observed their processes for a minimum of fifteen uninterrupted, record-breaking minutes, come back to us and we will send you into the next phase of your development, E-Man[SM]. But we ain't, as the coach said, there yet.

Cost Management: Understanding the Supplier's Process

Systems capabilities, powerful human assets, and management focus all connect to competitive cost management, not simply traditional cost cutting, or the Lopez approach to negotiation, but total cost management. But very few purchasing departments have excellent cost management, the ability to understand what materials, parts, and assemblies *should* cost, not the price at which they are. Valuable comparative data include a breakdown of every element of cost on each item purchased. Top Ten company Honda of America excels in this area, with John Deere coming up fast. To develop that rich database of strategic information, most plants must start at the beginning of the buying cycle, at the quote form. We have seen different plants operating with very different quote forms—some simple one-pagers, others elaborate descriptions that resembled complex contracts.

Even the Biggest System Starts with the Quote

The best building block for creating a strategically valuable cost system, one that becomes a decision tool, is a simple three-page quote sheet (see Fig. 4.3) that all suppliers must complete in great detail, describing every cost and every step in the processing of the part. If the part commodity is steel, the data will include, for example, the cost of the steel, the net and gross weights of stampings, as well as the quantity and reason for scrap. Added to material costs are setup charges, tooling costs, maintenance, and the like. The goal in cost management is proficiency in cost analysis that can be used well at the start of mass production, or before that, in development, design, and prototype stages of product management.

Because real savings lie in the development of new products, your strategic intent must be to develop good data and Best Practices with the fewest and the best suppliers, covering the fewest number of specifications for steel and other parts, to simplify the design, and to use existing skus wherever possible. Companies that do this well routinely lower the cost of new products by 20 to 30 percent. Clearly, new product savings cannot be realized or institutionalized without superior cost management resources and tools.

Cost Tables

Honda of America has the advantage of working with a relatively young supply management organization, so from its beginnings Honda managers have worked with good cost information. Their outstanding development and use of cost tables, as well as financial summits called *jicons*—open-book meets to share and review financial data—establish a benchmark that few North American organizations have approached. Honda purchasing engineers work hard with suppliers to develop complete cost tables because they need to understand as well as the supplier how costs are developed for the bidding process.

Stamping buyers, for example, must understand each cost breakdown in the purchase contract; when a customer pays the supplier $.10 each time an 1,800-ton press cycles, plus the cost of the raw steel for each hit and the amortized cost of the tooling and setup charges, the total part cost buildup clarifies the supplier process as well as quality and performance.

Part Quotation Form

New Part Number:
New Part Name:
Decision #:   Revision #:

Type of Quotation:
Plant Location:
Old Part Number:
Old Decision #:
Quote Currency:

Old Revision #:
Commodity Code:

Supplier Name:
Supplier Location:
Supplier Number:
Date Issued:
Quote Number:
Page:

Raw Material

Type / Grade	Supplier	Country of Origin	UOM (Unit Of Measure)	Usage measures input a	Usage measures output b	Usage measures loss a - b	Price/ UOM c	Input cost a x c	Scrap cost (a - b) x c	Scrap value d	New Total Matl. Cost (a x c) - d	Old Total Matl. Cost e	Cost Difference ((a x c) - d) - e
								-	-	-	-		-
								-	-	-	-		-
								-	-	-	-		-
								-	-	-	-		-
								-	-	-	-		-
								-	-	-	-		-
								-	-	-	-		-
								-	-	-	-		-

Subtotal A:

Process Costs

oper. #	Process Desc. (assy, paint, etc.)	Machine Size and Type (tonnage, etc.)	Burden Cost/hr. a	People # of People b	Labor Cost/person hr. c	Output Pcs. per hr. d	Scrap % e	New Total Proc. Cost a+(bxc)/d*(1-e)	Old Total Proc. Cost	Cost Difference
								-		-
								-		-
								-		-

Process cost (total of list on page 2) (Sub-total B addl)

Purchased Components

oper. #	Part Number	Part Description	Supplier	Country of Origin	Cost / Piece a	Pieces per Assembly b	New Total Comp. Cost a x b	Old Total Comp. Cost c	Cost Difference (a x b) - c
							-	-	-
							-	-	-
							-	-	-
							-	-	-

Subtotal B:

Process cost (total of list on page 2) (Sub-total C addl)

Acquisition Fee % on purchased parts: 0.00%   Acquisition Fee on purchased parts

Subtotal C:

Supplier Assumptions

Total Production Costs (A+B)	
S.G.A. & P% 0.00%	Manufacturing S.G.A. & P per piece
Subtotal C:	
Packaging (if not provided)	Type:
Transportation (if not provided)	Provider:

Est. Order Qty.
Pcs per Pack:
Part Weight:
FOB point:
Effective Date:
Local Content:
Lead Time

Comments:

Grand Total

Tool Cost

Issuer	Approval

Figure 4.3 Detailed Supplier Quote Form Capturing All Cost Drivers

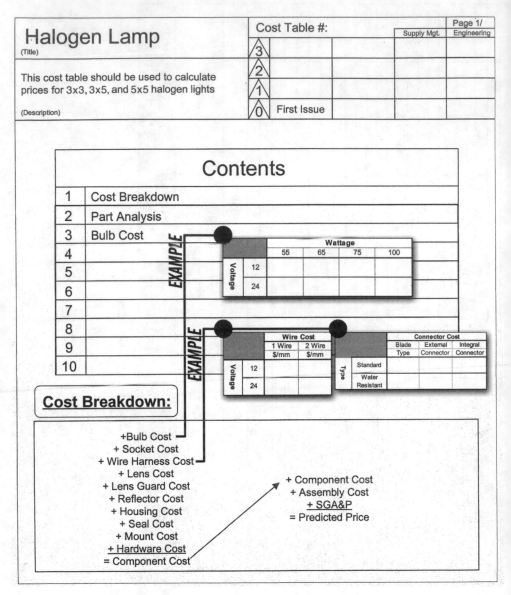

Figure 4.4 Cost Table

Bad performance or uneven quality should jump out of cost buildup data, and the details must be there to allow planners to go below the surface and search out root cause. Basically, suppliers in the stamping business are raw material converters and processors; they process and deliver from a customer's raw expenditures. Best

Practice customers like Honda, Chrysler, and John Deere are contracting for the specialty conversion processes, but most North American purchasers operate as if they were buying finished product only. They do not recognize that in the flow of material from raw through conversion into the hands of customers, the processing, not just raw material price, is key to arriving at competitive prices.

Profits, Not Leverage

Cost buildup expertise, especially in the hands of excellent purchasing engineers working with high-level systems, is a competitive advantage well understood by all Japanese producers. The strategic intent is not, however, to squeeze suppliers out of a healthy profit, because world-class producers want all members of their enterprise team to be profitable and strong. But they must be sure that suppliers are charging the right fees for processing and conversion work.

The best cost managers in purchasing therefore understand more than the technology of steel conversion; they also become very knowledgeable about suppliers' internal financials—their SG & A, labor costs, turnover, logistics issues, and even the level of activity of work for other customers—because all these factors determine suppliers' profitability picture. There is more to purchasing planning than spending money. The more an OE knows about its suppliers, the better the relationship.

No Respect

The most frequently heard complaint about purchasing's position in most traditional organizations is that they "get no respect." Although this complaint has assumed the noise level of a low, constant whine, most Best Practice organizations still struggle with the issues of how to compensate, recognize, and position purchasing professionals so that they can do the best possible job for the enterprise. But the Top Ten companies have made tremendous and very visible gains.

Why would top management choose to support engineering, or

sales and marketing, rather than purchasing, when 80 to 90 percent of the cost of their product is controlled by supply management? When purchasing gets pushed into lower levels of an organization and ignored, results are limited to mediocre, tactical performance in strategic areas.

Political networks and vested interests are tough to dislodge, but there is always truth in the numbers. Twenty years ago Xerox might have been included in a list of best U.S. manufacturers, although the beginnings of its downfall were already in place. Japanese competition, namely, Canon, was set to eat Xerox's lunch, and management never looked, never asked, never even suspected. Production and supply chain had been marketed to outside experts by Xerox management; the real strength they needed was not there. The company was doomed by its blindness. A few studied reviews of competitors' costs would doubtless have clarified their vision, but they chose to stay inside and market their way out of the hole. It didn't work for Briggs and Stratton, for U. S. TV producers, for many North American small electronics producers, and it didn't work for Xerox.

One approach to bringing the "truth in numbers" message forward is through computer assists. Indeed, an approach that three of our Top Ten winners, most remarkably IBM and American Express, have taken is to beef up computer systems.

Big Bucks Solutions?

Companies that want to improve purchasing power with good systems, like 1999 *Purchasing* magazine's Medal of Excellence winner IBM, use systems to improve positioning. Sometimes big installations provide the answers, and sometimes companies lever off-the-shelf packages with remarkable, quick results.

Interestingly, the cost of most SAP installations can be justified by the large purchased dollar savings that come from the added information availability. A $350 million system, for example, could be the biggest single purchase ever made by a producer, but the software recovers the cost of lost, or unconsolidated savings opportunities.

Three outstanding companies—Monsanto, IBM, and Bristol Meyers Squibb—have paid for major system investments by centralizing purchasing operations and information. We estimate that companies will find savings of at least 15 to 30 percent through smart system implementation and other Best Practice changes. The exact percentage of savings is unknown; we feel the only way a producer can begin to realize the potential is to start managing costs.

For example, in the nondirect material area, IBM has saved for the fourth year in a row a cost reduction percentage that has grown from 6.5 to 11.5 percent, and they continue to surprise themselves. Total spend on nontraditional purchases and indirect materials and services represents for most North American producers low-hanging fruit—an amazingly easy source of billions of dollars of savings that can be realized only with better data. John Deere, for example, buys $2 billion of indirect materials; a 26 percent savings of the total calculates to over $520 million, cash that can easily be freed up for working capital or new product development.

Users and Givers

Some producers use their gains to enrich teams' capabilities and speed growth and learning. Some companies, however, simply pour savings back into further cost reductions, never realizing the burst of energy that comes from redeployment of resources into new initiatives; they are the ones who believe they can *save* their way to success. We don't recommend this approach for anything but sheer survival, and we predict that few organizations, GM among them, which dedicate their hard-won savings to no-growth initiatives will survive to realize their limited gains; it's a no-win exercise.

Users, or takers, don't give back. They fail to see the opportunities for the entire profession that are created when leaders distinguish themselves by setting examples of creativity, courage, and resourcefulness. In Chapter 7, we profile managers like Harley-Davidson's Garry Berryman, IBM's Gene Richter, SmithKline Beecham's Willie Deese, and other seasoned professionals who give back to their professions even as they live their dreams. In-house MBA programs in supply management, fellowships and internships, supply management journals, and research projects, as well as off-site conferences and guest speakers all move teams forward as they raise the bar for entire industries. In the automotive world, Honda and Chrysler have set new standards for employee development and professional advancement as their individual performance skills have been enriched.

We believe, however, that most traditional organizations still fall into the "taker" category; and when the profession stagnates, as purchasing has for the past fifty years, while manufacturing and engineering have steadily advanced, making up for lost time takes enormous energy and overtime. We think the best approach is enlightened self-interest—invest in practices such as conferences, development, training, systems, and people that your best competitor would kill to own.

5

FUTUREWORLD

Five hundred years ago there were no submarines or Gattling guns, anti-
septics, refrigeration, rivets, safe sex, big theaters with twenty movies
playing simultaneously, Esperanto (thousands of languages was fine,
and so was Latin), public libraries, gas lamps, railroads,
washing machines, Kleenex, typewriters.
One hundred years ago we did not have electronic fuel injection, rayon,
penicillin, Post-it notes, electric vacuum cleaners, face-lifts.
Fifty years ago we did not have color TV, wireless telephones, manned
satellites, nuclear power stations, heart transplants, the Bullet Train,
minicomputers, Velcro, birth control pills, stereo lithography,
cat scans, the Global Positioning System.
Five years ago we did not have digital cameras, the Palm Pilot, on-line
grocery delivery from electronic warehouses, Pokemon, teenage
cosmetic surgery centers.

A Bridge to Lean Manufacturing and Beyond

The future of supply chain and the short-term future of manufacturing is completely dependent on procurement professionals' understanding and building a bridge from traditional practices to lean

manufacturing, and then another span beyond, to e-manufacturing^{SM} by the year 2020.

Unfortunately, lean manufacturing is practiced in no more than 15 percent of North American companies, and there are misunderstandings about its application, although Jim Womack's important book *Lean Thinking* established the concepts and cited good, familiar examples—Wiremold, Lantech, Critikon, Pratt & Whitney, and others. Since *Lean Thinking* appeared five years ago, more companies have focused on lean manufacturing, sometimes as they redesigned procurement, and sometimes not. Few have successfully taken lean principles to all the suppliers in their chain, although many big companies have worked hard to institute good lean practices at a few spots in the enterprise.

Since that book appeared, these same companies have struggled to find ways to root lean manufacturing in their organization and spread it beyond the shop walls into white-collar areas like order administration and engineering, as well as supplier and logistics operations. The well-known pioneers notwithstanding—Wiremold and Lanatech—most companies have not enjoyed deep or wide success.

The Lean Manufacturing Challenge

What is lean manufacturing and how can supply management facilitate or absorb its principles to build a bridge from customer to supplier operations, as well as a bridge into the future of the supply chain?

For the answer to these questions, practitioners must recall the origins of lean manufacturing—Henry Ford's production system, Taiichi Ohno's work at Toyota (of which Just in Time was only a piece), the quality crusades, MRP, and the interest in agility and flexibility.

Ford

Take just one idea—a little idea in itself—an idea that anyone might have had, but which fell to me to develop—that of making

a small, strong, simple automobile, to make it cheaply, and pay
high wages in its making.

–Henry Ford*

Henry Ford created great new ways of producing vehicles that allowed his company to leapfrog an army of small competitors by making volume his killer app. Volume translated to command of the market—in time to produce a vehicle. But Ford worried about the whole process; he was an entrepreneur whose technical interest was matched by his passion in other areas—labor management, material planning, and product breakthroughs. Just twenty years after founding his corporation, Ford workers succeeded in producing vehicles *eighty-one hours—about three days*—after receipt of iron ore. Seventy years later we are still puzzling over Toyota's three-day car concept, although pieces of the process have been cut away and generally speeded up.

The methods that Ford pioneered to produce *his* three-day car are similar to what we now call lean manufacturing, namely, standardization of work process, employee involvement, zero quality defects, and secured supply sources. Today the words he would use to describe his operations might be slightly different, but basically Ford was aiming for simplicity and speed, and in his era, he met those goals so well that even Toyota's Taiichi Ohno is reputed to have credited Ford with inspiration for the Toyota production system.[†]

Ford's first moving assembly line was built in 1913, the same year that pay was set at $5.00 a day, a breakthrough that Ford himself cites as proof of the value of his approach to production, and his belief that workers should be able to buy the products they built! Five years later the company had accumulated enough capital and market to build what became the world's largest industrial complex for its time, the River Rouge plant.

By June 1924, just sixteen years after the first of its type of vehicles was produced, Ford could claim its ten millionth unit; two years

---

*Today and Tomorrow, Henry Ford (in collaboration with Samuel Crowther), Portland, OR: Productivity Press, 1988, p. 2.
†Ibid.

later the number had risen to thirteen million. Ford had what seemed to be an open-ended market and the seemingly unbounded opportunity to perfect his methods and improve vehicle technologies.

By the time Ford's market had stumbled and shifted away from the Model A, the automotive industry had gone global. Ohno and others who sought inspiration from the U.S. giants took the vertical integration idea into a different form, outsourcing to kieretsu in Japan and less tightly knit supply chains in North America. This change was pivotal in the development of the purchasing profession, because buyers were forced to go outside, learn the landscape of their supply base, and become extremely skilled at "feeding the machine."

One by one the supply chain learned new approaches to faster, higher-quality production—just-in-time, kan ban, quality methods, root cause, problem solving, Design of Experiments, material requirements planning, and finally simplicity under the labels of agility, flexibility, and lean. By the year 2020, manufacturing and procurement should have incorporated all these improved production techniques so that inventory moves smoothly in and out of processing operations controlled and directed by very smart systems.

Here is where the disconnect now appears—the systems to manage material and processing flows are in design and should be usable within the next twenty years. Lean manufacturing will have been augmented with smart pull systems to track and direct material flows through very flexible processing operations, in response to market requirements. That's the overall goal that all progressive manufacturing professionals understand and are working toward, a goal that is making its way through the tiers of the supply chain. It is procurement's role to make the transition to lean, and progressively to move advanced systems through the chain.

From Pull to Lean to Smart Systems

Supply base professionals are still working with outdated systems, while manufacturing—about fifteen years ahead—has unplugged or limited the use of MRP/ERP software solutions.

Let's start with what lean manufacturing really is and what it requires of the supply chain. It is important to be clear about how supply management can facilitate the principles of lean; without supply chain support, lean practices are limited to disconnected pockets of good process, episodic forays into blitzkrieg kaizen activity.*

Lean manufacturing works on pull—the pull created by actual customer orders as they flow through a process, all the way back to raw and component materials. It's a complete reversal of the top-down planning that MRP systems tried to satisfy.

Pull systems typically operate on elements well described in the Toyota Production System, including kanban, a container or card system that triggers replenishment from upstream operations; the 5's to cleanse and maintain the process; one-piece flow and lot size of one vs. MRP batch and queue, assembly line mode. High-quality performance becomes critical to maintaining flow, whether the material is moving from one cell to another in an assembly line, or farther back, from a third to a second tier supplier, for example.

As many practitioners have discovered, pure JIT, or very lean operations, leaves little room for recovery under catastrophic conditions—disruptions like strikes, fires, and earthquakes require superhuman recovery efforts. Despite the glorious story of Honda's recovery from the WEK fire and Toyota's similar, but more expensive recovery from its brakes supplier fire, companies like GM and others have suffered seemingly irreplaceable losses from recovery supply chain disruptions. Purchasing becomes the most important link in the chain when accidents happen, and all the linkages that should have been established with suppliers must be relied on. When there is no inventory in the pipeline, and suppliers can respond quickly or alternate sources are found, lean or JIT systems work.

However, in a less than perfect world, supply chain pros plan for disruptions. Honda's final assembly plants are fed by an off-site warehouse that contains no more than twenty-four hours of certain parts and assemblies—just enough to keep lines running and to stage materials for smooth deliveries. The cost of line-down situations has

*See *The Kaizen Blitz*, Laraia, Moody and Hall, John Wiley and Sons, 1999.

been estimated at approximately $26,000 per minute, and since most line-down situations last well over that period, purchasing is designed to intervene immediately.

Understanding what the end customer wants is key to building a system that can pull the entire value stream through many operations and many tiers of procurement. By value stream mapping—the quickest way to learn this approach is to do it, starting with *Learning to See*, published by the Lean Enterprise Institute in Brookline, Massachusetts—lean managers can identify and remove waste at all levels of the enterprise.*

Learning to think lean means taking lean concepts to suppliers, because with the outsourcing shift, they generally represent 70 to 80 percent of the value of a product. Though good supplier development is not cheap, neither is reengineering manufacturing processes. Co-author Nelson projects a three-to-one payback on investments in supplier engineers.

Effective supplier development is more than getting cost reductions for a particular part; it means helping suppliers take costs out of their processes. Effective supplier development looks at all of a supplier's processes to eliminate waste and gain improvements in quality, delivery, cycle time, and costs. This requires supplier integration at the earliest stages of new product development; shared information, resources, and savings; and dedicated resources to identify and close performance gaps. In other words, it requires the manufacturer to treat suppliers as if they were a department within the company.

For supplier development—whether the goal is kaizen activities, or new product design, or new process layout—there must be a committed collaboration between customer and supplier, approached with mutual benefit in mind. This may require the supplier development engineer to spend weeks or months in the supplier's factory, working with management and production floor personnel. And it may require both parties to open their books to the other.

---

*For the other basics of lean—poke yoke, takt time, standardized work, set-up reduction, and the visual factory, we recommend *The Kaizen Blitz* (Laraia, Moody and Hall, John Wiley and Sons, 1999) and *The Visual Factory* (Michel Grief, Productivity Press, 1991), or *Visual Systems* (Gwen Galsworth, Amacom, 1997).

No two companies approach supplier development exactly the same way. However, the most effective projects follow the same general twelve steps to supplier performance.

Examples of successes derived from application of these steps abound. A tillage equipment supplier whose sales to Deere totaled about $6 million per year—more than half their total revenues—was having trouble with on-time delivery. As a result three factories could not meet dealer orders. Repeated attempts to work with the supplier failed. Finally, purchasing told the supplier that Deere would send no new quotes until it made significant improvements.

That worked. The supplier agreed to a supplier development project. First, the customer and supplier spent two days mapping the supplier's manufacturing processes. They found

- a purchase-order-to-shipment time of 62 days
- only 86 high-volume parts compared with 597 low-volume parts
- material acquisition problems due to low-volume production needs on 597 parts
- lack of materials standardization
- non–value added job processes
- lack of parts tracking

The findings prompted targeting a handful of areas for particular emphasis: steel code consolidation, part cancellation due to obsolescence, and delivery tracing and development of manufacturing cells to reduce operation cycle time. The results were impressive, including:

- On-time delivery to the supplier's primary customer rose to 96.5 percent.
- Past-due orders to all customers fell to $31,607 from $261,702.
- Part numbers fell by 10 percent.
- Manufacturing cells increased productivity.
- The supplier installed a system to monitor performance of their own suppliers.
- The supplier realized their most profitable year since 1990.

The key to extending lean manufacturing in this case was mapping, and human factors—trust, cooperation, and communications. The cus-

Manufacturer and Supplier

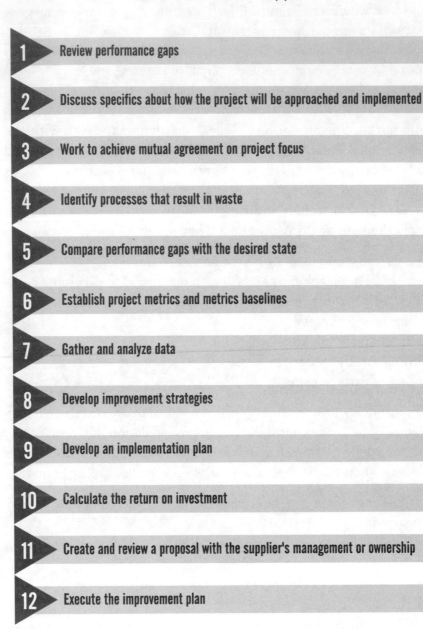

1 Review performance gaps

2 Discuss specifics about how the project will be approached and implemented

3 Work to achieve mutual agreement on project focus

4 Identify processes that result in waste

5 Compare performance gaps with the desired state

6 Establish project metrics and metrics baselines

7 Gather and analyze data

8 Develop improvement strategies

9 Develop an implementation plan

10 Calculate the return on investment

11 Create and review a proposal with the supplier's management or ownership

12 Execute the improvement plan

Figure 5.1 Twelve Steps to Supplier Performance*

*R. Dave Nelson, "Manufacturing Solutions," *Automotive Engineering International*, August 1999, p. 68.

tomer built a bridge between customer and supplier operations that should continue to carry improvements deeper into the supply chain.

From Supplier Development to the Boardroom

IBM's transformation is a glimpse into the future of procurement for large, winning enterprises. In the midst of the redesign of IBM's corporate structure, Chairman Gerstner consolidated the corporate spend under a single chief procurement officer, "the god of the spend." Internally, it was a "shock to the system."

IBM's board of directors actually delegated the entire outside spend to Gene Richter—in writing. Richter in turn empowered his financial gurus to pay bills and his commodity teams to go buy commodities, a loss of power for the general managers who would have previously held the purse strings. In terms of what purchasing will look like in the future, this model seems very possible—a policy literally derived from the board of directors, directed specifically to one high-level officer with total responsibility for the spend in a complex, many tiered organization. It's a shift away from concern with purchasing policies and procedures, right into the corporate boardroom, and it's a clear indication, we think, of how spending authority will be realized not too far into the future.

Other examples of boardroom intervention in run-of-the-mill operations exist. Certainly Thomas Stallkamp's move into purchasing from the parts supplier divisions, and then into the role of president, highlighted the financial accountability and influence of procurement. Both Stallkamp and Richter understood how to communicate the strategic importance of purchasing in a way that board members understood and seized as an opportunity.

Creating the Seamless Process Requires Structural Changes

The future will be one of integration brought about primarily by systems and the Web, but also formed by powerful enterprise leaders, like Stallkamp and Richter. The implication is that the career life of a tactical purchasing person, someone who expedites and sends out releases, is limited, because expediting as a recognizable activity will have evaporated in the future. Evidence of this shift is clear at successful companies like Honda and John Deere, where expediting has been broken out and separated from the rest of the purchasing organization to become more of a full-time tactical supplier interface position. Those jobs will dry up.

Blurred Boundaries

Responsibility for supply management, including world-class logistics and production planning, will include everything that touches materials and material processing; all these previously siloed functions will dovetail into a single seamless process, if done right. The supply manager's role—from working new models and developing the supplier, all the strategic initiatives, including cost and quality issues, both of which are strategic—will become to decide on the source and to cost and order parts on a large blanket order. The next step would have been for a tactical purchasing person to release orders against a manufacturing plan, and to expedite the parts in or out as the schedule changes. Transportation clerks and expediters would then bring in the orders.

But in five to ten years, tactical purchasing jobs will have been eliminated by the production planning process—a pull system. Once a supplier has been selected, production planning will schedule all materials in, and with little or no expediting materials will move through the ultimate world-class logistics system.

Integrating and improving logistics beyond simply the movement of materials, will be a breakthrough for 99 percent of purchasing organizations, because most global organizations do not have an overall logistics strategy or perspective. Inbound freight is therefore typically the responsibility of the purchasing department because buyers traditionally are concerned with expediting material inbound. Buyers have over the years tried to lose this headache by shifting the logistics responsibility to suppliers, typically for a 5 percent fee; the problem with this approach is that they are almost never buying high-level service performance.

Suppliers are less concerned about cost and time-effective timing of deliveries, so that most shipments arrive LTL (less than truckload). There is enormous variation in pricing of freight charges, especially for materials arriving from overseas. Good logistics pros understand the schedules as well as the business plan, and they buy what makes the most sense, "round robins" or "milk runs," for example. These improvement approaches sharply reduce inventories, the difference being inbound shipments of one or two days' inventory at maximum, compared with days or weeks under traditional practice.

Inbound

By the year 2020, purchasing professionals doing logistics will have the opportunity to ship via "fast freight" ships—water jet propulsion systems that should reduce time between continents to under four days. Air freight will lose its attractiveness for a higher proportion of shipments.

Outbound

Obviously, outbound material will be improved as well—about 3 percent of most companies' total spend. This is another area currently managed by the wrong department. When inbound and outbound freight are handled separately, outbound is controlled by marketing, and time, rather than cost, becomes the main objective.

Many factories have a small group of planners with no purchasing experience who buy outbound freight service. With no purchasing oversight, they tend to be influenced by trucking companies, and they perform a somewhat narrow slice of the strategic material movement function. Beyond being simply tactical, their processes do not include consolidation, forward planning, optimization with inbound freight.

Proof of this are the empty trucks passing each other on the highway; the opportunities are enormous, billions of dollars of savings each year in North America alone. But this consolidation problem will be solved with good systems and smart data analysis; suppliers own some of the data, production owns a few pieces, and sales and marketing and dealers own other pieces of the freight bill.

The current enterprise, at all levels, has no way to tally all the logistics charges for comparison against better routes. However, at John Deere, out of the total spend of $8 billion in 1999, $866 million, or 11 percent, is dedicated to material movement—inbound, outbound, premium charges, customs, and freight forwarding. The word *logistics* causes many purchasing pros to run for cover, but the short-term opportunity for even 5 percent savings at Deere amounts to about $50 million. Over the next five to ten years the winning enterprise will have taken all the cost benefits and moved to the level of intelligent system simulation—best way—for freight movement.

What happens when no one owns logistics? No one pays attention, and material accumulates in trailers used as warehouses—at a cost of $1,000 per month per trailer. Or the material stays in constant motion—inventory on wheels—with the added expense of freight charges tacked onto in-process cash investment.

John Deere managers have seen this logistics transformation first-hand. At one point seventeen different entities received and paid a variety of freight bills—from suppliers, or the consuming plant, and occasional freight consolidators (all of which were LTL). Further, payment was made by an equal number of systems—the supplier and the customer, as well as third parties. The work was handled by so many different areas that it belonged to nobody: it was no one's job. Until a new manager, a Toyota veteran, came on the scene, and consolidated and rationalized the material movement supply base, just as most companies consolidated and rationalized material suppliers ten or twenty years ago.

For lack of consolidation of control, logistics will remain an expensive orphan to the enterprise—farmed out to purchasing, manufacturing, marketing, sales, even customers. But by 2010, winning enterprises will have consolidated their gains and moved to high-tech transportation options at less expense than traditional methods. With little analysis, opportunities continued to appear, including outbound round robins that by delivering to dealers once per week saved almost half a million dollars per year at John Deere, more than enough to justify the creation of a director of logistics.

With a director of logistics and thirty-eight professionals, plus a system, for a total cost of approximately $4 million, management expects Deere to realize at least 10 percent in savings, or a 10 percent payback of $50 million, an easy decision. The compensation package to get started with a director totals approximately $250,000, and the expectation is that this new group will realize $86 million in savings over a three-year period.

Smart Logistics

Deere continues to search for opportunities by benchmarking the best, starting with Don Schneider, of Green Bay, Wisconsin, owner of Schneider Trucking, a $3 billion per year business that specializes in "smartness." Schneider's glass-walled headquarters resembles a commodity exchange as planners intent on computer screens—each dedicated to specific customers, like Walmart, Sears, and Maytag—continuously run optimization routines, planning and replanning the best way to organize truckloads in each cubic foot.

The optimization goal is always to create truckloads, and the result for their customers is an automatic 20 to 30 percent savings, the actual difference between truckloads and LTL. It's the cheapest way to get materials over the highway. Schneider extends his smart approach to material movement into the trucks; each driver is a business in itself. Schneider truckers are problem solvers on wheels, knowledgeable about products and business issues, as well as moving product from here to there.

Centralizing and consolidating logistics has cured another inherited vertical integration problem—the fact that management often doesn't hear the possibilities when they are presented. When outbound, inbound, and separate plants come together under a single management structure, management listens because of savings and the opportunities for lean, improved operations. Operationally, the director of worldwide logistics now reports into the worldwide supply management director.

Interestingly, in the world of professional associations, purchasing and supply chain is represented by fifty thousand members in the National Association of Purchasing Management (NAPM). But logistics professionals, members of the Council of Logistics Management (CLM), who number only ten thousand, hold significant power over the direction the profession is taking. The makeup of the CLM, however, tends to be higher-level executives, and interests go in a more strategic direction.

Logistics and Lean

Twenty years from now material movement—cost and times—will determine competitive enterprise advantage over production performance, quality, and purchased price advantage—long settled issues. The Web will have made every home and every downtown depot a material movement center. Producers with foresight will prepare for the upheaval by investing brains and systems in logistics simulation and data analysis, well in advance of 2020.

Just-in-time methods have their limits, as does lean manufacturing. Too much attention to peeling away all excess inventory is like an athlete with no fat cells, no reserves for sudden bursts of energy required in any race. Japanese manufacturers struggle with the inventory/no inventory balance, and smart logistics systems are one way to build freedom into the lean equation, without investing in hard physical assets. The objective is to be able to call on people and shipping methods whenever they are required, before suppliers even know of the problem. Smart logistics can provide that forward capability.

Again, by 2020, we will have seen the end of fragmented functions throwing designs, problems, and costs "over the wall." Manufacturing and purchasing in the 2020 enterprise will more resemble manufacturing and purchasing that Honda developed in the late 1980s.

Lean Purchasing

Dedicated suppliers, part of the enterprise team responsible for all strategic parts, will achieve tremendous gains. The National Institute for Supply Chain Integration, (NISCI), a North American–headquartered organization of top producers, including IBM, Daimler/

Chrysler, Hewlett-Packard, and Trane, is developing an image of the supply chain of the future, which doesn't resemble today's producer-plus-tier one configuration.

Rather, NISCI thinkers expect that the entire supply chain will be more visible, more clearly defined than today, and producers will clearly see, track, and manage suppliers deep in the chain at the tier three and four levels. Mike Doyle, NISCI CEO, predicts that there will be more intra-enterprise collaboration on problems such as new model development. "We think we are doing well getting tier one involved. Well, twenty years from now we will be working with several layers of the chain simultaneously, because lean is not just the level of inventory between you and your supplier, but the level of inventory over many links, or the absence of inventory."

Doyle believes the path to leanness will lead through simulation and other advanced thinking tools. Models taken from other industries, like aircraft and air traffic control, will be important to develop a realtime economic value-added model between several links in a supply chain. The idea is to highlight the difference in the supply chain between a snapshot and a movie, and to see what happens when one element changes. Current experiments centered on linkage—how to link these businesses literally in real time—are the answer.

Although the systems piece may seem "kind of obvious," says Doyle, "I don't know anybody that has them wired in that tightly—the closest would be the pc market. Those guys have fast turnaround, their whole product life cycle is one year." For now, "if we think of an extremely well-run factory with integrated, well-designed systems—we may call it ERP—the goal is to give the appearance, through the system of tier two and three and even four suppliers working right in the producer's factory, an image of distributed manufacturing only partially completed by companies like Dell, EFTC, and others. In fact, a manufacturing schedule should not look any different to a supplier than it would to an internal department, a weakness in all enterprise systems today."

CEO Doyle predicts that the same gigantic leaps will carry supply chains forward around engineering systems. Without (paper) prints, for example, engineers on both sides of the supply chain will simultaneously access designs. The work becomes virtual, especially around new products, and the benefits will cascade throughout the enterprise as drawings and other design decisions can be simultaneously transferred to suppliers.

From the prints, immediate transfer of tooling requirements, for example, will enable machine tool producers to finalize designs as products move quickly in parallel through the cycle. Although this approach is now partially implemented with certain big producers like Chrysler and Boeing, systems will simplify and make valuable information available to even smaller producers throughout the supply chain. The side benefit, of course, is that dedicated suppliers will be even more tightly linked to their big customers.

The Cost of Technology

Boeing's 777 innovation, and Chrysler new product platform work, have all enabled the giant breakthroughs that take an idea through modeling of the part, into electronic drawings that can be quickly transferred back and forth for multiple iterations. When this type of idea flow is affordable and consistently used up and down the supply chain, the process will resemble today's Internet access that is enabled for virtually the cost of a pc itself (the system becomes a giveaway to entice purchasers to sign up for multiservice packages).

Cifunsa

Generally accepted applications like Catia and ProE will become more easily transmitted as bandwidth capacities increase. Globally, design communications are extremely important for suppliers like Cifunsa in Saltillo, Mexico, that must communicate with many different customers around the world in different languages and time zones. Good systems are not only the answer for Cifunsa; they become the competitive advantage that sells their superior process quality and costs abroad. They make the buy decision easy for big customers.

Cifunsa's factory is the best casting plant that co-author Nelson has seen, but as a certified supplier to John Deere and the Big Three, they have taken systems to a new, advanced level. From one room filled with various suites of software, they can talk with their customers as they transfer most of their design work "over the wire." The process is actually more cost-effective than sending prints back and forth by air, especially on items as complicated as engine blocks. And it is ten times speedier than telephone communications with paper transfers.

Next to Cifunsa's software lab is a room filled with plastic prototype equipment, a modeling room par excellence that is also tied in to ProE and Catia. Deere's choice of this company as a casting supplier is at this time unique—not only are they the best and the least expensive in the world, but their factory processes are better than anything purchasing executives have seen in Japanese plants.

Foundries used to be hot, messy, smelly places where art and science mixed to produce sometimes perfect castings. Honda's foundry in Anna, Ohio, however, is nearly perfect. Environmentally its odorless, high open spaces resemble a laboratory more than a furnace. Few workers are required to run the operation, and quality is exceptionally high. Cifunsa's foundry, however, is cleaner than the Anna plant, a proven new level of global excellence.

Global Excellence

The lesson to be gained from the Cifunsa experience is that consistently high and predictably perfect performance levels are not beyond current capabilities; by the year 2020, they will be globally available in many industries. A public company, Cifunsa started as a family-owned operation mostly known for engine blocks, although they also produce castings. Success has grown this company to total sales of approximately $450 million, 85 percent of which is generated through twenty-nine part numbers. Cifunsa produces approximately two million blocks per year for its worldwide automotive customer base, at a high level of quality that has earned the company Ford's Q1 award, General Motors's Spear 1 and Supplier of the Year, and Chrysler's Pentastar.

As the engine business has changed technically, the supplier has moved forward as well, and so it is not difficult for North American assemblers to place an order, work through design issues, and go to full production from thousands of miles away, with the safe expectation that they will receive a set standard of quality.

Order transfers from Deere to Mexico pass through a contracted EDI third-party supplier; this service will be superseded, of course, by better Web-based communications, which we expect will be ready within the next five years; security, speed, and bandwidth barriers will have been solved and data transfers will be transparent to customers and suppliers alike.

The Cifunsa/Deere experience may seem innovative and progressive to some companies, but most big producers have moved into second- and third-generation purchasing and design systems, and within ten years their small and medium-sized suppliers will all be on line, in parallel. Cifunsa's attention to software extends to an innovative program to track training, developed in-house, that monitors training for three to five thousand employees, a focus that has continued to yield high-quality results.

Our view to the future is that remote, distributed, perfect manufacturing will evolve on the Internet, but data transfers must and will become more secure for intellectual property and bandwidth challenges.

Human Challenges Beyond Lean and Systems

As predictable standards of quality go global, and smart logistics and pull systems make superior products available globally, the role of purchasing professionals will also "get smarter." Essentially, the skills currently valued in purchasing will be turned "on their heads."

From being heavily weighted on the tactical side, with little time left for market research and analysis—procurement's most important work—the professional will flip to most intelligent, forward-looking work around specific commodities and processes. Just as very successful marketing and sales professionals today understand their market trends risks, so will purchasing pros.

Figure 5.2 Procurement Flips from Tactical to Strategic

In the future the supply chain manager will be a superior sleuth, capable of running down data showing the percentage of his buy compared with total production for his country, his region, and the world. He will also be able to name the manufacturers and their relative production costs, usage patterns, volumes, types of material, grades, sizes, and colors.

For plastic injection molded parts, for example, the purchaser must develop a mental database of worldwide resin producers—where resin plants are located for particular specifications. Location in this and many other commodities is, of course, the prime determinant of logistics costs. There may be thousands of suppliers of polypropylene, but if the buy is for a highly engineered thermal plastic resin, one that is very heat resistant, for example, there will be fewer locations and greater competitive demand for the superior producers. This is a strategic, rather than tactical skill that must take priority over other operating issues; in twenty years the job will be 90 percent strategic. Buys will be made not simply for parts built inside customer plants but for suppliers that do processing using consigned materials. The new professional will represent and understand the entire global plastics supply chain.

Targeted Sourcing

The second necessary piece of strategic expert information management is an understanding of technologies, like plastic conversion technology worldwide, including all the variations on molding processes, as well as the rankings of the best players in cost and quality. With a few thousand dollars, anyone anywhere can set up a molding machine in their garage and hang a sign out that says Superior Custom Molding, but as Nypro has proved many times, there is an enormous range of capabilities and quality among producers, and the only way to do research in the new manufacturing era is to visit and benchmark the best plants.

Within about five years, however, on-line quality certifications around various suppliers will be as available as on-line parts catalogs. The next generation of parts producers who dedicate technology and production resources to specific industries and even specific components—like dashboards for automotive—will come on-line shortly after Web-based certification protocols are in place. We call this targeted sourcing, and we think preparation for this phase starts with good people and systems. The market will accomplish the rest.

Matt Lofton, a veteran LTV steel salesman—the best salesman in the world!—is a model for the new purchasing professional. Lofton brokered the steel buy for Honda of America's first assembly plants, when Japanese steel was not enough, and when quality issues presented a challenge for North American suppliers. Matt's ability to understand the customer's growth plans and quality requirements, which were at that time considerably higher than Detroit's, enabled the transplant to bring more production to the United States, despite US Steel's uncooperative stance. Lofton became the solutions broker, and he set the standard not just for deep and wide market knowledge but for high-level industry management and growth that produced strategic results. Lofton's reputation precedes him in all negotiations, as well as simple inquiries.

This is now a challenging transition. In many large companies, like IBM and Allied Signal, the movement of strategic information out of plants into a central "brain trust" has been painful but necessary. Local focus prevented any single operating officer from assembling the entire picture puzzle; within five years, however, systems will have eliminated the local expertise advantage, and the resulting information consolidation will save producers billions of dollars.

Marketing strategy, for example, does not originate at fifty different producing plants; it's a top-down effort rolled out to various producers; supply management will undergo this same transformation. Supply chain sourcing knowledge has to be organized centrally—not necessarily in a single headquarters at the top of the mountain, but in a single controlling management system, a virtual focal point.

Consortia

Where small and medium-sized suppliers have limited leverage, they will team up with other buyers in consortia. Although this is certainly not a new idea, the nature of consortia will change dramatically as supply chains will come together, forming larger entities, all Internet-enabled.

Things could get nasty. Imagine a top auto producer who has reached a sourcing agreement with a very high-quality, high-delivery plant in Mexico. Could that customer have suppliers about which no one else knows? It is indeed every producer's goal, and for years this type of secrecy has not been possible. If a supplier is world-class, it's a challenge for customers to keep a secret and keep other customers away. In electronics, for example, where certain components are commodities, it may be difficult to reserve enough capacity to render suppliers captive, but with some enterprises ten years out, that is exactly what will happen. It's all part of the enterprise-against-enterprise competitive challenge.

In the resin business, for example, although all good buyers will be expert at plastics technology, and certain technical information will be commonly available, there will be certain protected converters who do some things so well that the enterprise will find a way to lock them in from a data management perspective. It's a competitive advantage that companies will kill to preserve over the life of the new products, at minimum.

Transactional Superiority

North America enjoys transactional superiority, a communications infrastructure facilitated by on-line business and multiple communications systems not equaled by regions with less mature infrastructures. At times, we may want to "turn off the bubble machine"—unplug the answering system, the fax, the cell phones, and messagers and pagers, but these intrusive devices have proven to be a North American business advantage. Transaction speed kills slows businesses, and it bypasses slower decision making like certain Asian and European models.

Lock-in

One approach to guaranteed lock-in is complete or partial ownership of suppliers. Honda of America created suppliers in North America as it geared down parts shipments into the United States from Japan. The landed costs and logistics speed made sense. Toyota has taken the same approach to building a captive, high-performing enterprise, as have some German companies that take an ownership interest. When customers have an equity relationship, their influence extends into how and where the supplier technology will be used. In the United States the relationship between Delphi and Visteon seemed to point, before the spin-off, to some innovative ownership arrangement. Market dynamics may be hard to predict, but customers will continue to work at protecting enterprise interests through information, technology, and physical ownership control.

Not all businesses are big enough to demand a supplier's full production, but where a strategic gap exists in the enterprise "talent pool," the Japanese approach to creating a good supplier will be more common ten or twenty years from now. Government restrictions, currency shifts, and other previously impenetrable barriers will not interfere with winning enterprises as they lock up their resources, especially around proprietary, differentiating technologies.

At John Deere, for example, electronics that manage crop data through on-board computers are a strategic advantage; the device that collects data, predicts crop yield for each square foot of soil, and recommends fertilizer mixes, depth of planting, and weed control—every factor that can be programmed to optimize yield—is a key strategic factor that must be protected. Deere's answer has been to buy an electronics business, a big step beyond partnering. Other electronic management ideas in process, such as when to change engine oil, warnings on wheel bearing wear, and so forth, will be available to Deere as soon as its electronics producer can create the solutions, and the solutions apply to anything that moves.

Flexibility

The reality of the three-day car, the two-hour VCR, and the one-shift engine drives producers to design for faster production of short lead time items. Instant communication inevitably speeds up, but it is effective only with good relationship builders. These professionals carry a specific skill set that centers on understanding the business acquisition model. For companies closely joined at the hip, it will not be unusual or difficult to perform regular jicon-type reviews on a rolling three-year plan of twenty-seven different business planning items. The objective is to understand your partner's every need—whether there should be, for example, a new plant in the works or a new process. The relationship builder will be positioned to monitor and encourage an outward focus, because as general managers of manufacturing outside their own operations, they will have the ability to source success.

Will the relationship builders be engineers? Most of them will be, and as business development managers, they will need strong analytical as well as human and systems skills. These professionals run the Big Board, watchers and monitors of your business's health, around the world. Currency fluctuations are no mystery, as is the magic of business valuation.

The Center for Advanced Research Future Study Project

NAPM'S Center for Advanced Purchasing Studies in Tempe, Arizona, runs many benchmark and research programs around purchasing issues. A 1998 study looked at trends that concern the profession five and ten years into the future.* Results focused in on eighteen purchasing and supply executive issues.

Outstanding among the eighteen issue findings are these points:

1. Strategic Sourcing—Supplier assessment and evaluation will become more detailed and precise. One focus group response put it this way: "I'm not thinking of a supplier evaluation as a static document where you use the same formula for every supplier, but you measure the supplier based on where you're at with that particular supplier and that particular relationship."
2. Demand-Pull Purchasing—Here the findings were alarming: "Most firms were skeptical that demand-pull systems would ever be fully implemented." Tell that to Toyota!

Respondents seemed to feel that the main challenge would be getting systems across key supply chain members to work together. Although we well understand the technology of Internet applications in demand pull, we also recognize the inevitable power, the pull, that larger enterprises will use in twenty years or fewer to crush competing chains. These giants will not be limited by open-ended, common access to the Web; they will have designed and installed "armored tanks"—locked systems—no one sees in, and no one gets out, to absolutely guarantee security and competitive advantage. No one said the next twenty years in purchasing would be pretty or pleasant!

A Stretch Vision

Two Robinson sisters, Merle, age five, and Ruth, age three, sat on the porch of their farmhouse at the top of a hill, in southern Indiana's Pike County, overlooking a country road. The road was unpaved, although it was at that time, 1910, a main highway, so you could hear a wagon or even a person approaching on foot, even from a distance. One hundred years before this hill had

---

*CAPS Research Study, "The Future of Purchasing and Supply, A Five- and Ten-Year Forecast," Center for Advanced Purchasing Studies, Tempe, Arizona, 1998.

overlooked a swamp, but the land had been dredged, and soon neat patterns of barns, chicken coops, farmhouses, and orchards spotted the reclaimed landscape. Merle, the middle child, saw dust swirls down on the flats; soon she heard a loud sputtering rumble, and she called to her oldest sister, Hazel, age seven, who was behind the barn, "Get out here quick! There's something coming!" Hazel had heard this before, and she was busy with the chickens. "Just a minute," she called back, as she lay down her bucket and closed the gate.

Things didn't usually move all that fast in Indiana, and by the time Hazel rounded the porch, the thing, the auto-mo-bile, had sputtered past the farm and was on the downhill run to Evansville, leaving nothing but a few puffs as proof of its passing. Hazel was surprised that the Thing had gone by so everlastin' fast, and she thought, "Surely I could have seen it if I had just hurried."

Two days later, another opportunity to witness the Thing presented itself. This time, all three girls were ready, as not one, but two vehicles passed each other going in opposite directions on the state road. The girls were awestruck on the porch. "Do you suppose we will ever see that again in our lifetime?" Hazel wondered aloud.

–Dave Nelson (whose mother, Hazel Robinson Nelson, was tending the chickens when the first auto-mo-bile passed by)

We want to provide a stretch vision—at a minimum of ten or fifteen years out, twenty if possible (in *The Technology Machine: How Manufacturing Will Work in the Year 2020*, we skipped to the year 2020 because we knew a shorter span did not contain enough movement—not enough contrast from here to there). Some of the visions of work life that far out are shocking, and some may not seem technologically possible, but many of them are already here. Then we want to illuminate the gap between then and now so that forward thinkers can develop the first steps to get from here to there.

Why twenty years? Japanese companies are known to have 50-, 100-, 500-, and even 1,000-year plans in place. The exercise of envisioning the supply chain five years out is wasted energy, especially for such a complex, organic entity, because five years is just about now. Ten to fifteen years represents nearly one generation of leadership, but it's still not enough. Twenty years is the absolute minimum stretch of the imagination that we must use to describe the future, at least most of the landmarks. At that point, although we may not understand all the vehicles that will take us there, the new crop of professionals will have learned to speak a different language, and their work structures will be less inherited and more of their own thinking. They will absorb technologies, and the successful ones will use these new tools to bridge what may appear to many to be an uncrossable chasm.

A handful of recognizable changes clustered around technology, people, and organizations bear watching, although they move so quickly that it will be hard for the eye to capture more than a sense of their direction and speed. The main issues around our stretch vision for the new procurement professional lie in these areas:

1. E-commerce and Son of E-commerce

For many years in traditional organizations, e-commerce stood for EDI (electronic data interchange), an awkward data transfer protocol for certain limited applications, the first step beyond faxes and MRP systems; now, in many but not all companies, e-commerce means simply buying off the Web. But obviously e-business technology will be developed well beyond simple data protocols, even five years from today. More important than the mechanics that technologically enable mega-speed and access, however—the bits and bytes—are the implications and impact for procurement and the organizational structure twenty years out.

New technologies, just as the telephone and cell phone did in their time, have the potential to redesign the supply chain, but only the potential. Technology unleashed, or technology unharnessed without enlightened, progressive management and trained professionals, will not improve and solidify supply chain gains. Too many examples of unrealized technological potential exist—nuclear power, for example. One can certainly not argue the physics of the breakthrough, but as Chernobyl and Three Mile Island demonstrated, our human structures are incomplete and not strong enough, or perhaps not flexible enough, to manage the accidents and inevitable fallout. The supply chain, like every other technology user, needs to develop management leaders who understand and move technology forward to fit their applications. Unfortunately, few of those technology management leaders work today in the supply chain area.

2. Procurement Systems

Systems continue to be a severe disappointment. In the purchasing and supply chain area, good simple solutions are hard to come by. They are either expensive or too complex—or both—but solutions to systems needs for the 2020 winning enterprise will be completed within the next five to ten years. Other industry sectors like aerospace and banking, as well as commodity trading, contain completed elements from which purchasing software gurus must "shamelessly copy," and until the systems that drive the enterprise are as dynamic and technologically advanced as the products they service, progress will be halting and overly expensive. Unfortunately, although we have seen brilliant examples of innovative systems solutions in companies like John Deere, IBM, American Express, and Flextronics, these solutions were developed primarily in-house, independently of big software houses with whom the responsibility and the power to provide answers truly lies. We'd like to tell procurement managers which packages to buy for various solutions, but that is not possible yet, and if we were to take the risk of naming names, users might well be disappointed.

3. New Boundaries

By the year 2020, the line between supply chain and manufacturing responsibility will have blurred and reconfigured so that manufacturing—actually, processing of material—will fall into the domain of procurement. This is a reversal of generally accepted top-down hierarchies. The redefinition of all procurement positions therefore yields fewer, but broader, technically more proficient positions. The new profile should inevitably rise higher in the organization as it covers material movement inbound, processing, and outbound finished product.

The additional challenge lying in wait between the current state and the 2020 future state is that another clear boundary will also blur and cause anyone with shortsighted vision to want to reconsider their position. The boundary between planning and execution will dissolve as realtime, on-line process control systems and simulation take over. Leading-edge examples in industry illustrate.

Nypro, a high-tech Massachusetts plastics producer, is headed by engineer Gordon Lankton, who raised the company from the ranks of dozens of competitive, low-tech plastics commodity producers into the heights of world-class, super-high-quality producers. The traditional approach to plastics manufacturing would require much monitoring and tweaking to reach very high-quality levels. But Lankton believes in the value of realtime process control, and he has invested in automated equipment and much training and development for employees to guarantee that level of performance. Inside Nypro's refurbished carpet mill in Clinton, Massachusetts, you will not see walls papered with static process control charts or many visible statements recounting historic performance levels, because the purpose of a realtime in-line process control system is to set a direction, like an air traffic controller, and from very frequent readings and feedback make appropriate adjustments "on the fly."

Procurement on the Fly

That same on the fly approach to buying and moving materials is what purchasing needs to develop and adapt; the methods will come from other industries, like oil, brokerage, plastics, and steel. And the implications for redefinition of purchasing and manufacturing (or processing) roles are ironic because, as Mike Doyle, CEO of Chicago's NISCI, observes, "This is ironic—it jumps off the page—

we in purchasing have worked all our lives to get control of the buy, to stop the 'buy-around,' and to force people in the plant, on the floor, to quit doing the buyer's job and let the buyers do it." There has been a long struggle between purchasing and manufacturing to set boundaries.

But life comes full circle. After fighting to raise the level of professionalism in procurement by pushing for new levels of accredited professional training and performance, followed by the application of so many effective techniques that we have come to love so well, like outsourcing, supplier development, and quality metrics, professionals are facing another juncture. Purchasing and manufacturing job functions will be combined, and once again, manufacturing will inevitably be involved in the buy, and not just for new products or special projects. *You just can't keep a good manufacturing guy down! Or out!*

It's a Horseshoe-Shaped Journey

NISCI's Doyle thinks one explanation appears from the idea behind this common saying, "the space between sanity and insanity is small, but the distance is large." Doyle believes the twenty-year journey will take the shape of a horseshoe; the distance to go from one end is long, but the space looking across from one end to another is small. If we could find a bungee big enough to propel all the travelers over the chasm—the shortest distance from one tip of the horseshoe to the other—that would be a mistake, because as we travel the more roundabout route, we inevitably solve problems, change institutions, pick up new fellow journeyers, and solidify cultural intelligence. The idea is to lose bad habits and develop new organizational structures as we move; some of them will be unrecognizable to many of us now, but they will make their appearance as the market and the journey require it.

Look at what we have glibly labeled "manufacturing," for example. "What we have been saying to ourselves is that we need to be more open. It was always OK for manufacturing to do the buying, if they had been trained and if they were sensitive to the professional tech-

Figure 5.3 The Horseshoe-Shaped Journey of Transformation.

niques they might have used. And if they could have had the vision or the view of the whole, instead of just one piece." Doyle is referring to the common problem of shortsightedness: "With technology now we can go anywhere in the world, and we can see the whole."

When procurement has brought in different disciplines, the ability to see has improved immensely. For the new professional with fine background and preparation, it is foolish to believe that rotations in and out of purchasing don't work. We have come, as Doyle would say, "on a very long journey from one end of the horseshoe to very close to where we started, but we could not have jumped that gap. Too much got done by making the journey the long way." Certain traditional tasks, for example, were eliminated—the tasks associated with sales and purchasing have been eliminated.

Elimination of Jobs

"In my future there is no such thing as a buyer or sales guy. What were they, anyway? They are the communication mode and the channel. The buyer/seller channel can be replaced by technology—we won't need people to serve as technology boosters." It's an amazing transition that proves again how we seem to come full circle. Their replacements, however, will be technical experts and relationship builders par excellence.

Henry Ford Is the New Profile, an Entrepreneurial Model

At the turn of the ninteenth century, when Henry Ford pulled together the resources and manpower to organize his company, he was heavily involved in production, as well as design, sales, marketing, even purchasing. The level of his involvement was so great that a corporate myth tells the story of how, when he died, workers had to hurry to retrieve the steel orders for next month's vehicles out of his vest pocket! Although this is just a corporate myth, bits of organizational wisdom illustrate widely held beliefs and practices, and Ford exemplified this entrepreneurial approach to starting, running, and never quite handing off a complex operation.

Doyle links this fable to his belief that some of the best professional buyers in the world are entrepreneurs. Who could not say that Michael Dell is not a first-class purchasing buyer? Entrepreneurial professionals like Dell would not call themselves buyers, but "if you look at their handiwork, by gosh they have done it well."

"It is a flaw of the purchasing community," warns Doyle, "to think we know everything. We have still to make the whole business process simple enough—because great buying is great entrepreneurship. An entrepreneur has to think about everything, and a buyer should be thinking about everything—of course they don't."

Data Central

In the year 2020, there will be a small cadre of people in large companies who are supreme managers of data and keepers of the information so critical to enterprise survival. The other dimension relates to the depth of the supply chain, the information technology that must be wired up to take control deeper and wider. Technology has always advanced in stops and starts as pure innovation is transformed into practical applications that become commercial successes.

Doyle compares the innovation that must take place behind the supply chain to other big technology steps—Wilbur and Orville Wright's airplane, for instance. He believes that although the basic enabling technologies to simulate or design a high-performance supply chain have been created, their practical applications are not available. He cites other high-technology sectors, like the aircraft industry.

Although Orville and Wilbur "invented" the airplane and flew it for a few minutes at Kittyhawk, it wasn't until 1920 that commercial aviation became practical and profitable. Three ideas came together to make the aerospace industry possible:

1. retractable landing gear
2. movable wing flaps
3. the variable pitch prop

Without these three inventions, commercial aviation would not have happened, because aviation wasn't practical with no flaps to slow down an aircraft for a safe landing. Retractable landing gear solved the problem of how to carry and land with great weight aboard. And the variable pitch prop enabled big planes and big cargos.

Supply chain technology is at the same impasse as early aviation, "searching for the proper compliments of inventions," says Doyle. "We are searching. And of course at NISCI that's what we are trying to do. One of these days between now and 2020, maybe well before, these inventions will have occurred. The Internet may well be one of them—but we are not done yet—we still need an invention to measure total economic value across the supply chain, and we need a way to understand supply chain architecture."

Learning from Wall Street

Technically, these are big challenges, but Doyle adds one more everlasting challenge, finding a solution to the trust/culture/people processes, working in a complex chain. Without a common scorecard, like Wall Street's giant score-keeping machine, human behavior even in the supply chain is free to wander.

No one on Wall Street has the opportunity to ignore the market, and the same overriding concerns for good metrics should rule the supply chain—as soon as we decide how to measure it! Supply chain metrics are now focused on micromeasures, without a single, simple tool that evaluates an entire chain's performance profitability, speed, or even innovation.

Expectations for corporations differ from industry to industry. Intel may be expected to earn a 40 percent return, while Ford would be pleased to show a 5 percent return, and part of the difference in returns comes from capital needs going forward. Further complicating the formula, the behavior of Wall Street is linked to emotion and whim—with a bad public relations event, a stock dives, despite its calculated value.

Doyle believes that the brightest brains value and track corporate performance on Wall Street; by 2020 the sharpest minds will be focused on supply chain performance and valuation. "We are close, and by 2020, some enterprises will in fact operate just like Wall Street," with their own Big Board, their own valuations and formula for calculating expected returns and speed, and their own "fund managers." Unfortunately, the gap between chains for companies that perform like Blue Chips and the others struggling to find a position "will be almost uncloseable, because companies will have traveled around the horseshoe—they will be over there waving at us—you can see them, but you can't get there."

NISCI, according to Robert W. Hall, founder of the Association for Manufacturing Excellence, is in its own transition, always working on the edge of uncertainty and chaos. It's an uncomfortable feeling, "tiptoeing on the leading edge of what's knowable. You can't tiptoe there without falling off either way, but you can't stay there either. It's an unstable place—why be surprised to feel the earth moving under your feet? Accept it as normal—the earth moves a lot there." "This will be," Hall warns, a "very shaky deal."

There is one more reason why building bridges to the next era is a lonely, confusing business—the masses will never go there, only a few brave souls. It's the story of NISCI and earlier breakthrough groups who find themselves in a frightening place, who don't know where they are going, don't know how to get there, "but with a great group of good people—all frightened together as the earth moves under us, we are learning a lot and having a good time."

Stability will not come to NISCI until the organization has matured to the level of NAPM, the National Association of Manufacturers, or APICS. By nature and by design NISCI is a very unstable place where people who are very curious about what comes after, what comes next, are comfortable to be—they are brave enough or stupid enough to stand at the edge of the chasm.

Groups like NISCI are a necessity that will lead, drag, and otherwise persuade many big companies to start their journeys. Would it be cheaper, faster, and better to do this together, or does it make more sense to do it alone? Doyle and his members obviously believe in group efforts.

We await a combination of two or three critical ideas to come together and render a big idea viable. With Henry Ford, these were spark arresters, the carburetor, certain types of steel, and the moving assembly line. Before the conveyor, cars were bin-built in a bay, but Ford knocked the bays down and loaded up production. McCormick's real contribution was not the reaper but the standardization of parts. In the semiconductor industry nothing happened for the first fifteen years until the first chip was developed. All the big breakthroughs needed to be "commonized" to have real impact.

Quiet Progress

Progress will be unseen. Doyle likens it to a group of explorers viewed across a canyon. After the good-bys are said and the emigrants set out on their journey, we tend to forget them. We don't see them again until they show up on the other side of the canyon—all along the way they continue out of sight. "Today," says Doyle, "even if we were to abstract away from the Top Ten, the really good people sometimes hide what they do in plain sight—what they are doing is not easy for other people to see, and really hard for the others to duplicate. They don't have the interconnectedness in their head—they see the piece and parts, but 'what does that have to with building cars?,' they ask."

Good News and Bad News on the Horizon

The future of supply chains is filled with good news and bad news, and the bad news is quite frightening. "Somebody will have to break the news to the world pretty soon—there are big structural problems in our economy, very serious fractures." It doesn't take much imagination to know that over 50 percent of our companies are classified as small and medium-sized, between three hundred and five hundred employees. As big customers continue to consolidate the supply base and reduce suppliers, half of that sector goes away, or slips into the margin. The problem is, says Doyle, that "a. that's the sector that's producing employment, and b. that's the sector that's produced innovation. Whoops, we won't be doing that! The 70's shakeout of middle management will be 'Boy Scout Camp' compared to what's ahead."

Seeking a Safe Haven

Where to run? Working for a big company, even a Raytheon or GE, will be safer because for the vast majority of smaller companies in small-town America, there is no outplacement, no lifetime pension—businesses will one day just shut their doors. And your next job won't be in that town.

So the prediction is for another major displacement of families, a commercial real estate shakeout caused by loss of bricks and mortar retail strip malls and shopping centers. When this shift rolls across the economy, in the next five years, and it compresses the middle of the chain, there will be significant ancillary effects, the replacement of once powerful sales venues with bits and bytes.

Although we certainly won't buy Starbucks over the Web, color auto dealerships gone, as well as banks and libraries. Although 70 percent of book buyers have not purchased yet over Amazon.com, it may be years before retailers and commercial real estate moguls realize the full horror of their circumstance, but it is coming.

In Search of the New Giants

Fifteen years ago a small group of professionals ran innovative big purchasing organizations that were the first to understand JIT, concurrent engineering, and quality methods—men like Ken Stork, director of procurement at Motorola, Jim Sierck at Allied Signal, and Gene Richter at Black and Decker. The next generation is moving in—professionals like Thomas Stallkamp, Dave Otterness at Flextronics, and now Richter's successors at IBM.

Where is the third generation and when will they arrive? And will we recognize them when they appear?

6

COST MANAGEMENT IN THE EXTENDED ENTERPRISE

Best Practice Leaders: IBM, Honda, Whirlpool

When manufacturing began its JIT transformation in the 1980s following pressures from the Far East, accounting concepts soon came under fire as well. Managers began to doubt the value of classic cost accounting methods, especially variance and burden protocols. They began to think that their systems were inflexible and untimely, but they struggled with a lack of appropriate substitutes. Specifically, the detailed accounting for labor and material costs missed the mark and proved to be less of a guide to the right decisions than a way of dissecting history, assigning costs (or guilt), and classifying administrative charges. As much as procurement and manufacturing cried out for decision tools, what they got instead from software packages was seas of detail and a dearth strategic information.

Traditional Cost Accounting vs. the Newcomers

The struggle continues today, although companies like Hewlett-Packard and others turned temporarily to the new gurus of accounting for answers, Robin Cooper and Ted Kaplan of Harvard for Activity Based Costing, and Tom Johnson of Portland State University, author of *Relevance Lost*.

What they found was still, however, not a rethinking of the accounting systems they needed for decisions but a small system whose application as activity-based costing allowed them to compare individual projects, not the full answer they needed, but an improvement just the same.

Two additional big shifts in manufacturing management further increased the need for new metrics systems—the shift from high-labor to low-labor content, as well as the growth of outsourcing. When labor accounted for 50 or 60 percent of input to finished product, it was important to measure it accurately and frequently. The relative wage rates of various workforces—domestic and overseas, or union vs. nonunion, or even high vs. low skilled— seemed to be a determining competitive factor.

In parallel with the focus on wage levels, all the industrial engineering time study work that contributed to building a base of standards—how best to perform work measured in discrete time slices—reinforced the hope that management could control product costs if only we could measure them better—in more detail. Work from Frederick Taylor, the Gilbreths, and generations of industrial engineers that helped us consolidate control of cottage operations became barriers to supply chain flexibility.

Systems That Failed Manufacturing and the Supply Base

Clearly, the accounting systems that failed manufacturing won't work for supply management either. Although purchasers must inevitably understand the labor cost buildup at their suppliers when they evaluate price opportunities, traditional cost accounting will still not give them all the answers they need, but certainly there will be reams of numbers and pounds of data.

The problem is that prices move so quickly, and global currency and other strategic issues move so quickly, even the Best Practice purchasing operations are challenged to manage their information pipelines. But that is exactly what the winners in the next twenty years must become experts at doing—watching and responding to macro shifts as they manage the microprocessing costs. It's a seemingly impossible challenge, given the calcified accounting systems they have inherited and the simultaneous lack of appropriately powerful cost management systems all organizations are crying for. But Best Practice winners like IBM, with their commodity managers, and American Express, with their supreme money flow "engineers," have succeeded in this difficult area.

A few Best Practice organizations understand the scope of this very difficult problem, although not all of them have succeeded in assembling an answer that will carry them strategically and tactically forward without some missing pieces. IBM under Gene Richters is a leader in cost management; Honda, for other reasons, particularly its work developing the supply base, is another cost management leader.

The "Good Enough" Answer

It may be that as processes move toward 100 percent reliability, and as the leading enterprise groupings form over the next five to ten years, the systems so desperately needed, along with the professional expertise to run them, will be created to take second and third tier contenders into mastery of new cost management techniques. However, given the "barriers to entry"—professional commitment to specific accounting methods, regulations, and so on—we think that the winners in this challenging race will be the innovators, like IBM, who figure out a system that works "good enough for now," something strong enough to supplement—rather than do an end run around—the current cost management approaches. Very few companies have successfully attacked current cost management machines and won, and we don't advocate spending energy to achieve that.

Look to Practical Solutions, Alternative Accounting Methods

Instead, we recommend that supply management take a hard look at alternative systems—smart solutions that move purchasing into a commodity management way of thinking. Study the best cost management leaders, look at how their best suppliers arrive at costs and monitor them daily, and push on in that direction. A word of caution: do not expect the end producer's and the supplier's cost management approaches to mirror each other, especially at the first, second, and third tier levels.

Every single respondent in our Best Practices survey placed cost management in his company's top-three strategic issues. Undoubtedly cost management means different things to different organizations. To some the focus is on actual cost reductions through continuous improvement, consolidation, or other economies. To others cost management means the systems by which we measure and track costs. Either way, as manufacturing discovered fifteen years ago, supply management executives do not have all the tools at hand to strategically manage and redirect costs.

Big Board Tools

By the year 2020, however, we believe they will, and the immediate challenge is to get from here to there without launching another systems crusade. The survey also highlighted management's awareness of cost as a key differentiator in supply base consolidation, and as processes become more consistent and predictable, cost management systems that will perform as well as stock and commodity market systems, the Big Board, will become available.

The infamous Ignacio Lopez, GM's long-departed purchasing hatchetman, did indeed force badly needed cost reductions on his North American suppliers; other big producers have survived massive cost reduction drives, Honda (the 1998 Accord's 30 percent cost-down), and IBM, both Best Practice leaders, included. Each took different approaches toward the management and development of its supply base, as well as various internal staffing approaches toward managing the challenge.

For the next five to ten years supply management's challenge will be to achieve intelligent cost reductions by a combination of smart cost management, well-trained and resourced purchasing profession-als, and innovative but not comprehensive cost management sys-tems. Having seen the Lopez, the Honda, and the IBM approaches, we think leaders will find a way to achieve enterprisewide price per-formance without killing themselves and their suppliers in the process.

And remember, all North American purchasers, and European companies as well, typically leave billions of dollars on the table—low-hanging fruit and ongoing creative cost management quick hit opportunities, at a minimum 10 to 20 percent of their total spend. The opportunities from a little intelligence applied in the right spots are that great.

Where to Start? Benchmark the Best Practice Leaders

When IBM began its total transformation, purchasing and supply management did not go untouched. Gene Richter created global competitive awareness that enabled the turnaround; continuous innovation fuels IBM's ability to respond in markets that have bypassed lesser competitors.

Big Blue and the Big Board

Remarkably, IBM procurement has developed an ability to see inwardly, but also, through Richter's leadership, the company has developed a very powerful external commodity market focus that constantly evaluates and positions IBM in world commodity mar-kets. In essence, the way IBM manages price negotiations and swings resembles more of Big Board commodity trading—extremely fast and high-energy price competition and tracking—than traditional purchasing concerns over supplier's individual price deals.

Mike Heinrich, IBM's director of finance for global procurement, based in Somers, New York, reports on a dotted line into purchasing chief Richter. John Prophet, whom Heinrich describes as a "veteran benchmarker," is titled manager of competitive measurements. Basically, Heinrich's finance group provides Richter with a scorecard telling him how well the procurement team is doing. Although the scorecard does not track every item in the parts list, with a spend of $40 billion, it hits a significant percentage of the monies procurement spends.

Price, Price, Price

Heinrich describes his job this way: "What I track is a limited set of goals—*price, price, price!*", the belief being that if the group hits the market on the price parameter, they will hit the corporation's overall strategically competitive targets. Surprisingly, Heinrich elaborates on his obsessive devotion to the numbers: "I only care about better price—not terms and conditions and deals that you negotiate, just price." Richter has other staff people concerned with the suppliers' quality level, delivery performance, and technology leadership. "If we can find a way of measuring what is happening to price on our commodities, and compare that to what is happening in the market, you are seventy-five percent there. The other twenty-five percent—trying to get good deals, moving liability to a supplier, or negotiating certain other terms and conditions like local warehousing or line-side stocking—all this should be done, but it's not what I am interested in tracking."

With that overriding mission, Heinrich's commodity experts search out industry metrics that tell what a particular industry—silicon wafers on the production side, for example—is doing; C++ programming skills would be a commodity tracked on the nonproduction side. Analysts would be interested, for example, in the hourly rate for programmers, which might be established by research to be in the $10 range, and they would trace changes over the past quarter looking for significant trends.

The group breaks the total $40 billion spend into some thirty-eight commodity groups and tracks $30 billion in total, $20 billion on general, and $10 billion on production. (The rest is OEM manufacturing, like subcontracting, on which it is very difficult to get industry data, including some delegated procurement, insurance, and corporate treasury items.) Production hosts twenty-five commodity councils; in the nonproduction world, customer solutions and in general—from electricity to programmers to office suppliers and software—items that do not have part numbers. To date twelve general procurement councils have been established, and each of these commodities has a sourcing structure—a council chair and dedicated sourcing buyers. The goal is to optimize IBM's leverage in those commodities as an IBM company, not as a series of divisions; as a worldwide entity, the council can of course optimize IBM's purchasing power.

Data-Intensive Searches

The starting point is the end-of-December monthly cycle on the production side, and quarterly on the general side, although managers are looking for ways to get onto a monthly cycle here as well. Production commodity price data are maintained electronically on-line from accounts payable, but on the general side obtaining the price data is a manually intensive task.

Obtaining the market data is all manual. Planners might use Dataquest or outside consultants who research and organize data that IBM planners then review to establish the industry line. This mammoth process might also involve site visits to suppliers by consultants. Reports are made typically around the twentieth workday following the month, or December's data won't be published until late in January. The rate and pace of technology change and the challenge of trying to figure out the true takedown rate—even part numbers can change midyear—further complicates this critical mission that proves that price increases don't necessarily reflect true market price trends.

Market Cost Comparisons Count

John Prophet and his team of three update the database and the part numbers so that when an analyst pulls from accounts payable files, the record reflects current parts. It's a time-consuming task; much good data come from talking with buyers. Clearly, IBM is proving that it is important to track the parallels between absolute prices and industry average prices. The goal is to know as much as possible about prices, especially when certain products are treated as industry standard commodities, like drams, whose cost buildup often holds very little relationship to market prices.

Dual Tracking

Plans are in the works to change this process in the future. In 1999 IBM started dual tracking; the costing consultant delivers not just the industry average on the fifteen megabyte chip, for example but the best price the suppliers are charging to large OEM manufacturing. IBM can then compare IBM prices on an absolute basis to the best, not just the industry average.

This year saw dual tracking on four commodities—memory, storage, LCD flat-panel displays, and monitors. Data include the best prices the competition is getting vs. the IBM price, so it is important to look at the lowest price the industry is paying, compared with IBM's price; IBM buyers factor in sourcing policy as well. Not being willing to put all their eggs into one supplier's basket, buyers may choose not to take the absolute lowest, maintaining instead three or four suppliers to protect the supply chain. By spreading the buy around, IBM can compare their average price to the lowest price. The goal remains to drive IBM's best price to the level of the industry's best price. Logistics, warranty, and other terms and conditions are not included in the comparisons so that planners can work with pure price.

Cost Reduction

Cost reduction goals, what analysts think an industry will do, and IBM's percentage of the total industry spend, are developed by commodity because industry pricing changes daily. All production councils have been challenged to improve the price IBM pays by more than the average change in industry prices. At the end of the day, councils are ranked against their peers.

Council members are primarily procurement buyers with titles ranging from senior buyers or quality professionals, with an occasional engineer, up to the executive-level council chair.

Big Blue's Biggest Opportunities

It's a global game, and IBM purchasing executives cannot see a single area that doesn't show opportunity. Commodity managers stay focused by working within a measurement system that ties merit pay and year-end bonus into a comparison of how they perform relative to other councils. All commodities have an equal opportunity to succeed or fail—no area carries a special performance handicap, or one that is expected to fall short. This is, according to IBM management, a "very dynamic measurement—we measure against what is going on in the market."

Forecasting Total Takedown Rates

So much for internal measures. Externally, IBM purchasing wants perspective from managers on what the total takedown rate is going to be. With an industry declining 10 percent per year, for example, if IBM buyers can get another five points, the goal becomes a 15 percent point advantage. The object is to maximize the total takedown.

Developing Cost Detail—The Supplier Quote Form

When most companies think about cost management, they completely focus on current cost control, linking into current operating plans and the strategic plan, but they are missing half the picture, because there are two approaches:

1. current product cost control
2. future product cost control

The best companies maintain two separate processes that come together to manage total costs. On the current cost approach, shift the emphasis from typical accounting variance reporting to a system that measures the impact of cost reduction activities on product. The goal is, rather than talk about how a company has managed to reduce total purchasing costs by $6 million in a year, for example, to relate cost reductions to specific reductions on the new sport utility vehicle, or the new van. The reason is that Best Practice companies are more concerned about cost impact in the eyes of their customer—what is the sticker price going to look like after this improvement program? This approach requires most companies to rethink their approach on gathering and organizing of critical data, and it all starts with the supplier quote form, a document that feeds all the other purchasing product cost systems.

The Supplier Quote

Most companies that are doing a superior job of cost management, particularly Honda, and now John Deere, try to accumulate as much detailed information about their suppliers' process and other costs. Both Honda and Deere believe that the foundation of a good cost system is the supplier quote system. The supplier quote is the second step that can be performed after a company has been able with raw data analysis and some computer assist to categorize all of a company's buy by commodities. Decentralized organizations have to complete the extra first step of consolidation and translation, but once the consolidated data have been accumulated, it is easy to select the top suppliers for further examination.

Big decisions break down into more manageable pieces with the right data, and the three-page quote form allows producers thinking of moving production to Mexico, for example, where labor cost is about one-tenth North American rates, to understand the trade-offs. The supplier quote form is designed to be completed on-line on the system, with the supplier and buyer on-line and looking at the same numbers simultaneously.

With good data manipulation assists, it should be possible out of the total usage for steel, for example, to boil data down into categories of top suppliers, steel grades and types, sometimes by product using the steel, or even regions. Interestingly, although Honda has more information on suppliers than any of its competitors, they do not retain "goes into" data for each model and each commodity type. Instead, they have established a "rep" vehicle, a common one that represents the entire line; from the rep unit, changes in cost profiles can be added based on exceptional characteristics.

Working with a Rep Machine

Starting with a high-volume model—at John Deere such a model would be a tractor from the 8000 series—analysts begin to follow and understand every price nuance on the breakdown of that tractor. Each point opens up opportunities for further discussion, and as they work the issues on various components, they begin to understand more about the total cost for that model.

The organization will begin naturally to shift their focus—to realign—as people understand more about the costs on the rep machine than they knew about traditional, nonrelevant costs. The foundation techniques may be the same—comparison between plan and actual, for example—but now the systems are changed to reflect accounting information on the rep machine, rather than total variance. The shift builds bridges between the new approach and the traditional system.

This approach works particularly well with new products; if a supplier needs to modify a design, tallying up the cost changes with the quote form should be painless. Some suppliers can take advantage of customers under the traditional methods of costing new products by fattening their bids on productivity factors, and if no one examines the detail, many past and current sins will be buried in product changes.

Cost Tables

The next step, after the supplier quote form has been completed in detail, is to work with major suppliers to reach an agreement to develop cost tables. For example, during a John Deere analysis project, graduate students were assigned to review steel buys. Although the company buys thousands of different grades of steel, with good analysis they were able to easily recapture 10 to 15 percent of the total steel buy.

Ten to 15 percent savings is not unusual following this degree of analysis and collaboration. Matt Lofton, an executive at LTV in Cleveland, estimated that companies can find 10 percent reductions without any serious effort. They simply, says Lofton, "have to look at buying in a different way. They must organize and prepare, but they must also cause the steel companies to see a buyer as their best customer."

Rationalize the Spend

Bad customers, in the eyes of steel suppliers, buy very small quantities of an endless variety of product; producers can't make good profits from this kind of business. Lofton urges smart customers to tackle the analysis that will enable them to consolidate and rationalize their spend. "Anything you touch will turn into gold, particularly for the one-time deal. Do it once, get it done right, and don't repeat the exercise every year."

Co-author Nelson believes that of the three basic requirements for good purchasing—supplier development, strategic sourcing, and cost management—cost management, a strategic concern when well designed and executed, will carry Best Practice leaders into success year after year. Nelson estimates that it takes four to six years to complete training and job experience on all three points. A new purchasing training program at Deere in fact puts new hires into a certification program that covers cost management and lots of practice—data gathering, analysis, and decision making—under the wing of an experienced mentor.

Managing Like a Commodity Trader

Big Board action should be the driver of all new cost initiatives in supply chain management. But learning to work like a commodity trader with limited visibility to the markets is impossible without on-line resources. IBM, Flextronics, and Deere are all working toward that very aggressive, high-level approach to buying. It is the only way to manage global market issues.

Honda purchasing lived through the impact of currency fluctuations in the 1980s, and the lessons from that challenged management to look at procurement in a whole new way. They decided to build up the Marysville complex from a knockdown (KD) assembly plant supported by components shipped in daily from Japan, to a self-reliant assembler supported by local suppliers.

In 1982, when Honda was producing cars from kits, the exchange rate was about 250 yen to the dollar; as the yen continued to fall, local content had to increase because it was not possible for Japanese automakers to sell cars priced competitively with their high domestic parts costs. Localizing became more important as the yen continued its fall. Inevitably, it became more and more difficult for automakers to sell finished product that would have been designed and quoted years previously at a higher cost.

Good tracking by rep machines, the 98 Accord, for example, allowed Honda executives to anticipate currency changes and to prepare for them at home in North America. When steel prices drop or a resin plant burns down, purchasers need to have a Big Board in place—a comprehensive realtime system that will help them anticipate, see, and react to big swings.

Whirlpool's Unique Approach to Cost Management

Whirlpool competes in a global $80 billion business that, like the auto industry, is undergoing massive consolidation and many strategic moves; products in this business must be very efficiently manufactured. The company claims number one position in the race, with 14 percent worldwide share; the top five contenders hold 41 percent share. Whirlpool employs over fifty-eight thousand employees in more than 170 countries, supplying ten key brand names through $7 billion in purchases. In six years, Whirlpool has dramatically shifted its business from a North American focus to a global one, and purchasing has picked up new challenges as well.

The Value-Added Challenge

Whirlpool understands that to create sustainable competitive advantage, they must combine four critical elements:

1. Product innovation and leverage
2. Talent development
3. Global leverage of procurement best practices and suppliers
4. Capital utilization

Roy Armes, Whirlpool's corporate vice president of global procurement operations, believes the company gets their competitive advantage from their ability to integrate manufacturing, product development, and procurement. The organizations are integrated in a cross-functional way; moreover, both procurement and global product development report to Armes's boss, the executive vice president and chief technology officer of Whirlpool. "We think our ability to effectively integrate our manufacturing, product development, and procurement organizations results in a competitive advantage—that's probably one of the biggest contributors to our success."

Quality Initiatives and Integration Are Key

Whirlpool has gotten very serious about achieving superior quality. Their quality method, dubbed OPEX, is one of the areas in which Armes believes they have developed strong competency and advantage. "There are three or four areas where we feel we have developed competency and competitive advantage—first is cost management, which is managed by developing strategic relationships while at the same time allowing room for creating a competitive environment within our supply base. Another is quality improvement through the use of our OPEX initiative. The third and very valuable element is manufacturing, product development, and procurement integration. Integration is what's really delivering a lot of these results, a cross-functional effort that leverages design, manufacturing, and the supply base to achieve unprecedented performance."

The idea, says Armes, is to set up and operate a global organization that delivers regional value. "In procurement we refer to this as being center-led, but regionally executed. Basically what that says is we develop our programs in procurement from global best practices, internally and externally, which is coordinated from the center, then implement and execute them regionally." The goal is to drive consistent execution globally to optimize value.

This unique approach has significant leverage across the regions. For companies still struggling with the central/decentralization quandary, Whirlpool has been there, done that, and they think this approach can work particularly well in a large enterprise. For companies that have inherited a matrix organization structure, in which there are too many bosses to report to, trying to tear down barriers and concentrate on value and optimizing efforts is easier with a streamlined, unique organizational approach.

Quality Results

OPEX, which is similar to the Six Sigma program used by a few major companies, applies various classic quality tools to the supply chain to drive significant improvements like these:

1. Field failure costs increased six times in a couple years around a specific electromechanical assembly found in refrigerators; in fact, this problem was one of the top ten failures in the field. "Our approach," says Armes, "was to work directly with the supplier. We mapped the process and system—not just the components—of our system, all the way from the supply base to putting it into our product. We found a degree of variation through the process that resulted in a loss of process control, which drove and contributed to these field failures. By establishing the appropriate measures and clearly monitoring them, we were able to better control our critical variables. This one project alone resulted in a 98 percent reduction in the internal reject rate, and an 87 percent reduction in field failure costs.

Whirlpool was able to realize savings of $1 million within a six-month period.

2. High scrap rates for a supplier's co-injected part improved through the application of the OPEX tools. Scrap was reduced by over 85 percent, and resulted in almost $500,000 per year savings in rejects and productivity, as well as an admirable improvement in delivery; along with cycle time reductions on the plastics press, all added up to a windfall of savings.

OPEX tools used to generate these project savings, and hundreds of others, include thought mapping and process mapping, where the process is better to understand how this part, a component, or a system is really working. The measurement system is also evaluated to determine the appropriate process metric to control critical variables. Design of Experiments, a tool that has been around for many years, helps Whirlpool better understand these process variations. Other tools are used in the development process as well, says Armes, "such as statistical tolerancing, to see if we are getting the most robust process and design; FMEA, Taguchi, etc. All these tools help us to understand the variables and to become more proactive in the design process. While many companies utilize these tools to some degree, selecting the right tool for the situation will help expedite the quality improvement process."

Armes and his colleagues also believe that procurement, along with product design and development, plays a key role in global value chain leverage.

Supplier selection, design standardization, and supplier technology management, including teams that evaluate and optimize component and subsystems, all contribute to Whirlpool's improved cost management position of its 55 to 60 percent purchased parts spend.

Says Armes, "The costs of major appliances have changed very little in the past twenty years, while feature and quality levels have improved substantially, a good indication of the competitiveness in the industry. But it's also a testimonial to the value being created for the consumer."

The most critical factor that has driven Whirlpool performance, according to Armes, is the manufacturing, product development, and procurement integration as it relates to material cost and supplier initiatives. Marketing also helps identify where the highest value opportunities exist. When purchasing addresses these areas, they are armed with quality and supplier development tools, as well as superior metrics. Supplier improvement projects generally lasting from three to six months produce even more gains. Integration extends to co-location approaches because many suppliers are co-located with Whirlpool engineering, such as their suppliers' packaging engineers.

On-line Auctions, Innovative Cost Management

While most purchasing organizations continue to work on new approaches to cost management—anything that does not speak only to material variance—the Web's influence is felt here too. Although cost management typically focuses on breaking out the elements of cost, then negotiates each element with the right suppliers, the result being a cost table that delivers prices, the e-Auction concept is gathering speed. An e-Auction is generally designed to work price, especially in commodity markets, but cost management requires a great deal of relationship building and trust.

E-Auctions require an efficient marketplace and good preparation for bidding; to date, auctions of course have not been cited as good approaches to trust building, but they work well for targeting reductions on certain products. United Technologies has found both approaches useful. Because auctions are so much faster—and exciting—we believe they would today be "the Lopez weapon of choice"!

AT Kearney Develops E-Commerce Auctions

Experts at AT Kearney predict a dramatic increase in worldwide e-business that will end the traditional procurement function. The world's top one hundred companies will do $400 billion of business-to-business transactions via the Internet by 2001, an increase of more than 1,000 percent compared with 1998. Along the way, pur-

chasers are shedding suppliers that don't add value to corporate purchasing performance, according to an AT Kearney study released
November 2, 1999. Projections are for one-fourth of many companies' external expenditures to be conducted via the Web, compared
with less than 2 percent in 1999.

Tom Slaight, a vice president at AT Kearney based in New York,
declares: "According to these findings, we believe the traditional procurement function will cease to exist while the remaining strategic
supply management and innovation component will become a
boardroom level competitive weapon." Slaight cites the following
reasons:

- Seventy-six percent of CEOs from participating companies said
  they expect procurement to contribute to shareholder value,
  compared with only 12 percent of CEOs with the same expectation of the function three years earlier.
- Corporations plan to decrease their procurement headcount by
  roughly 25 percent in the next two years, mainly in the transactional area.
- The number of companies that outsource day-to-day procurement activities will double by 2001 to 37 percent.
- One-third of large companies, or twice as many as in 1999, will
  use strategically managed consortias by 2001 to leverage their
  buying power.

"Companies facing the make-or-buy decision increasingly choose
to buy," Slaight said. "Leaders are buying more strategically, from
fewer suppliers, with fewer people."

The consulting firm also studies Best Practice models. The study
evaluated companies on 28 Best Practices in procurement. Companies were rated for each Best Practice by assessing the degree to
which they identified a practice as critical to their success, how well
they applied the practice, and the impact of the practice in delivering
clearly measurable benefits—reductions in cost and time, and
improvements in service, quality, and so on.

"We found that procurement leaders today are leveraging supply
markets for innovation and revenue generation, *while followers still*

focus on cutting costs," said Niko Soellner, global head of AT Kearney's strategic sourcing practice. Leading companies increasingly look at supply markets as "value levers" to help improve overall corporate performance. Outsourcing of noncore activities is on the rise, as is the volume of the typical company's external spend across industries.

The study indicates that excellence in procurement has a substantial impact on business performance. On average, compared with the remaining three-quarters of the study's participants, the top quartile of Best Practice companies recorded a nearly one-third higher rate of profit growth: a twofold advantage in the reduction rate for cost of goods sold and five times higher growth in return on equity.

At the same time, participating CEOs made clear that their expectations of suppliers have risen. They increasingly expect suppliers to drive innovation and to support customers' marketing efforts, not just reduce costs. For a supplier not seen as providing extra value, the outlook is grim. The study, which analyzed how the 162 companies manage the combined expenditure of $520 billion annually across almost every product or category, shows that companies plan on average to eliminate more than 25 percent of suppliers within the next two years.

U.S. Companies Are Global Leaders in E-Business

The AT Kearney study shows that U.S. companies are the most aggressive in reshaping procurement. For example, U.S. companies that participated in the study expect that by 2001, orders for 29 percent of their total external expenditure will be placed via the Internet vs. 20 percent across all companies participating in the study worldwide and only 14 percent for European companies.

With leading companies in the automotive, telecommunications, and other industries, the firm is employing Internet technology in business-to-business actions that helps clients achieve multimillion dollar savings and reduces purchasing cycle times, while sourcing products and services globally from larger networks of suppliers.

AT Kearney is pioneering a Web-based approach to fast, competitive pricing, an on-line auction; this method can save smart buyers

20 to 30 percent on their normal buys. The cost of conducting the auction is approximately $50,000, in addition to preliminary setup work; advance preparations for the event can take two to four weeks. It is important to prequalify all bidders who will participate, because none of the entrants will participate if they see a "low bid rabbit" on line.

The firm assisted Visteon Automotive Systems to conduct an Internet bidding opportunity for seventeen prequalified suppliers from around the world. The suppliers were vying for nearly $150 million in contracts to produce four different types of printed circuit boards. The ninty-minute auction, and the qualifying process that preceded it, reduced costs and shaved weeks off the sourcing time line.

AT Kearney also conducted an Internet-based auction for Sprint that attracted eighty-five qualified suppliers vying for more than $75 million in telemarketing service contracts for the global communications company. The four-hour auction streamlined the negotiation process by at least three weeks, facilitated the introduction of additional diversity suppliers, and improved the average proposal prices by 5 percent through the realtime, on-line bidding process. As a result of the sourcing process, Sprint expects to realize many benefits, including significant overall cost reduction and service improvement.

Before the Auction

Well before the auction date, a team worked with Sprint purchasing and marketing specialists to develop a request for proposal specifying the capabilities required for quality delivery of twenty-six categories of telemarketing services. The request for proposals (RFP) also outlined the rules of the upcoming on-line auction, highlighting the elements of what would be a winning proposal.

Using nonprice parameters including service, quality, hiring processes, training, and technology, as well as indicators from AT Kearney's strategic sourcing process, the team developed a list of qualified suppliers to receive the RFP. Suppliers who responded to the RFP were contacted and encouraged to log onto the auction Web site before the event, to become more comfortable with the process and to see the lowest qualified bids that would start the auction.

During the Auction

Suppliers didn't hesitate when the auction opened at the designated day and time: bidding began immediately, with 250 bids in the first fifty minutes. Sprint and Kearney knew the source of each bid, but individual suppliers knew only the amounts. From their Web browsers, suppliers monitored the lowest current bid and submitted new bids accordingly. Data were refreshed by the minute; quartile reports, generated hourly, alerted suppliers to their relative position for each of the twenty-six subcategories of spend. An 800- number help line gave suppliers immediate answers and assistance throughout the auction.

Sprint participants from marketing, purchasing, finance, and other interested departments viewed the proceedings from a computer projected onto a large screen, and the auctioneer and members of the Sprint team coaxed and prodded bids through Internet messages, telephone calls, and e-mails—some addressed to all participants and some to individual bidders.

An onscreen prompt built into the program ensured that suppliers reviewed their bids for accuracy before hitting the "send" command. Sprint and AT Kearney were notified as each new bid was entered and implications for savings were calculated instantaneously.

If any supplier entered a bid in the last five minutes, the auction was extended by ten minutes to allow everyone the opportunity to respond to competition. Originally scheduled for three hours, the auction was extended for forty-five minutes to complete the bidding. During the course of the auction, eight hundred bids were submitted.

After the Auction

As price was only one of the factors to be used in determining the final list of preferred suppliers, the team used the RFP responses and the results of the auction to select a list of finalists to participate in a site visit process. Suppliers who fared well were invited to continue in further discussions on a range of issues. In the end, sixty new suppliers were involved in the action, including eleven minority-owned suppliers.

Implications

Clearly, the auction has potential to create a new competitive landscape of Internet auction providers. New robust technologies must be available to make auctions effective for both buyers and suppliers. Pioneers believe that Internet auctions will become the preferred channel for all goods and services, but suppliers must also become convinced that there are sufficient benefits for their participation, and that their systems can support this high level of performance and negotiation.

With this method, suppliers don't need special software or fee-based connections, just a Web browser and password, to participate. Any laptop connected to the Internet will link suppliers to the auction. "Not only are the savings great, but Internet auctions are far more effective than traditional snail-mail paper negotiations for client and vendors. Both sides say . . . the process is easy to use," says Slaight. The auction is expected to replace round-one negotiations with suppliers, cutting 70 percent from proposal cycle times.

Buyers also reap additional savings because more suppliers are involved and the realtime auction spurs competition, causing even incumbent vendors to provide better pricing, says Slaight. New suppliers see value in obtaining business on the Web with lower selling costs, while incumbents see the opportunity to increase their business from a broader appreciation of their value. Although the Kearney Internet Auction uses downward bidding to promote competition, the lowest price doesn't always win. Quality and service factors are used to preselect suppliers before the action, then become tiebreakers after the auction is completed.

Suppliers benefit because auctions facilitate efficient market making—reducing their cost of sales, and providing a level playing field for qualified competitors, introducing them to potential new customers, and helping them better understand the markets they are selling into, says Slaight.

Auctions are basically a "gateway to the world" that enables remote suppliers to participate as easily as local ones. "Because auctions are non-emotional and prevent favoritism, the level playing field enables smaller companies to compete with larger rivals and newcomers to take on incumbents," Slaight believes. The flexibility of the Internet auction allows it to be used at all stages of the sourcing life cycle, including category sourcing and category resourcing and for recurring bids based on available production capacity.

"In addition to streamlining the purchasing process and broadening a company's potential supply base, Internet bidding identifies real supplier interest instead of flashy sales messages. Open communication from the beginning helps a company create the type of fact-based relationships with suppliers that can lead to breakthrough ideas and true competitive advantage, according to Slaight.

Buyers report surprise benefits. When they prequalify suppliers, for example, they downgrade the importance of certification. Certification, says Slaight, builds in a switching barrier; suppliers, he says, love certification, because it "keeps my competition out." In fact, suppliers can gradually and imperceptibly increase price—the customer may actually not realize how much more they are paying for an item if the supplier can concentrate on overwhelming them with information, emphasizing the deal they are getting in quality and service. Costs inch up. But if the Internet can replicate the intent of certification—a big if—experts are hopeful that buyers will be even better positioned to make smart choices.

The Three Types of Cost Management

Timothy Laseter, a Booz Allen consultant and the author of *Balanced Sourcing*, now believes there are three types of cost management:

1. Bottoms-up cost models. Honda excels at developing details through supplier quote sheets and jicons (cost management meetings conducted by customers with suppliers).

2. Parametric modeling, using multiple regression to evaluate cost drivers. McDonald's discovered from building a cost model showing multiple suppliers that by adjusting the multiple factors implicit in chicken farming—feed mix, humidity, breeds—farmers could discover the optimal mix to use as the price of feed changes. Boeing and Whirlpool have also developed working parametric models. At Whirlpool, analysts considered different types of compressors across the globe, looking at performance of various cost drivers like efficiency and BTU ratings.

3. Industry dynamics—modeling how costs ought to behave. In a true commodity market, where capacity, availability, and industry trends dominate—microprocessors at Intel, for example—the goal is to forecast how costs will behave. IBM uses data on industry dynamics quite well to go beyond traditional purchasing questions.

Laseter recommends starting simply—don't try to design an overly complicated cost model; get a handle on the cost drivers in the commodity, and triangulate the data by obtaining validation from multiple sources wherever possible. Finally, be sure to consider total cost, not just product cost.

Value Analysis and Value Engineering

Finally, can a company do a good job on costs without formal value analysis or value engineering? Because real, lasting cost savings come early in the new product development cycle, value engineering work is always a part of Best Practices for companies like John Deere and Honda. Value engineering occurs mostly during this phase; when Deere prepares to make a new lawn tractor, for example, with all detailed available information in place, it is important to get the engineers together to look closely at opportunities like molds and tooling.

The tools for Best Practice cost management are unfortunately not fully developed, although Best Practice leaders like IBM, Honda,

John Deere, and AT Kearney have each created workable systems that have allowed them to achieve dramatic results. Certainly as traditional cost systems are replaced by Web-based bid and sell routines, and as more companies develop enterprisewide pricing intelligence, cost will cease to be the number one worry of all procurement professionals.

7

THE PROFILE OF THE NEW PROFESSIONAL

They Build Transformations

The strategic results that enlightened companies need the most cannot come without high-level, innovative vision and guidance from a new breed of purchasing professional, leaders like Garry Berryman at Harley-Davidson, Willie Deese at SmithKline Beecham, Thomas Stallkamp (former head of Chrysler purchasing, later president of the company), and Gene Richter of IBM. Each of these supply management leaders migrated from other areas into procurement, and each worked huge changes in a very short time.

The transformation that each of these leaders worked on their organizations lifted the companies above the average and moved them along a continuum of progress that highlighted their leader's vision and direction. We believe that each one of these leaders knew *before* taking executive positions exactly where they wanted their group to go; they developed and held specific strategic goals that they deliberately unwrapped and instituted as the best approaches to success.

With these leaders, nothing happens accidentally. While they may be unable to control commodity market prices or delivery glitches, they make no mistakes about how to reconfigure an organization for performance, and how to hire and train the perfect people to do the job. The influence of a handful of visionary leaders, like Richter and Stallkamp, can move an entire profession; the influence of well-heard supplier executives carries change into the fabric of the enterprise and makes it more lasting. In many industries, the changes have been slower and less marked, but they continue to build, and as movement happens, new leaders will emerge, and better professionals will appear to take decision points. It is inevitable.

A Shift in Vital Statistics

Purchasing magazine has conducted a survey every other year since 1987 to examine the personal and professional aspects that characterize the purchasing/supply management professional in the United States. Many practices have been revisited since 1987, the height of just in time and quality initiatives in manufacturing. Since 1987, compensation, span of control, spend, and other vital statistics have significantly shifted power in the direction of professional purchasers. Let's look at the specifics:

- More companies are shifting professionals from other functions into purchasing. Nearly half of those surveyed were assigned to purchasing by their companies, rather than choosing it as a professional step. In the last survey, only 39 percent of respondents had been moved into purchasing by a company assignment.
- Routine paperwork is still the bane of purchasing pros, typically taking about one-third of their time
- Purchasing managers and supervisors oversee an average of four subordinates, down from the average of seven in the previous survey.
- Purchasing's role in design and development continues to grow.*

*Source: *Purchasing* magazine, "The Profile of the Purchasing Professional," Kevin R. Fitzgerald, July 15, 1999.

Clearly, the *Purchasing* survey shows progress in daily operating functions, even in the expansion from pure procurement to new product involvement. But the survey tracks shifts along a known set of criteria, and we believe the real leadership change occurs when brilliant, visionary thinkers bring breakthrough innovation onto the scene. Although they may excel at these specific performance criteria, what marks the leaders is the high level of innovation and energy they bring to industry.

The Innovation Imperative

One characteristic not included in the *Purchasing* survey that we strongly believe distinguishes each Best Practice leader is an ability to find new ways to bring old adversaries together, to leapfrog internal and market limitations, to set a new standard for performance across industry lines. The focus on lean manufacturing—still a relatively new idea for most North American companies not well understood in practice by either manufacturing or procurement as it is carried into procurement—is an example.

A very generous estimate is that 15 percent of North American manufacturing companies actually embrace and employ lean manufacturing techniques, although lean is far superior to what is typically done in those businesses. Lean companies like Honda and Toyota, which are pushing lean values and practices down into their supply bases, can easily document quality metrics in the 100 ppm range or better, performance to a narrow delivery window of 99.9 percent or better, and drastically reduce costs with no sacrifice of profitability.

Furthermore, lean producers have discovered how to redesign their material flows, especially in new product introductions, to take significant time out of the new product introduction cycles before volume production begins. They may have even discovered, like Harley-Davidson, how to eliminate prototype builds. Yet all these lean improvements require a new breed of materials specialist. And that's where the innovators come in.

Lean Based on the Supply Chain

Lean manufacturing in high-performance organizations cannot happen without extremely powerful, intelligent procurement. Otherwise, improvement is simply shop floor kaizen, possibly extended to white-collar areas like customer service and logistics, but shop floor just the same.

Fifteen years ago North American managers could count on the fingers of both hands the number of well-recognized purchasing leaders—the list included Ken Stork, director of purchasing at Motorola; George Harris of TRW; Jim Sierck at Allied Signal. These leaders were "early adopters" who made the pilgrimage to the Kawasaki plant in Nebraska, or they had made trips to Japan, where they marveled at the difference between traditional American manufacturing practices and Japanese zero-inventory approaches. They were easy converts to just-in-time manufacturing because, as early adopters, they could "see" the potential in new ideas; they could connect the dots and move from concept to implementation without the aid of consultants or cookbooks. Early adopters lead the way whenever big changes sweep industry; early on they can make the connections between a brilliant concept—just in time, for example—and the necessary changes for complete execution.

These leaders appear to be acting on blind faith. They "know" that if they go in a certain direction—reducing safety stocks, for example, in the just-in-time framework—they will save money and force quality improvement. Early adopters rely more on their own vision and experience, rather than needing a series of well-documented, detailed implementation examples to move on an idea. Tom Gelb, head of Harley-Davidson manufacturing at the time of the AMF buyback, was such an early adopter, as was Stork at Motorola. Blind faith carried them, and networking with other early adopters—telling and retelling "campfire stories"—sustained them.

The just-in-time and lean movements were led by early adopters who attacked waste in manufacturing and understood some of the supply chain implications in these new approaches, although they may not have been able to impact immediately. As converts they started to raise the bar for material management. They rationalized the supply base as they introduced point of use certification of suppliers to eliminate inspection and queueing of in-transit material. They battled for quality standards in the midst of compensation schemes and utilization/efficiency formulas and other organizational barriers that derailed progress. They took excess inventory out of the aisles, racks, warehouses, and trailer trucks where manufacturers had built accumulations of forecasting and push system "mistakes." They attempted to move outside of manufacturing to influence other functional areas like logistics, purchasing, and order administration. They believed that if they could just take safety stocks and other cushions out of the system, producers would expose the problems just below the surface, and, leaders would then be quick to jump to the solution. But they were wrong.

The just-in-time pioneers made tremendous progress in manufacturing, and they laid the foundation for better purchasing, but they were not lean, and they did not quite succeed in mapping excellence throughout their enterprises at all levels. It may be that suppliers were not ready for the same performance levels that original equipment producers were working toward; it may be that the infrastructure to support lean, enterprisewide progress was not in place; or it may be that a handful of leaders was just not enough to take Japanese management techniques into all corners of the organization—there were too many internal "messes" to clean up and not enough time even to look beyond the production walls. They were also unable to integrate software systems—technically the software industry has lagged production requirements—leaving most of their breakthroughs to be hardware- rather than software-focused. For whatever these reasons or combinations of reasons, manufacturing progress stalled after the initial breakthroughs of just-in-time.

Around the time of the publication of the lean manufacturing bible, Jim Womack's *Lean Thinking*, astute manufacturing professionals realized that fixing production was not enough. Manufacturing as an increasingly narrow slice of the whole production continuum could be well improved with a few pull approaches learned from the Toyota production system. The opportunities that

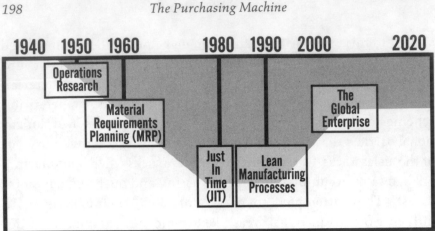

Figure 7.1   From JIT to Lean and Beyond

would clearly yield much bigger savings, however, lay on either side of the manufacturing process, in the supply base, internal and external. The time for another generation of pioneers, early adopters and innovators, has arrived.

Innovators and Integrators

The profile of new leaders for this next phase in Best Practice enterprise development is one of remarkable innovation, as well as an ability to integrate. Each of the new supply management leaders has transformed his purchasing organization and taken it steps above other areas in the company. Harley-Davidson, IBM, American Express, Flextronics, Whirlpool, Honda, and Chrysler can all point to powerful supply management innovators that have mapped a course to take them into the next big wave of enterprise performance.

Leadership Transformation No. 1—IBM

IBM and Chrysler are equally impressive purchasing turnaround stories. Each represents innovation in the heart of companies that were brought back from the dead. IBM, however, made the greatest and, possibly, the most painful changes by transforming itself in fewer than ten years from a high-tech giant into a flexible, fast multiproduct provider.

A challenge such as the one IBM met and beat defeated other high-tech contenders, NCR, Apollo, Prime, and Digital Equipment Corporation (DEC), for example. Their vertical integration posture was so deeply entrenched that it could be changed only too late and with great pain, yet IBM's procurement transformation was accomplished with trust and respect. The key was centralization. For decades Big Blue had relied on internal developers, manufacturers, and component suppliers for closely held manufacturing expertise. For some time, the size and strength of this behemoth isolated IBMers from new ideas and external challenges, but the clone industry changed all that. When the price differential in an ordinary office PC reached two to one— IBM prices coming in at roughly twice the clone's—the price tag eliminated the closet advantage of the IBM name and any supposed proprietary software benefits. The exodus began as soon as the first clone hit the market.

IBM's challenge penetrated all areas of the organization, from the consulting groups to manufacturing and procurement. Gene Richter, however, as the new head of procurement, had an idea about what transformations the company needed, and where, to rebuild a more profitable engine. Centralization, rationalization, and outsourcing were the starting points.

Centralization and Outsourcing

. . . we woke up. We realized that we couldn't be expert in everything.

–Gene Richter

Outsourcing meant shutting down many internal IBM plants. The pain continued for months as the company freed itself of dedicated hardware facilities and began to specialize in customer-focused information solutions. Purchasing, especially with the hiring of veteran Richter from competitor Hewlett-Packard (Richter had also earlier participated in the great success of Black and Decker), began to assume a higher leadership role. In 1986, 28 percent of IBM's revenue was spent with outside suppliers; ten years later, that percentage grew to 49 percent; by 1998, it was 51 percent.* Moving the buying authority from decentralized groups of buyers into a central procurement organization was Richter's first and biggest contribution to the transformation.

How did Richter manage to pull the purchasing dollars back into central control? A carefully worded letter from the top started the reintegration process. IBM chief Gerstner clarified the move that put Richter in charge of all buys; Richter in turn appointed certain managers throughout the company to sign off on all purchases. There were strings attached to each authorization. The manager had to report to Richter key data on the purchase, who did not often authorize anyone outside of purchasing to spend. The eventual effect was to take back all spending and put it in the hands of central purchasing. Centralizing allowed management to get their arms around the numbers, consolidate the spend, and analyze and prioritize future spending.

Centralization allowed IBM to organize along commodity lines, dubbed "commodity councils." For travel and expense, for example, one of the twenty plus commodity groups brought under control, hiring a vice president from United Airlines, one from Marriott, and another from Holiday Inn changed the way purchasing companies conducted outsourcing; the objective became high-level negotiation and consolidation for leveraged price advantage, an impossibility with decentralized, data-poor buyers. Seventeen commodity councils have also managed to rationalize the supply base by reducing the number of suppliers; in 1993, IBM had about 4,900 production suppliers; in 1999, 85 percent of the $17.1 billion spend in production purchases went to fifty suppliers. The same approach worked equally well with other commodities like insurance and benefits. Hire high, position the professional as a vice president or higher, and stand back.

To an outsider, the IBM org chart might seem complicated, stud-

---

*James Carbone, "Reinventing Purchasing Wins the Medal for Big Blue," *Purchasing* magazine, Sept. 16, 1999, p. 39.

ded with experts of all kinds, and it is true that the organization is relatively large and sophisticated. But hiring experts in the field—the best and the brightest—soon led to being best in class. In 1999 IBM was awarded the *Purchasing* magazine Medal of Professional Excellence, a tribute to Richter's vision and innovative energies.

At his previous Hewlett-Packard position, Richter had enjoyed a relatively free hand. At each stage, as he moved from Ford, to Black and Decker, then HP, and IBM, he learned and grew and developed strong people. The results have taken IBM through the pain of restructuring into a leadership position that has advanced purchasing's use of the Internet, thus saving money through consolidation and central buys, and generating revenues as well. The creation of a new Procurement Service Group is taking the responsibility of purchasing out of the hands of clients like United Technologies; *purchasing has become a revenue generator.*

Other innovative initiatives credited to Richter's leadership include a supplier ombudsman and Customer Solutions Procurement, a new group, part of the Global Services division. This group runs a $21 billion spend with about 1,500 buyers and staff. Customer Solutions Procurement provides IT solutions for corporate customers, purchasing everything from workstations and software to peripherals. Solutions may in fact be acquired on behalf of the customer from IBM competitors, the ultimate in customer focus and service.

Again, this group is drawing on the leveraged buying power of Big Blue to accomplish big results for customers. And their creative approach to filling customer needs is another example of the swing from a traditional buying mentality to IBM's transformation into a solutions provider.

The Ombudsman Solution

In 1993 in the book *Breakthrough Partnering* we recommended that customers move to engage the best suppliers and draw on their expertise by working hard at communications. We introduced the concept of the world-class customer, an organization so attuned to the general health of the enterprise that it could not help but work hard at communicating and partnering with its suppliers.

World-Class Customers

Some companies, like Motorola, Honda, Solectron, and Harley-Davidson, are world-class customers; they continue to struggle with communications and other issues so dear to suppliers' hearts. Their success is reflected in the preference of their best suppliers to do business with them rather than their competitors. Supplier surveys, like those pioneered by Motorola with its entire supply base, followed and improved upon by Solectron and Honda, were key to opening and building trusting communications. Most suppliers have problems with their customers from time to time; not all suppliers, however, feel protected enough to take these issues to a positive resolution with their customers. Sometimes there is too much at stake to risk the wrong response.

But enlightened customers like Motorola, Honda, and IBM understand and are committed to the benefits of proactive communications because they understand how dependent they are on supplier expertise, and they understand as well that suppliers want to hire themselves good customers. Issues about payment, confidentiality, quality requirements, and other sensitive topics require well-considered responses for the good of the partnership, and IBM believes that a thorough approach to the process prevents bad results.

IBM purchasing is an innovator in buying on the Web as well. By removing paperwork from the traditional buying process (old estimates of traditional transaction costs, per transaction, ranged from $30 to $125 per transaction), purchasing saves money and, most important, frees buyers' time for more strategic activities.

Clearly, the five years Richter dedicated to transformation of procurement at IBM prove that purchasing's strategic contribution to corporate growth and health is nearly limitless. The innovative introduction of new groups and practices has become a model for revitalizing stalled-out companies.

Leadership Transformation No. 2, Daimler/Chrysler

The transformation of Chrysler contrasts with IBM's later complete reinvention of its business. Although the automaker stayed in the same industry as it struggled to make its comeback, the company basically had to refocus on its supply base. Chrysler's reputation among suppliers and others in the purchasing world had been, even as recently as ten years ago, at the bottom of the pack. Thomas Stallkamp's predecessor, David Platt, came from the old school—the "kick 'em in the head," approach to vendor management. As his successor, Stallkamp, formerly head of one of Chrysler's parts divisions, an internal supplier, had experienced his share of abuse; he had developed a sympathetic understanding of the difficult position suppliers daily found themselves in. The new purchasing chief learned the hard way the value of treating suppliers with respect and the benefits of working with them; it almost seemed that overnight he promised the supply base: Chrysler was going to become a different kind of customer.

In an amazingly short time suppliers noticed the change in attitude from Chrysler. In the years before GM's infamous Lopez came to Detroit, Chrysler had engendered an equally bad response among suppliers; heavy-handed tactics included pitting one supplier against another and being less than forthcoming about new product planning and strategic growth initiatives. Word got out that there was new management in place, and within a year or two, the company started to build a different attitude of trust among suppliers. Other automakers took note. Chrysler was beginning to provide serious competition for good suppliers; the net effect was to raise the bar for all automotive customers to become better partners. In fact, supplier surveys for some time have placed Chrysler in front of another medal winner, Honda of America, for supplier relations.

Cost Reduction and Sharing Savings

Thomas Stallkamp did not take a warm, fuzzy approach to supply base management. A clear-thinking "car guy," he understood the competitive pressures Chrysler faced and the role outside sources and expertise could play in the company's revival. Key to his strategy of treating suppliers with respect was his SCORE sharing program and the right of last refusal. The SCORE program drew on supplier expertise to reduce costs and improve reliability and quality. The SCORE program rewards suppliers when they send in suggestions for specific cost-reduction ideas; if their suggestion is accepted, suppliers keep half the savings.

It is interesting to compare the shared savings programs of Honda and Chrysler; Honda's supplier development program does share supplier cost savings, but the transplant did not have a program in which suppliers could bring forward any cost reduction idea and receive credit for it.

John Deere has also developed a savings-sharing program called JDCrop, a program modeled after Chrysler's SCORE. Deere saved $51 million between January and September 1999; the five-year total is $200 million.

Business Guarantees

Like all top automakers, Chrysler wants to stay with its best suppliers. To reinforce the small and medium-sized suppliers' commitment to the partnership, Chrysler offers a right of last refusal. This means that suppliers knew they "had the business," or it was "theirs to lose"; but before the customer began the process of moving the business to another supplier, they promised to communicate with the supplier and discuss the opportunity or changed requirement. Suppliers come to understand and trust the rules, knowing that they would have the opportunity to make changes in contracts, pricing, and the like, rather than face huge, overnight changes in their own revenue base, a bad practice the old Chrysler procurement group was famous for.

The contrast between these two innovators, Daimler/Chrsyler, the turnaround king of the auto industry, and IBM, a company that continues to surprise us, is a lesson for any traditional procurement group thinking about taking the first step toward Best Practices. There are many paths to success; the most important decision is to take that first step. While IBM started fresh—first centralization and rationalization of the supply base, then careful selection of the best suppliers in each commodity—Chrysler improved on what they already had, rebuilding the corporate image along the way.

Leadership Transformation No. 3, Harley-Davidson

Garry Berryman, vice president of supply management at Harley-Davidson, a veteran of two other procurement transformation stories—John Deere and Honda both—has taken the best of his earlier experiences, implanted those ideas in Harley-Davidson, and built a structure to support permanent adoption of Best Practices. Berryman is also an innovator in the midst of Harley and supplier professionals that still carry the mark of energetic upstarts.

Harley enjoys a taste of the outcast culture that to the outsider clashes with a solid Midwestern ethic, but the combination seems to fuel new products and new ideas. John Deere people have a particular, and peculiar, purchasing personality—Midwestern and stolid, with a certain honesty and straightforwardness that marks a high level of integrity. If an Iowa farmer says he will do something today, it will be done, in contrast to a mercantile approach that changes with the wind. Berryman's approach to suppliers is honesty combined with all the power of Honda's supplier base development skills—the Honda training, philosophy, quality circles. It's a powerful all-American brew that has allowed Harley to put many new concepts in motion, including supplier advisory councils, procurement engineers, new software, and a new organizational structure.

One of Harley's most innovative changes has been to bring supplier engineers into Harley to test their own products. For example, if a supplier creates a new tool, a new coating for a tool, or some other production product, traditional procurement practice could take years for approval; the internal wheels move slowly, especially when internal engineers are busy working on current issues. This "hurry up and wait" game for new tools frustrates suppliers. Berryman cuts through the roadblocks by giving the tooling supplier engineers their own Harley office and documentation that they use to prove the value of the tool. Proving the tool therefore becomes the responsibility of the supplier engineer, who may work with the foreman or other production personnel to complete the project; the engineer stays full-time on site until testing is done, and the data that he gathers tell their own story. If a supplier, for example, claims to have a coating that causes a tool to last 40 percent longer, they will decide together what kind of testing should be done, and the engineer goes to work. The supplier engineer becomes head of the project team, and he removes much of the aggravation created by the competitive *selling*, rather than proving of a new tool. By freeing up Harley engineers, average time to run the test is cut by six to nine months, and if the tool is indeed as strong an improvement as the supplier's pitch claimed, the company will have earned tooling savings as well.

Leadership Transformation No. 4, SmithKline Beecham

Willie Deese, SmithKline Beecham's senior vice president and director of purchasing, is a charismatic leader who would shine anywhere he landed. A veteran of a tough and chaotic Digital Equipment Corporation's (DEC) outlying internal supplier group in Springfield, Massachusetts, Deese started at the bottom in 1976 as a co-op student from North Carolina and rose to site manager. DEC in the 1970s was still a star performer—stock splits and revenue growth made millionaires of many assembly workers and stockroom clerks. But the rainbow came to an end when the company's suicidal reliance on proprietary technology, combined with founder Ken Olsen's single-minded dedication to mini's, backfired. Olsen never believed in PC's; rumor has it that when Olsen belatedly announced DEC's PC offering, Rainbow's foray into personal computers, Steve Jobs wired a black funeral wreath to headquarters at the Mill.

Although the end result was clear, it took some ten years for DEC to find its sad resolution in the arms of Compaq, the next generation's troubled giant. Olsen's moral parameters did not include layoffs, and this ethic prolonged the company's end. Management danced around necessary decisions with nearly catastrophic results. Big mistakes layered on bigger ones as an exodus began, led, of course, by the best and most marketable executive talent, Willie Deese among them. Deese moved from DEC to SmithKline, then in early 1996, to their largest customer, Kaiser Permanente, where he created a corporate purchasing organization. One year later Deese returned to SmithKline to take on a powerful and difficult corporate leadership role.

Deese heads a worldwide purchasing group responsible for $6 billion of goods and services ($1.7 billion of raw material and packaging, $800–$900 million in capital equipment and construction; the balance is in all other noninventory goods and services ranging from computer equipment to temporary personnel, fleet, events and travel management, marketing and sales, and advertising and promotion) that runs well with a mix of strong characteristics—empowered professionals, thorough analysis, knowledge management systems, and rigorous internal and external goals and tracking metrics.

"More and more," says Deese, "the spend is being managed and led by purchasing. For example, we now co-manage marketing and sales expenditures. And the way we do it all is with cross-functional teams—we call it category management (formerly commodity management). We are very structured and analytical, and that is the way we buy goods and services around the globe."

Key to this data-driven strategy is a knowledge management system showing what SmithKline buys, from whom, and at what price. Deese believes that to effectively manage procurement on a global basis, managers must be able to answer these four seemingly simple questions:

1. What do we spend?
2. With whom do we spend?
3. What do we pay?
4. Where is this material bought around the globe?

It's a shock, but Deese believes that 80 percent of global procurement groups cannot answer these questions. The reason is that they have very different information and financial systems on a global basis; a part number for an ingredient common to global production might well appear with four or five different sku's. Glucose, for example, is used in seven different SmithKline locations, although the chemistry and the supplier are the same. Answering any of these four questions is impossible without basic system consolidation, a challenge for even producers dealing with a handful of components. SmithKline's Deese realized that his organization needed information, not just data, to systematically improve costs, so he called for the creation of a powerful, unique computer system to bring in the right numbers.

Spendtrak

SmithKline's answer, Spendtrak, a software system developed in-house that cost $1.2 million to create in nine months (says Deese, "we said we needed it quick"), from spec through implementation, helped purchasing to reduce their spend by $200 million (out of a total $1.7 billion). Spendtrak developed over thirty different commodity categories—sweeteners, corrugated, excipients, flavors, and so on—over twenty major and approximately thirty-five smaller countries around the globe. The new system significantly shrank the time to gather data, then offered a launch pad on which to develop category management strategies.

Follow the Numbers

"We get price arbitrage out of it. We can look at any given item across the globe, compare pricing among different suppliers in different countries, ask why, and move it." Deese is pleased because the system allowed planners to perform analysis that proved that SmithKline was paying a premium for many goods—sometimes 15 to 20 percent. "We knew that because we were in the pharmaceutical industry with large profit margins, we were not receiving the best pricing for our size and scale in the marketplace," says Deese. With a target of 21 percent cost reductions over a three-year time frame, and an ability to compare costs and suppliers and move commodities, just as a broker moves stock buys from one source to another, Deese believes they are on target. What started as a five-year program—to reduce cost by $200 million—was completely met in three years two years ahead of schedule and below budgeted cost. "We have probably lost 7–10 percent of the suppliers—they opted out, but in the major areas we are now working with about 2,000 globally who represent the bulk of the spend. It was a quid pro quo—the suppliers that worked with us, we were sure to give first preference with new products—they had first opportunity."

Spendtrak facilitates global collaboration because supply management pros work through the system on global teams. The beauty of the system is that it allows managers from India, South America, North America, and Europe to go on-line and see, for example, what's happening with glass contracts, or the comparative prices paid in London vs. Latin America.

A Strategy Shift, Innovation Through Knowledge Management

What's next? Deese believes the next real frontier is e-commerce—"the Internet will transform buying and selling relationships." SmithKline is piloting electronic auctions and looking at operation resource management systems; one developed internally will go to a commercial solution. Purchasing has been challenged to further reduce costs on packaging materials by $200 million over three to four years; on the noninventory side, managers took on a challenge to reduce goods and services expenses by $250 million. Each of these reductions funnels cash back into the business. "We are generating savings to help fund our R & D efforts, to buy additional advertising and promotion, which drives the top line of our company."

Category management at SmithKline is another of Deese's innovations. Category managers—commodity managers in other industries—totally understand the cost structure of their products, the industry, and the technology of that product, so that when they construct a procurement plan, they are presenting the complete picture of that commodity—past, present, and future. Planners look out five years and evaluate various decision options, the costs that affect the supply chain, for example, and purchasing's alternatives; planners look at various options to improve cost, quality, and delivery on a specific product over a five-year period.

John Bolla of Pittsburgh, a ten-year purchasing veteran, is SmithKline's third-party purchasing category manager; Bolla has also handled other commodities, including plastic packaging, but his concentration on third-party contract manufacturing is critical to SmithKline's cost reduction in the marketplace. Bolla manages negotiations and strategic issues for seventeen suppliers, of whom five make up approximately 70 percent of the spend. Preliminary work in this commodity group allowed SmithKline to reduce the supplier headcount, while purchasers studied the market, trying to determine which supplier could manufacture a breadth of products, rather than a single hit. Again, it's a matter of taking successes from a few big products in the group; Nicorette gum and the Nicoderm patch, two of the heavy hitters, make up approximately 70 to 80 percent of the total spend.

Virtual Plant

Category managers deal with the strategic arm of purchasing, sourcing, negotiation, pricing discussions, and the contract; purchasing's tactical arm reports to the operations group. SmithKline purchasing takes a unique approach to third-party contract manufacturing, treating it in an organizational sense as a virtual plant. Bolla expresses it this way: "We have virtual plant logistics people in operations that manage schedules, planning and forecasting, so that we don't have category managers tied up doing tactical things."

Still, bringing third-party contractors under control continues to be a challenge. SmithKline has worked creatively on its 21 percent-over-three-years cost reduction target, although Bolla reports there are still some roadblocks in the third-party group; many of the suppliers that have been managed by the commercial business have a different approach to supply management, "impediments to the business." For some products, especially ones like Nicorette gum, that cannot be purchased anyplace else in the world, "we have to work a little harder at total cost of ownership, total cost of value—it's more difficult than traditional purchasing"; joint teams help reduce supplier costs. Bolla relies heavily on the Spendtrak system, "a tremendous tool." Generic drugs and private-label gums, for example, will make the marketplace still more competitive; consumers will have more choices, and purchasing will have more challenges. The power of Spendtrak will be essential for intelligently managing cost pressures.

Category management can be a stepping-stone to a director slot either of an area or a region. Still, the current position calls up many new skills and energies in a way that the traditional buyer position cannot. Category managers can expect to spend 45 to 50 percent of their time on the road, visiting suppliers and exploring new ones, and they are constantly under the gun to innovate.

Poster Sessions

Deese empowers and excites employees because he believes in actively supporting knowledge sharing. Periodically, managers present their success stories at poster sessions, worldwide conferences where commodity managers share their stories. Deese likes the recognition factor, as well as the worldwide networking that these three-hour sessions facilitate. Attendees move from booth to booth and see what has been accomplished, a street fair of improvement. Deese believes in giving professionals the resources and the opportunity to exercise their strength, and the poster sessions show the powerful result of his charismatic leadership. Some of the success stories might be as simple as a project in which all the plastic syringes from around the world are consolidated for pricing; another project consisted of a homegrown laptop program to compare prices. The last poster session hosted thirty different booths, all data-driven but all designed to reward innovation and information gathering par excellence.

Deese encourages people to "show their stuff"; he believes recognition will carry the company into their next round of heavy market competition, including pressures from "the other drug company down the street, Bristol Meyers." Sharing stories at poster sessions turns into recognition for Best Practices—success breeds success. Deese has run sixteen different sessions; each booth stays up for over three days, giving all attendees time to absorb the stories.

The Tough Part—People

Deese knows his people are doing transformational work. "Everywhere I have gone and done this—in three different companies—we have had the same exact kind of accomplishment," but there is a difficult side to it. "We have anywhere from 30 to 50 percent people turnover. And the reason is that you are now asking people to step up their performance by [an] order of magnitude—it's exponential. We are looking to save big amounts of money, as well as asking people to deal with very high-level professionals in the supply base, and to perform analysis at a much higher, more detailed level. Sometimes people opt out, and sometimes you have to make tough decisions." High-performance purchasing requires a different kind of purchasing professional, certainly not someone who "places and chases." Key to being successful is the ability to influence peers, senior management, as well as external senior management in the supply base—"the premium," says Deese, "goes way up on the ability to lead and facilitate cross-functional teams. Not everyone is cut out for it."

A certification program in category management, an internally developed exam, and some on-the-job training helps bring new people up to speed. The average age of new hires is the low to mid-thirties; compensation ranges for someone fresh out of college from $30,000 per year up to $100,000-plus for a top line, experienced category manager. "We expect big things from these folks," reiterates Deese, because "the average category manager has to reduce the cost of his portfolio by $1 million per year, and that is not necessarily easy in a regulated environment."

"They Have a Challenge the Minute They Walk in the Door"

Performance measurement is equally tough. A commodity manager's ability to hit target represents 30 to 40 percent of his or her annual merit and bonus rating. Once managers reach grade 7 and above, they become eligible for bonus and for stock, and their stock and bonus rating is impacted by their ability to hit target, a number that is tracked religiously. "We realize," says Deese, "that you can't hit targets unless you are tough, and we give them a lot of support. I view my job as looking out into the future, at what will be required from business and technology—I work hard at putting plans and strategies in place, and removing roadblocks and barriers so that people can do the work."

What's Next for SmithKline

Category management was a major change for SmithKline, says Deese: "Two or three years ago purchasing was not viewed as the core. We have changed that—we understand that this is a large part of the cost basis of the company."

"We think we are doing some innovative things in supply management," declares Deese. "Our key drivers were that we wanted an ability to connect procurement on a worldwide basis—have people from India, South America, North America, Europe—all go on-line with Spendtrak and see, for example, if there is a contract for glass, and the price. We knew we had to have executive management in our company involved, and so we do supplier forums around the world—typically we have the CEO and other executives from suppliers participating with our senior executives as well. This is the way we have put it all together—we really involve and engage the entire company." The benefits are far-reaching in SmithKline, he believes, because even the involvement of marketing and sales has changed—"it's phenomenal!"

Deese says, "We never stop—we believe the next real frontier is e-commerce and the Internet. It will transform buying and selling relationships, so we are piloting electronic auctions and other e-Tools."

Leaders in the Supply Base

It's easy to look for innovation leaders only in big producers—the Hondas, Chryslers, and IBMs seem to take up all our attention. But there are many faster, brighter, and, by necessity, more innovative leaders working in small and medium-sized suppliers. Peter Bemis, the president of Bemis Manufacturing in Sheboygan Falls, Wisconsin, is an example; Bemis calls their work "success by association."

The Teardown

When John Deere was looking to raise productivity and lower the cost of some of their lawn products, Bemis had a solution. Out in the country, Bemis set up a skunk works in a warehouse where teams could go to work and focus on tearing down a line of Deere garden tractors. Teams of engineers and suppliers, several subteams, as well as industrial designers arrived on site for several days of brainstorming. The results they came up with included reengineering concepts to reduce part count, consolidate, and provide subassemblies directly to the Deere assembly line that raised Deere productivity. In three months using multifunctional teams—not only engineering but quality managers, engineers from Deere's Horicon works—personnel tore down the unit piece by piece.

Horicon engineers gave the team good numbers to start from. As engineers came up with concepts for improvement, they classified brainstorms as "reach," "stretch," and "leap." Reach ideas were easily attainable; stretch would require additional engineering work to validate, and leap ideas represented "out of the box" thinking, concepts that industry had not seen before that would require more investigation validation and time to develop. The goal was to bring real value to the marketplace.

The team presented results to Horicon management; for each concept the exact benefits, investment required, and cost savings were presented. The team had torn the tractor down into seven sections; the hood assembly, for example, a "reach" concept, yielded projected annual savings of $629,000. Other sections were equally promising; the instruments pedestal, projected savings of $552,500; the steering wheel came in at $45,500; seating, $184,400; mower deck, $706,000; fuel delivery system, a "reach" concept, saved $105,400.

Bemis's contribution of co-injection technology—the encapsulation of an alternative material on the inside of an aesthetic material—changed the way hoods were produced and lowered cost as it improved impact strength. Other components—the grill, the bumper, and various sections of the hood assembly—yielded big savings with relatively low investment. At the end of the teardown project, the consortium team presented a number of solutions for reducing Deere's total cost by more than $2.2 million per year.

Bemis, participated on one team, described by an engineer team member as "just a team member—Peter has many skill sets, is very creative and innovative with engineering concepts," although Bemis's academic degrees are in business and philosophy.

"The idea of a supplier alliance isn't earth-shattering," said Bemis. "What has been remarkable, though, is watching the idea be put into practice, and then watching the practice produce measurable results that single suppliers acting alone could not have delivered."

Together with Kelch Corporation, an injection molder also head-quartered in Wisconsin, Bemis launched the Consortium, a supplier

John Deere LT Teardown

Developed "Reach, Stretch, and Leap" Concepts for Each Region of Tractor

- Steering Wheel
- Fender Deck
- Mower Deck
- Fuel System
- Frame
- Instruments/Pedestal
- Seating
- Hood Assembly

Consortium Identified New Opportunities to:

- Reduce Deere's Vendor Base
- Substantially Decrease Number of Parts
- Free Up Line Capacity
- Leverage Latest Advances in Materials Engineering
- Capitalize on Advances in Supplier Technology
- Maintain or Enhance Product Aesthetics
- Get Improvements to Market Quickly
- Savings Exceeding $1 Million per Year

Figure 7.2 Reach, Stretch, and Leap Innovation Ideas

alliance offering OEMs new product development assistance. Bemis believes the Consortium's premise is simple: synergy works better, faster, and at a lower total cost. "We bring people together across conventional boundaries, identify synergies between competencies, and leverage them to everyone's benefit."

Alliance Keeps OEMs and Suppliers Lean

Dennis Nourse, president and CEO of Kelch, says the Consortium "increases the supplier's chances of surviving vendor consolidation efforts." Nourse added that the Consortium approach "allows both OEM and supplier to stay 'lean and mean'." It's a familiar enough scenario: where price-per-part and quality are comparable, suppliers make the cut based on their ability to add unique value. That could mean engineering or materials expertise, advanced technology, exceptional capacity, or some combination of all these attributes.

"A number of our competitors have responded by trying to sustain a host of in-house competencies beyond the core functions of their businesses," Nourse said. "This, of course, adds overhead, making it more difficult for them to reduce the OEM's total cost without sacrificing their own profitability."

Nourse contended, "The Consortium concept lets suppliers sidestep this dilemma. Each supplier contributes unique value toward total cost reduction, without the burden of 'one-stop shop' overhead."

Beyond the Teardown

Bemis noted that the Consortium's model allows for the roster of participating suppliers to vary based on the needs of a particular project. "We had injection molders, materials suppliers, an industrial design firm, and key OEM representatives. Future Consortium projects could conceivably include competencies ranging from rubber molding to steel stamping to upholstery manufacturing." In fact, additional consortium projects were completed with Whirlpool, Carrier, and Kohler.

The constant, Bemis and Nourse agree, will be bringing together OEMs and suppliers who share common concerns. "Specific expertise aside, the Consortium can be only effective if participants bring similar concerns to the table," said Nourse. "They have to have a passion for new thinking. They have to value cross-functional collaboration. And they have to be willing to sacrifice no small number of sacred cows along the way."

Transformation Leadership

The best organizations have the best leaders, and the best leaders hire and develop the best people. Best Practice organizations are instantly recognizable by the excitement that bubbles up among empowered, involved professionals.

Ten years ago we might not have been able to recognize a really good company until Honda showed how purchasing should really be done. Co-author Nelson remembers from his Honda days that what made the company grow so fast was management's drive to involve and empower their workforce right down to the line worker. The local supply base was grown and improved at the same time with intensive supplier quality circles and training initiatives. Purchasing was equally empowered, growing from ten associates in the early eighties to over three hundred less than ten years later.

What makes these new supply leaders great? They are innovators and integrators, able to see beyond traditional practices to a few important market challenges. Typically, they have a sixth sense for talent and devise innovative methods to empower, recognize, and reward high performers. As integrators, they are not afraid to bring together suppliers and customers, and they pioneer new communications devices, like the supplier survey. They may come from the supply base, or their career path may have taken them through manufacturing or logistics, but they probably did not come out of purchasing. And many of them are engineers with strong technical foundations, managing organizations that are becoming more and more technically process-oriented.

8

SYSTEMS—BEYOND EDI

Becoming E-Enabled

Today, two major challenges exist for all organizations—speed and information access. Tomorrow, one additional challenge—information (or intellectual property) transfer and ownership—will further complicate the role of systems in the extended enterprise. This consideration has been much neglected by the purchasing profession and software sellers for the past two decades; it will emerge "in your face" with every mouse click on the Net.

It has been possible for supply chains to operate with an odd mix of faxed, EDI'd, and various main software packages, with an occasional manual or small, innovative software program thrown in as long as a few human hands—clerks, expeditors, freight forwarders, and so on—were there to keep the pieces together. However, the 95,000 baud rate demands of most e-enabled businesses, drawing directly from consumers all the way back through the pipeline to manufacturing and purchasing, has restricted the effectiveness of even the smartest human systems aid—the speed just isn't there.

Thinking Beyond Lean . . .

This is a challenge that not even the urge to simplify will satisfy. Leanness unbundled from one organization to another is not the complete answer to the e-challenge. Let's look at two examples—automobiles and computers—that illustrate.

The typical automobile is assembled from five to six thousand components and assemblies supplied by three hundred to four hundred good first tier suppliers, who are in turn supplied by hundreds of second and third tier and raw material suppliers. Such a network that touches perhaps one thousand various companies, especially one in which the lower tiers are supplying more than one big customer, offers exponential opportunities for complexity. Schedules, quality requirements, management philosophies, technical specs, tooling, even trucking arrangements—all present a different picture of the extended enterprise capabilities; speed and transaction protocols represent a whole other cluster of complex parameters. It is impossible for even the best trained human minds to plan and manage such an operation. Chrysler, GM, Honda, Johnson Controls, and hundreds of other "purchasing-enriched" organizations prove this daily.

It won't be like this forever, however. A handful of very smart systems innovations can extend the power of the human brain—"wetware"—the same way ATM back-office software expanded the calculation and transaction capabilities of the bank teller; the same way control tower dispatchers and signalmen became air traffic controllers, and biplane pilots became 777 information monitors in the cockpit. Systems are a basic requirement for simply moving information: triggers, signals, exception reports, and midcourse adjustments; but systems can be "trained" to produce what-if scenarios, to reset the course under certain conditions, and to think ahead to what a network may perform, given various possible events.

When we presented the vision of smart manufacturing beyond lean initiatives, we envisioned a blurring of the boundaries between manufacturing and procurement. In fact, other boundaries blurred, all the way from new product concept through design, prototypes, and first-volume builds. Simplification in the procurement organization and in other production jobs will continue, even as information volumes increase exponentially.

Learning to Ask the Right Questions

Just as manufacturing has progressed into an e-enabled network of linked customers, suppliers, and freight movers, so has procurement entered a big growth time marked by the need to ask the right questions. Advanced supply chain organizations in the Top Ten seem to understand what questions they need to be able to ask daily; they seem to have identified the best source of information for answers, and they are constructing e-pathways to funnel the right information to their planners. This massive construction project is difficult for many groups to see, but the lines are there. Leaders like Joe Yacura of American Express, Dave Meyer of John Deere, and Dave Otterness of Flextronics are among the insightful few who see the possibilities for redefining their own jobs by building the systems they need to become information seekers, information managers, and information sellers. They understand that their organizations are no longer sources of bricks and mortar, metals and plastics. They are the key to money movement through the processing cycle, and they understand that the only route is through e-enabled systems.

Find Your Spot on the Continuum

Supply chain is on a continuum. It's not just about the systems transactions that we are trying to conduct; it's about the questions we should be able to answer—quickly and, repeatedly—how do we process and serve up the data?

And the Winners Are . . .

The best information technology procurement groups are IBM, American Express, Flextronics, Sun, and John Deere. But in the area of brilliant innovation and gigantic leaps at the feet of Goliath is the Arizona start-up, Intellimet.

John Deere and Supplier Auburn Industries

Question: Quick, what do Darwin and a robotic tuna have in common with vehicle frames and small metal parts?

Answer: Genetic algorithm software that "magically" schedules thousands of parts and thousands of operations across suppliers' machine shops in Nebraska and Iowa.

Fulkerson's Obsession: A Meta System

John Deere is a big, old company that loves innovation. Its founder was born in Rutland, Vermont, in 1804 and grew up in Middlebury, where he received a common school education and served a four-year apprenticeship learning the blacksmith trade. In 1825, when the Industrial Revolution was picking up speed, Deere began his career as a journeyman blacksmith, and he soon gained considerable fame for his careful workmanship and ingenuity. His highly polished hay forks and shovels were in great demand in western Vermont. But in the mid-1830s, a downturn and emigration from the East lured Deere West. He took with him a small bundle of tools and some cash, and left his wife and family behind; they were to rejoin him later.

The trip took the Vermonter by canal boat, lake boat, and stagecoach, and finally, like others before him, Deere found himself in territory settled by fellow Vermonters, the village of Grand Detour, Illinois. The blacksmith was so welcomed that within two days after his arrival in 1836, Deere had built a forge and was in business.

One of Deere's first breakthroughs led to the company's founding and a long series of innovations that won the company dominance in the world agricultural equipment market. The cast-iron plows that the Midwestern farmers had brought with them from the East did not work well in the rich, Mississippi Valley soil; every few steps the farmer had to stop and clear off the plow blade. Plowing became a slow and tiring task, and some farmers considered moving on.

But Deere studied the problem and became convinced that a plow with a highly polished, properly shaped moldboard and share would scour itself as it turned the furrow slice. In 1837 he made such a plow, using steel from a broken saw blade; he tested the innovation on a nearby farm. Deere knew that this tool would be so well-received that he started making it in anticipation of farmers' orders, another departure from blacksmiths' traditional practice of building to customer order.

The "self-polishers" made from discarded saw blades were in great demand, and suddenly the blacksmith became the manufacturer. On the plains there were limited quantities of the quality materials he required, so in 1843 the entrepreneur arranged for a shipment of special rolled steel from England. The steel's journey, like the company founder's journey before it, was long—across the Atlantic by steamship, up the Mississippi and Illinois Rivers by packet boat, and overland by wagon forty miles to the little plow factory.

In 1846 the first slab of cast steel ever rolled in the United States was shipped from Pittsburgh to Moline, Illinois, the site of the company's current headquarters and Deere's first big factory.

Ten years after developing the first plow, Deere was producing one thousand plows per year. Deere continued to innovate, making changes in design as he felt farmers needed them. Deere continued to fill worldwide demand for new ideas, and even during the Depression of the 1930s, the company achieved $100 million in gross sales for the first time in its history. By 1955 the Vermont blacksmith's company had taken its place as one of the one hundred largest manufacturing businesses in the United States.

Deere Optimization Innovation

In May 1997, the Smithsonian Institution honored Deere and Company's use of Optimax's genetic algorithm–based schedule optimization software by including it in the Institution's Permanent Research Collection of Information Technology Innovation. On the John Deere seed planter assembly line, more than six million combinations of available options can be specified when the planters are ordered by the customer. With this software the factory's daily assembly schedule—a complex, multivariate equation beyond human capabilities for solution—is created in minutes.

Bill Fulkerson is a twenty-year plus veteran of John Deere, a trained mathematician with a biology minor. Fulkerson has the innocuous title of staff analyst and an uncanny eye for innovation. He became intrigued with chaos theory after reading a couple of books during the companywide Christmas shutdown in December 1992. He readily absorbed the ideas of complex systems and became especially enamored of genetic algorithms. The company was assembling an increasing variety of new products while reengineering their order fulfillment process to reduce time to fill customer orders. Faced with what Fulkerson calls an "infinite variety" of products with an untold number of options that were impossible to forecast, the company experienced growing inventories of raw materials and unsold products.

Fulkerson had a visceral sense that genetic algorithms could help resolve Deere's scheduling problems. Perhaps genetic algorithms could be used to search for improved schedules, rather than relying on departmental schedulers with legal pads and spreadsheet templates.

It was worth a try.

In 1993 Fulkerson found a site on the Internet where scientists exchanged information about genetic algorithms. He posted a message asking if anyone knew anything about scheduling a production line, and one week later, he had a response. Bolt, Beranek & Newman, Inc., had used genetic algorithms to schedule work at a U.S. Navy lab. A prototype scheduling system was developed at John Deere to run on a PC located adjacent to the loading dock. Essentially the software played God (or perhaps more correctly, Darwin), running through up to six hundred thousand schedule iterations of a monthlong planning horizon of planter orders with each iteration seeking to "breed" an improved schedule.

The software product was called OptiFlex by its originators, the Optimax Systems Corporation of Cambridge, Massachusetts. The biological parallel is sexual reproduction; the objective is to search through strings of information (schedules) to reduce the impact of infinite variety on assembly-line effectiveness. "In the past," recalls Fulkerson, "our challenge was volume—now the challenge has become variety."

"Planters are ideal for this approach to scheduling," says Fulkerson. "You can configure a rectangular frame to handle from four to thirty-one rows." The assembly has seed boxes and seed delivery systems, a component of the variety. "It's like building a VW bug right next to a big school bus on the same line, the same day. We had the challenge of trying to level the work requirements on the feeder lines as well. Big frames take a long time to build up and cool, and we put in every constraint we had to make the software robust."

The use of genetic algorithms enabled John Deere to breed a better class of production schedule that met both market and manufacturing constraints while operating as efficiently as possible. The process starts with a population of schedules (say, ten or twenty) from which two parents' schedules are selected by chance, biased by an assessment of their fitness. Two new schedules are derived from the parents by breaking them at an arbitrary point and exchanging parts as in cellular mitosis. In the Darwinian sense, these children undergo natural selection, with superior children being introduced into the original population while the population size is kept fixed. The population becomes more fit at subsequent iterations, until there is little chance of further improvement, and the process halts with the fittest member of the population designated as the production schedule.

When asked "What's next," Fulkerson responds that he sees most manufacturing software companies racing to incorporate available-to-promise and capable-to-promise routines to take the traditional manufacturer closer to producing customer orders on demand, or mass customization. From there it's an easy jump for successful software providers to move from these strategies to promise-to-profit strategies (PTP). The reduction of capacity coupled with a flexible and agile response to demand variation sets the stage for achieving price realization above "cost plus" formulas. Yield management strategies that reward long-range purchase guarantees with lower prices and extract premium price for short-term delivery are on the horizon. Firms will reserve capacity for premium-priced, short-term production and manage long-term purchase contracts. In the end, not all customers will be of equal value to the firm.

Fast Forward to MIT's Dome, the Pratt School of Naval Architecture

Art not only imitates nature, but also completes its deficiencies.

—Aristotle

Across Massachusetts Avenue, not far from the famous Smoot Bridge, three stories beneath the big Dome, the site of dozens of brilliantly successful MIT hacks, including those positioning a police cruiser, a large plastic cow, and numerous other objects on the roof, strange doings continue to mysteriously advance the cause of "science." This time the subject is fish, penguins, and underwater propellers.

It's All About *Drag*

When fish swim, the movement of their fins is like the less efficient spinning of a propeller; the side-to-side flapping leaves little eddies of water—positive and negative "space"—that propel the tuna forward. But some fin energy is wasted motion, just as the energy expended to drive a propeller is not 100 percent effective. Marine scientists and naval architects for years have focused much of their design energy on improving the drag ratios and propeller systems in the vehicles they create. At some point, they decided to look to nature for a better way—better shape, better movement, better skin—to move the boat faster, with less fuel, through the tank.

MIT scientists discovered that the bluefin tuna is one of nature's most efficient swimming machines, capable of reaching speeds of up to forty miles per hour. Observers were puzzled, because the fish's swimming motion held an efficiency secret—visually, the tuna did not appear to be that efficient a swimmer. There was something they were not seeing.

That's where colored dies, computer modeling, and the MIT submersion tank come in. Self-guided robots and autonomous underwater vehicles (AUVs), the marvelous devices that locate sunken wrecks and pieces of broken aircraft, are important topics for underwater research; scientists want to develop better propulsion systems that will go faster and use less energy. This is just one piece of a rebirth of research in hydro propulsion technologies—fast ferries, fast boats, and, yes, fast fish.

Researcher David Barrett directed the construction of a robotic tuna, dubbed "Charlie," modeled from the body of an actual prize Atlantic catch; the Robotuna's forty-one ribs and eight vertebrae, and flapping fins, all covered with a blueish skin, were built to attempt to pattern a robotic swimming machine after the best characteristics found in nature. Millions of years of evolution have developed phenomenally efficient propulsion and agility for real tuna, and that's where Darwin comes in. Out of Darwin's fish population, only a few "fittest" fish are chosen through natural selection—the deformed or slower ones get eaten by bigger fish—to continue their line; succeeding generations evolve to better, faster, "fitter" fish.

Man-made propellers generally demonstrate 50 to 70 percent efficiency, but Charlie's robotic flippers, as measured through computer simulations tested in the tank, achieved 90 to 95 percent efficiency. Clearly, propulsion experts could learn much from natural and roboticized tuna swimming systems.

Color coding the wake created by Charlie as he flapped from one end of the tank to the other revealed that his side-to-side tail motion created a thrust jet that moved his body forward. Scientists also dis-covered from studying live fish that other body parts—backbone, stomach region—contributed as well to forward movement and to the tuna's total drag ratio. So the challenge became determining which of the millions of possible combinations of body movement worked best for Charlie.

Evolution Fast-Forwarded

The term *genetic algorithm* may sound a bit fancy, but the simple computer rules resemble evolution. The program uses a comparison of two values—parents to the child—and the question, "is it greater or lesser" (better or worse). If the child solution doesn't fit better, kill it and try the next calculation. The optimization program is basically a comparison routine that keeps comparing many variables one to another until the program finds the best solution to accomplish the objective—getting tuna through the water.

The program is not difficult to build. Step one is to define the pop-ulation, then specify the variables, then do a calculation of Charlie's speed, given one specific variable—no fin movement, for example. Ask which is better, the calculation result with no fin movement or the result of the second calculation, movement with one fin flapping a little. The computer (evolution) selects a value that represents "one fin flapping a little." Next, pick another variable—one fin flapping a little and the other flapping six inches every two seconds. Ask, "Is that better than the parent?" Yes. Continue iterative comparisons until you have evolved the perfect solution—a child—that meets all your parameters (travels forty knots through heavy seas for eight hours at a stretch), and you will have "evolved" the perfect swim-ming machine.

Although a human could do the optimization problem, it would take months, and the ability to change parameters is so limited that computer algorithms are the only practical way to run the exercise. Furthermore, making a slight change in variables is a characteristic scientists want to be able to do fairly easily for multiple what-if iterations. Clearly, the makeup of such a complex creature as Charlie would be hard for us to duplicate. But Barrett set seven parameters for movement in his computer-generated program, totaling some 282 million combinations of possible movement patterns, and let it run. The genetic algorithm cranked through millions of years of virtual evolution, comparing one generation to the next, and selecting the best swimmers (the survival of the fittest), to generate the best fin movement. Robotuna's resulting speed and efficiency did not reach nature's ultimate swimming capacity—tunas have been clocked at 250 miles per day—but scientists learned a lot about optimization. Better propulsion systems using less energy burned over a more torpedolike shape can stretch the terms of battery-powered underwater devices, for example.

One More Leap, Back to the Plains of Nebraska

An idea is a feat of association.

–Robert Frost

Remember our original question, "What do Darwin and a robotic tuna have in common with vehicle frames and small metal parts?" The common denominator is of course a genetic algorithm program, this one much cheaper and faster than John Deere's first $100,000 application. But the goal of each application—from seed planters, down through tunas and pikes, and back to John Deere equipment components—is finding the most efficient and fastest way, the "best" way, to handle huge product variety.

"Leanness" vs. Variety and Complexity

Let's move to John Deere supplier Auburn Industries' pioneering work in Nebraska. The same genetic algorithm software concept has allowed planners to crunch massive amounts of data—possible combinations of work centers and process flows that make up the "ideal" (in a Darwinian sense, "fittest") combination of possible routings of thousands of parts to form good combinations of machines in cells that carry the most common parts routings. This is why the exciting possibilities for genetic algorithms that duplicate millions of years of Darwinian selections are so important in a manufacturing community obsessed with anorectic leanness: *variety can be reduced or managed only so far into simplicity*. The market is demanding more and more complexity, and only the power of computing systems using intelligent data management, like Evolver, Deere's choice for their pioneering genetic algorithm scheduler, can handle the exponentially multiplied number of possible combinations.

Optimization

Dave Meyer is a supply base manager for Deere's World Wide Agricultural Division. Dave specializes in plastics sourcing on paper, but his real thing is innovation.

Dave has discovered another one of those manufacturing pioneers, a simple optimization solution to the complexity problem so many suppliers and their customers find overwhelming. Here is how it works.

Imagine a truck driver tasked with making deliveries to forty-one different towns in North Dakota; some towns must be visited before others. The driver's goal is to find the shortest route between the towns; he can adjust his schedule somewhat, but one of his constraints is that certain towns must be visited before others. It's a multivariate optimization problem that faces typical manufacturers every day. Enter Evolver.

Evolver is an off-the-shelf add-on software package available from Palisade Software Corporation (www.Palisade.com) that installs on top of Microsoft Excel; access is through MS toolbars. To use Evolver, the user first creates a model in Excel, including setting up parameters and any formulas or calculations. In the forty-one-town example, these would be the cities' locations, distances between all city combinations, and precedence relationships.

Evolver will create a certain number of guesses as to the best order of the cities—typically, says Meyer, fifty to seventy guesses would be enough for this size problem. Next genetics is introduced. Evolver takes 50 percent of the order from one guess and marries it with 50 percent of the order from another guess. A user-specified level of random mutation is then applied to the order and a new guess, or "offspring," is fully created with its own fitness score. We compare the new offspring's fitness score with their parents' fitness score, and if the new generation's score is better than that of their parents, we kill the worst and continue the generation/killing process until the program has bred better and better sequencing of the cities' delivery schedules.

Unlike real evolution, which plods through millions of years of living selection and "experimental" mutations, Evolver's software-based genetic evolution takes fewer than fifteen minutes to crank through this solution. Given the necessary start-up data, Meyer estimates most users can set up their model in less than one day.

Deere has successfully used Evolver in two different applications, the first internal to Deere for scheduling manufacturing equipment, to sequence various planter types through production and balance the load across different manufacturing cells. The second application is used with the supply base to change and improve plant layout and to set scheduling sequence for complex, multivariate parts catalogs, that is, to *manage*—not *reduce*—variety.

Many suppliers are typically set up to run parts in batches through functional departments—areas equipped with all drills, all lathes, all milling machines. Deere supply base engineers took one look at the clustered machines and batch production, and advised their suppliers that to reduce work in process and cycle times, they had to set up cells. The typical response, "But we're a job shop, there's not enough commonality, too many parts, low volume, cells won't work here," met with an atypical response from the Deere engineers: "We think they do, and we'll show you how."

Armed with a laptop loaded with Excel and Evolver, Meyer and John Knapp, Deere supplier development consultant, set out to provide the answer.

Four Thousand Planter Frames

Planter frames, the big add-on frames that drop seeds into furrows on a Deere tractor, take a lot of metal and assembly work—cutting, welding, bending, fastening. At Auburn Consolidated Industries' (ACI) factory, half the building was formed into customer-focused cells—welding through final assembly—and the front half, the problem half, was where fabrication and machining, lathes, press brakes, and other metal-forming equipment started the process. It's a vision of complexity that continues to defeat human scheduling capabilities.

But Meyer and Knapp argued that the 80/20 rule applied in this plant as well as most others, and they proposed a bit of analysis to prove their point. The numbers showed that two thousand of the four thousand parts represented 92.5 percent of the plant's production volume. Meyer and Knapp proposed that by concentrating on the top two thousand parts, they could decrease the analysis complexity without sacrificing accuracy.

The supplier furnished part number routings and the number of hours annually that each part used each type of machine, along with the numbers of machines in each machine category. All the data were cranked into the model, along with a few other parameters relevant to this supplier's problem. The replacement cost of buying an additional press brake, for example, was translated by the model into a factor that, should it call out the purchase of another machine, became a penalty cost. As simple as these numbers sound, getting them together can be quite an exercise.

Meyer suggested starting out with seven cells—trying to find seven different groups of machines and parts. The adjustable cells in the model were the machine combinations like a press break, drill press, a laser, or a drilling and milling machine, to see what the software said was best for the given population of parts.

Evolver's job was to adjust, take a guess, group machines in a cell, test the guess, run the parts across the virtual cell, and continue until the ideal population of parts across the ideal cell had been calculated for all seven cells. Capacity for various machines is factored into the formula, as is utilization. The program contains soft penalties for utilization over 85 percent while balancing this against underutilizing the equipment.

The model cannot throw all the equipment into all the cells because of the bonus and penalty points assigned for bad machine balance or new spending requirements. (If users need to buy a belt sander for under $100, the formula allows it.) The last factor is duplication; if parts are being duplicated in cells, a small penalty prevents the model from creating a good cell more than once—that would not be true optimization.

These factors are all tallied on a fitness screen, multiplied by a weight, and summed up into a fitness score. Understanding the relationships among the factors is the key to the model. This relationship is changed by adjusting the weight of each factor. "You're trying to get the model to make the right decisions. Evolver needs to know which is more important—adding forty parts to a cell or spending $4,000 on a new piece of equipment."

It's a complex goal to find the maximum number of total parts that will fit in cells without overusing the equipment, while enabling the best flow in the cell, with the least capital equipment outlay. This becomes the cell map for the new layout.

The second step is to define the specific drill press, milling machine, and press brake for the cell and determine the best way this cell and the others can be laid out in the facility. Individual machine capabilities may eliminate some parts from being run in the cell.

Time to Complete

From information gathering and analysis to moving equipment, phase one took five months. How does this new approach sit with supplier experts on site? According to Blake Beahler, Auburn Consolidated Industries industrial engineer, "People are generally happy— some grumbling—we just progress, we plod on. We set things up, and once it's running, if it breaks down for some reason, they start to gripe! Nobody likes change. Once they get adjusted, we're in. We're betting that one of the first results will be improved delivery."

What John Deere originally helped Auburn with, as part of their supplier development efforts, was moving to one-piece flow. The planter frame, whose weight totals nine thousand pounds, represented days of bending, welding, painting, and cutting, before it could be assembled for shipment. Auburn's upstream operations needed help, and Deere provided cell design know-how to change the batch process into something with more flow. Along the way, Auburn added point-of-use storage and kanban triggers; with one-piece flow, assemblers always found the right number of parts painted and welded to make a complete assembly. Planter assemblies contained 250 part numbers, over 2,000 pieces; the entire unit can be assembled in sixteen hours; normal headcount to assemble was ten workers; that number has been cut to five.

Auburn personnel were so pleased with the change from batch to one-piece flow that they implemented the same process changes in two other weld/paint assembly lines. When it appeared that they had truly achieved flow in half the factory, a disconnect with initial operations became embarrassingly clear. With batch in one half and its accompanying outages and delivery/quality issues, Auburn decided in the spring of 1999 to cellularize the remaining up-front, primary part manufacturing operations; of 2,000 total parts, 250 would be manufactured in-house, with the other third fasteners and wire harnesses, hydraulic components, and the like purchased outside.

"Intuitive Cells"

Planners attempted an intermediate exercise, developing "Intuitive Cells." By gathering experts on the system and defining good parts flows, and common routings, Auburn thought they were ready to set up cells. But, says Beahler, "we got cold feet—the more parts we thought up, the more parts we realized would not fit our flows, and the more we wondered how many parts we could really put into our Intuitive Cells. It was time to take a more analytical approach, starting with printed routings, about four thousand of them. Beahler remembers the actual complexity tally:

4,000 part numbers

250 whole goods run the previous year

75 work centers with routings

"It's overwhelming, the number of combinations. We called Deere—'we can't agree among ourselves on parts families—can you help?'" The first efforts to download the Auburn parts data from the MAPICS green screen system were awkward; data transfer took a couple months, plus some poking to "find the holes," for an additional hundred labor hours. Finally, Evolver, loaded to its data ports with routings and part number info, started to run. Two weeks later, the PC spit out the answer—"millions of years of evolution in a petri dish."

Beahler recalls that Evolver's cells were "surprisingly similar to the intuitive cells"; planners settled on four cells, an 80/20 split—80 percent of the parts fit nicely into these four cells. Planners played with the results and added a couple of small machines where needed, at less than $2,000 outlay. "One of the nice things about Evolver," says Beahler, "is that once you have the model established, it's just a spreadsheet, and you can make a change in the spreadsheet—see the calculation, and see the impact, see how many part numbers moved into the cell, and how many wouldn't run there. The only thing Evolver does is the random calculation and relative scoring. You go on faith that what it has is better than what it started with."

Don't "Just Do It!"

Auburn planners set to work with the answers they needed to physically move machines. Interestingly, from five months of data gathering down to getting it on paper, and setting up parts families, Deere's first advice to Auburn—"Just do it!"—was the reason they were willing to go to the Evolver approach.

Deere supply base engineer Mick McCleery believes that the key to supplier development is to "enable our suppliers to reduce their costs, but not take the price reductions off their margins. We have to show them how to reduce costs." One-piece flow helps, as does consolidation of raw material buys and scheduling and running production by parts families. McCleery believes that it's not always an easy sell—"I like going in and listening to them say, 'oh, yeah, JIT, that's when your supplier holds the inventory.' Then I know we have them—they don't know the difference between JIT, lean, kaizen, and lead-time reduction. Lead-time reduction represents a whole environment, from design to customer, and if you understand lead-time reduction you will understand the difference." It's very important, says McCleery, to start with a cell. "Manufacturing needs a system to find what makes sense out of thousands of part numbers."

Sun Microsystems

In 1996 Sun won the *Purchasing* magazine Medal of Excellence award for best performance in a number of areas typically neglected by other high-tech start-ups. But Sun saw themselves on another tier and dedicated high-paid resources to critical sourcing positions; the company's internal purchasing procedures were innovative and powerful, and supply management continues four years later to lead the way.

Randy Louie, director, strategy and business architecture, believes that Sun is "good at collaborating with the supply base, and good at dealing with the supply base all through sourcing, manufacturing, and delivery, and working with logistics suppliers."

The Scorecard

Sun uses Scorecard for its Top 40 suppliers to focus on product, process, predictability, as well as technology strategy and qualitative and quantitative input, like how well excess and obsoletes are managed, the ability to ramp and meet volumes. A share-the-gain program reinforces achieving mutual goals by encouraging everyone to make improvements on cost and quality, especially in areas in which both sides will enjoy long-term benefits.

Sun continues to innovate in the systems area. Mike Jester, application architect for worldwide supply base management, believes the company has enhanced suppliers' ability to communicate with Sun. "We have several different tools—some homegrown, and we are evolving some others. We use standard EDI, and we have done this forever, and we now have the Sun Exchange." Sun Exchange is a site with URL that allows partners to come on-line and deposit CAD files that can be picked up and downloaded into their own system. ASN, Sun's version of a supplier network, allows users to log on and take qualitative data from Sun's internal network. Specific plans are accessed by suppliers through this network—product migration strategies, for example.

"It's all part of building a method," says Jester, to go through the firewall, versus posting to a bulletin board, "going B to B. . . . The less friction, the better. We want to exchange processes with information—we don't need people to stop, capture the data, reform—send the message straight through." Right now, Jester points to a select set of suppliers who enjoy this special relationship and IT capabilities—Celestica of Toronto, an external systems supplier, Seagate, and Solectron.

SunSpot, a supply chain optimization program developed internally, evaluates flexibility in the context of high and low cost limits. The program helps planners develop a baseline to drive business up or down from within certain cost parameters, through several levels of the supply chain. Because most Sun customers don't simply "buy a box," product changes tend to resonate throughout several layers of the system and the supply chain; it's important to plan to key component levels.

Sun's Single Portal

MRP runs daily to keep the system in sync; otherwise, planners run to an Available-to-Promise protocol. If customers want product in five days, planning's goal is to build processes that respond in five days. Customers can order product using a credit card over the Web—lead times are published in SunStore and updated regularly. Configuration validation for customer orders and order tracking (same as Federal Express track and trace) round out customer e-commerce capabilities. The goal is to offer a single portal for all customer configuration, buying, tracking, and service issues, a simple objective complicated by the exponential possibilities incurred by Sun's supply pattern of multiple site sourcing.

E-Enabled Consolidation and Coordination

"We ship," says Jester, "from multiple facilities, and we have to integrate the system at customer site. We are developing with logistics providers a signaling environment to bring together the monitor and CPU and disk drive suppliers." Armed with an Execution Event Plan, the logistics provider knows how to pick up three different system components, and he knows the timing and the sequence. If a customer in Boston, for example, orders two boxes from California and one from Chelmsford, the logistics provider can put the whole customer order together—virtually—on his system, based on signals received just as he picks up line items from Boston's Logan Airport. "It's easy," says Jester, "if you know the sequence of events and you understand the times—there is a certain logical order that takes place—pick up the box, scan it, take it to the hub, scan, issue inventory receipt, allocate to a sales order, etc." Easy, yes, for a system, but not something yet achieved, like Evolver, by ordinary human wetware.

Intellimet

Although we have been looking at well-known leaders in supply chain using systems to achieve breakthrough improvements, companies like Sun, IBM, Flextronics, and American Express, we stumbled across a number of brilliant unknowns, Intellimet among them.

Delivering value from the supply chain is as challenging as eliminating nonconformance on the shop floor, and Intellimet thinks they have a powerful software solution to this growing problem. Lori Frantzvé, president and CEO of the small but fast-growing Arizona firm, knows from experience as an IRCA- and RAB-certified auditor that on-site examinations and evaluations of supplier companies can be a full-time occupation that tends to produce reams of data but few results.

To translate data gathered in traditional audits into actionable business intelligence, Intellimet created a patented "virtual assessment" technology that enables a customer to qualify a supplier's capabilities in multiple categories without ever leaving the home office. "It's a much more efficient method," says Frantzvé. "You examine your entire supply base in one fell swoop, then prioritize off-site visits to address problem areas or pursue opportunities for improvement."

"A Value-maker, Not a Deal-breaker"

United Technologies Corporation selected Intellimet technology after comparing the company's work history with AMP, Caterpillar, Deere, 3M, and other major manufacturers. The virtual assessment process enables suppliers to provide their customer with detailed information about operations without the pain and suffering traditionally associated with audits. "Our clients use virtual assessment as a value-maker, not a deal-breaker," emphasizes Frantzvé. "They can see how their key suppliers are performing relative to ISO, Baldrige, or even EH & S characteristics and then use our reports to root out risks and prioritize continuous improvement actions."

By using Intellimet's patented technology, a company such as 3M—which has close to one hundred thousand suppliers that require periodic review and evaluation—might choose to visit thousands of locations on a virtual basis. "We let you look at a long list of geographically dispersed suppliers in a matter of weeks or months, not years or decades," says Frantzvé. "Our clients can build the assessments to evaluate historic problems, current needs, future plans, or all of the above. Imagination and vision are really the only limits to the process."

Virtual Assessment

C. Powell Adams, now a distinguished professor of business at Elizabethtown College (Pa.), described his past use of virtual assessment as "one of the more ambitious and successful projects that I managed during my twenty years at AMP." After piloting Intellimet technology with over three hundred suppliers, AMP applied virtual assessment to over 90 percent of its production supply base.

According to Adams, his supply base managers and quality engineers at AMP obtained "consistent and accurate evaluations along with commentary to drive meaningful corrective actions. We more than achieved our goal of reducing the cost of supply base evaluation, increased the productivity and utilization of our quality engineers, and had a consistent and unbiased methodology."

What's next for Intellimet? By mid-2000, United Technologies will begin deploying Internet-based virtual assessments across each of its divisions: businesses as disparate and diverse as Otis, Carrier, Sikorsky, Pratt & Whitney, and Hamilton Sundstrand. "They have more than ten thousand suppliers with an average of three to four sites apiece," says Frantzvé. "The project is ongoing in scope, with no end in sight."

Flextronics

Flextronics, the world's third-largest supplier of electronic management systems, based in San Jose, California, is a company with a short but impressive history of visionary and innovative leadership. From day one of this start-up climb to tier one leadership, CEO Michael Marks's vision of his changing industry has positioned Flextronics ahead of big market swings. Starting with the company's creative approach to combining engineering with production for customers' geographic needs, Flex has continued to expand product offerings as its internal operations become even more creative. We named Flextronics one of our Top Ten because they think like David in the midst of a field of Goliaths—they succeed on smartness and innovation, not size, and they look good to continue that approach even as they battle for the number-one slot in their business.

According to Dave Otterness, director of supplier management, strategic materials, Flextronics is experiencing high "organic growth of 80 percent per year," supplying customers like Phillips, Ericsson, Cisco, 3Com, and Compaq rapidly with high-quality hardware systems solutions.

The company is very decentralized, yet Otterness is proud of how well "the supplier is represented across the customer base. We manage and contract for a high level of part numbers—higher value stuff—by developing sources. We contract with the suppliers, which assures the price; we use purchase orders to buy under the contract, at the price and technology negotiated by the customer." For this industry, it's another change in how to deal with the market; most earlier transactions in this business have been based on consignment, making companies like Flextronics more of a *process* provider. They want to do more for customers, like work with the supply base to develop technologies built into the product, thinking ahead to technical solutions that work in the supply chain.

System Must Guarantee Supply

"We absolutely must have," says Otterness, "instantaneous and assured supply. We concentrate on TAM, total available market, on every new product, because we know it has to come up *fast*." Systems in procurement are key to Flextronics's meeting aggressive time targets; the company uses Baan worldwide: "We were their fastest implementation—eighteen months," says Otterness, and the system is linked to an internal MDSS that is replenished every twenty-four hours, so that every commodity manager can see the whole picture on contract pricing, and other issues, as he needs it.

The decentralized approach means for Flextronics suppliers, says Otterness, that they must "win the business every day." In a tough market, "it's the integrity issue that counts. The business units have to trust that we bring the best value. People want to make decisions quickly—we are not bureaucratic in commodity management." Worldwide, procurement manages a $2.2 billion spend, over a lean representation of key commodity managers—five in California, five in Western Europe, six in Central Europe, four in Asia.

Otterness notes that not all decisions in this fast-paced setup are guaranteed to produce good results. Based on a bad customer forecast Flex signed up for an overbuy in Asia, just before Christmas three years ago. "I should have known better," says Otterness, with hindsight, "they were betting on the come." Under a one-day deadline, with limited material availability and flawed visibility to the customer's end market, the decision proved the wrong commitment at that time. The screw-up resulted in revisiting the supplier to negotiate a way to make them whole, with concessions for ongoing business deals. Flextronics personnel had to work with the supplier for six months to finalize the fix, a very good example, says Otterness, of the importance of integrity and being absolutely clear on supply issues, knowing at all times how much material you really have in the pipelines. "We're looking to understand not lost margin, but what is in the pipeline. It takes a certain amount of time to make sure the information is correct—what the supplier had in WIP, for instance. Our guys went and checked, it was true, got that first level of trust. That's where consistency and relationship count."

Purchasing continues to balance an amazing amount of risk. And the market they supply sometimes comes down to something as iffy as which Saturday morning commercial the kids are most attracted to—Sega or Nintendo. It's purchasing's job to have an ear to the TV, to anticipate the whims of even its most changeable consumer. Systems help, but still, says Otterness, "it comes to integrity and trust. If you don't have programs with suppliers and very good systems, versus pure demand pull, you're taking on a lot of risk."

Demand Pull and Variety

Flextronics's strategy goes to demand pull that provides suppliers with a weekly forecast. Their Baan system enabled this key activity worldwide, so that every Monday, at every Flextronics facility, preset formulas and transactions keep the pipelines loaded. Suppliers gain six months' visibility at a minimum.

Moreover, Flextronics planners key a sharp eye to quality. Inbound lot quality is tracked on nonstandard components, and internal defects per billion per supplier audits are used; from companies like Motorola and TI, the quality figure is in the five units range. It's a constant battle to manage huge customer variety—part numbers, shipments, upcoming products, and obsolescence. More than 80 percent of the business is full configuration box build, so Flex purchasing pros must be experts at buying fabricated material, as well as packaging, plastics, and components from resistors to power supply.

The Guadalajara plant produces Palm Pilots, boxes for Web TV, Phillips and Sony units, Motorola and Nokia. By building the local infrastructure, Flextronics is not only participating in huge market and customer growth, but it is also brick by brick, board by board creating a mature, capable production resource ready to service customers globally. Flex recognizes that building a powerful infrastructure builds good suppliers for other high-tech winners, Hewlett-Packard and Solectron, for example, as well. They are raising the bar for decentralized, global improvement. Inbound and outbound logistics suppliers— Fed Ex, MSAS, and Emory—are all tied into Flex through a Web-based internal tracking system.

American Express

American Express is included in our list of Top Ten procurement operations because of the brilliant leadership and creativity of its procurement head, Joseph Yacura. American Express's global procurement office, reporting into finance, manages the supply line for everything that the company buys worldwide, except TV ads and ad agencies, for a total spend of over $4 billion—travel, computers, telecommunications, temp agencies, recruiters, direct mail, even the plastic for credit cards. Yacura's background sparkles with creativity and drive; to an undergraduate degree in music theory and composition, he has added an MBA in finance, an MS in accounting, and most recently a master's degree in quality management. He also completed the Stanford University Senior Executive Program and sits on several professional associations, university and private company boards of directors.

Yacura believes that quality is the basis for any business moving forward, and that is where he dedicated much of his group's internal focus. He emphasizes identifying the internal customer and gaining a clear understanding of their priorities and needs. Several techniques are utilized to gain this understanding. One technique is an on-line survey to assess customer satisfaction and priorities. The results are tabulated and annual quantitative targets are established and incorporated into everyone's annual goals and objectives.

An internal customer toll-free "quality hotline" has also been established. Internal customers can call the quality hot line with any concerns regarding quality of either the global procurement organization or any supplier-related issue. All calls are recorded and classified on an on-line system; every call is closed out with the internal customer within seventy-two hours.

Focus Groups

Yacura's group also uses internal and external focus groups to assemble internal customers and, for the first hour, present the business plan and its supporting strategies, then leave the room and ask for a critique. Each table presents their reactions, and then, says Yacura, "we drill down and take that information, and anything we need to change, and we meet the next day with suppliers, and commit to changes." It's the PlanDoCheckAct cycle modified for this challenge—Present, Leave, Critique, Feedback, and Adjust.

Customers are also surveyed electronically, using a rating scheme that asks them how American Express is performing. Planners have created a quality hot line in the United States by which any employee can call toll-free and share problems. Again, it's Plan-DoCheckAct in action; the toll-free call categorizes the issue in one of thirty categories in a central database for further action.

The global procurement organization looks beyond the traditional roles of a procurement function and is exploring ways to expand its role in providing cost management solutions to its external customers.

With significant spending power, American Express has teamed with its service establishments to leverage buying power and reduce costs. A steakhouse chain, for example, has teamed with its supplier to reduce the cost of printing meal checks by accessing American Express's printing provider. The net result of over 12 percent per year savings has created a hunger for more creative opportunities from leveraging the spend.

"Our organization has taken the model of the Wall Street analyst," says Yacura. "We need to understand costs worldwide, and alternatives to secure our position in the marketplace, and we want to use technology to get there." Although Yacura's group may be doing traditional purchasing, with heavy focus on the customer—what the customer needs to grow his business—"much of what we are doing is moving from tactical to strategic planning. We have gotten ourselves out of a traditional paper-based acquisition process, for example."

External customers are restricted to buys from approved suppliers, and the technology assists moving procurement into a different public position. "Before, internal customers would come to us *reluctantly* to process an order. This process was providing limited value to the corporation and was viewed by the customer as a slow, cumbersome, and bureaucratic activity. We have reengineered the process and now internal customers place their orders directly with contracted suppliers. We now have leveraged our buying power, implemented product/service and delivery standards, while reducing administrative overhead and cycle time. Our internal customers have more control over the process and couldn't be happier. This could not have been done without increased communications and access to information that is now available through our systems."

Software—The Heart of the System

"We are pushing the envelope, abandoning the traditional mindset and becoming value-add consultants and advisers to our customers. If we can do this internally, we can leverage it to benefit not only the entire company, but also our external customers," Yacura reflects. The means to the end is simple enough, but the application is brilliant.

Lotus Notes carries a quality and value statement on-line; personnel conduct on-line discussions on specific topics—globally, complete with reference materials in major centers covering training, texts, manuals, employee development issues like position descriptions, and competency. Forty global commodity managers throughout the world are responsible for buying products and services. Their strategies, suppliers, performance metrics, critical correspondences, and so forth are all on-line.

The technology is offering increased market intelligence information, homepages, trade publications, call centers, foreign trade info—the more information available on-line the better the intelligence that commodity managers create and plan for. What American Express does extremely well—perhaps better than more traditional financial institutions like banks—is move money and make contacts.

With nineteen different procurement locations, Yacura sees an ongoing challenge with managing multilingual programs. Dealing with such global diversity—personnel fluent in English, Spanish, German, French, Italian, Swedish, Dutch, Mandarin, Japanese, and Portuguese—can be improved only with global technology assists. Lotus Notes "Guidelines for Outsourcing," for example, is building cross-cultural capabilities around supplier evaluation and tracking.

Artificial Intelligence System

Finally, a state-of-the-art artificial intelligence–based (AI) system has been created to help the organization retain valuable knowledge, a decision-making assist. The system is designed to help focus on the right questions, for example, in creating a statement of work for hiring consultants or systems programmers. The same logic can be used to create a set of performance metrics, or a total life-cycle cost model.

The system works to reduce cost and cycle time; there are many repetitive tasks of consistent processes, methodologies, and industry-accepted procedures and criteria that could leverage the power of AI. "When someone called procurement in the past," says Yacura, "it was the luck of the draw who they got—did that person ask the right question at the time? We are trying to put as much knowledge and learning into the system; we can focus on making change in the knowledge system, rather than bringing two hundred people in different countries up to speed. For areas like development of a statement of work, or supplier quality/performance metrics, AI is a perfect solution."

Yacura believes American Express is good at managing the financial aspects of a business, including its supply line. Another of his objectives—to be the best in the implementation of the corporate purchasing card—is a reflection of the company's eagerness to seize and perfect new technologies. "We are pretty good at managing globally—others are thinking about it, a lot of them have fragmented national operations. But we have benchmarked by looking at banks and financial institutions around the globe. We have always focused procurement differently from the way it is done in manufacturing—they're for the most part looking at improving the traditional processes. We are trying to take procurement into a whole new area. We see nothing but unlimited opportunities ahead."

Systems Are Key

We have looked at the best and most innovative systems that our Top Ten companies have to offer, and we are excited by the possibilities they have each created. Moving beyond MRP and ERP behemoths, each of our notable systems pioneers—Deere, IBM, American Express, Flextronics, Sun, and Intellimet—has approached e-enabling their businesses with, first of all, great innovation. We think these pioneering systems are what will actually move purchasing and supply chain management into the age of the extended enterprise. Trust and partnering work will take companies dependent on each other for success only so far globally. And the issue of leanness and simplicity in an era of unstoppable complexity will not go away or be managed into compliance.

E-Manufacturing (E-Man℠)

Advanced supply chain management and supplier production pros have no choice but to embrace e-manufacturing, the e-enabled capability that connects material sourcing, product design, and idea transfer, along with the more mundane operations in production, along the shared, global nervous system called the Web. At the front end of supply chain's management job lie the systems that simulate enterprise layout and customer activity patterns; next, we need systems to move CAD and other intellectual property files back and forth; the third requirement, setting up and managing the flow of parts through processing plants like Auburn Industries' machine shop, addresses lean manufacturing's failings and takes manufacturing into the next era, e-manufacturing (e-man℠).

9

LEADERSHIP FOR BEST PRACTICES

*The best way to influence top management
is to be top management.*
–George Harris, VP Purchasing, TRW (retired)

I*f you want* purchasing to take the leading, strategic role in your company's success, *you must leave management no choice.*

For generations, purchasing professionals have whined about their lack of visibility in their own companies, about being treated less than professionally when compensation and perks are handed out, about being the last to know of new strategic initiatives. And the truth is, they have deserved it.

The remedy for all these complaints, and for the bigger issue of using procurement as a lever to cut costs and improve efficiencies at suppliers' plants, is for supply management professionals to act like leaders.

IBM

Under the leadership of Louis V. Gerstner Jr., IBM's transformation is only beginning—although we may be unsure of the specifics of the numbers that will describe Big Blue and its partners in twenty years, business historians, according to *Industry Week's* John Teresko, "will marvel at the way he harnessed the technology power of IBM Corp. to help propel world commerce to a new economy—e-business".*

Gerstner is quoted as ascribing "nearly $20 billion of the com-

*Teresko, John, "Driving Success at New Blue," *Industry Week*, Dec. 6, 1999, page 56.

pany's revenue—about 25 percent of the total . . . to the Internet . . . in
December 1998 alone, IBM bought more than $600 million in goods
and services over the Internet. Procurement spends a significant
amount of total buy over the web—more than $600 million, and pro-
jections are for *savings of approximately $240 million in 1999 from
streamlining and offloading procurement processes to the Web."*
Clearly, IBM purchasing is leading the company into e-commerce
with the new systems it has created for e-commerce buys.

Begin with the End in Mind

—Steven Covey

———————

Every business entity that progresses has the stress of external challenges to urge them on—demanding customers, shifting markets, and
technologies. But we are recommending an internally generated discipline to hone individual responsibility and performance—Best Practice levels of performance that raise purchasing managers in the eyes
of executives. Suppliers constantly struggle with the challenge of
becoming the supplier of choice; major producers constantly struggle
with making their product the consumer's all-around choice. And
purchasing professionals must learn how to be the kind of resource
senior management turns to, a valued performer on whom they can
depend, someone whom CEOs and presidents absolutely need, whom
they willingly approach with, "I want you on my team."

It is not management's responsibility to upgrade purchasing's profile. Management makes strategic decisions every day, sets priorities
every hour, and every time, whether they raise the stake of purchasing in the company, they are making a yes/no decision about its value.
It is the job of every manager within the extended enterprise to
improve his or her department's position, and the path to visible leadership is perfecting at least two or three of the twenty Best Practices.

Three Steps to Supply Management Power and Visibility

Your job as a supply management professional is to leave the CEO *no
other choice* but to include you. You must become so valuable to the

organization that without your input, strategic guidance, and high-performing and consistent daily operations, your company would be unable to compete. Furthermore, all your good acts and focused activities must be known and valued throughout the enterprise—talked about—not simply taken for granted as meeting the expected levels of the profession.

Three steps will increase your value to top management:

1. BEHAVE IN A MANNER THAT SURPASSES MANAGEMENT EXPECTATIONS.

Supply managers do have a choice about how they are perceived. Senior management loves employees who arrive with solutions, not more problems—"we are shutting the line down, the parts arrived bad from the supplier" and "we can launch the new model next month, but it's gonna cost you" are bad messages that put you in the negative position of being *one more problem.*

Rather, your message should be good news about improving delivery from 97 percent on-time complete to 99 percent, with no incidence of lines down. Or you should be able to report 100 percent of suppliers delivering uninspected material in the 99.9 percent range. Our conversations with leaders from Top Ten procurement executives at Harley-Davidson, SmithKline Beecham, John Deere, Honda of America, IBM, Chrysler, and NISCI emphasize that they only speak in numbers, and they only take issues to their senior management, or to their people, that are well expressed in scenarios based only on corporate numbers that express financial position and change.

2. THINK OF YOUR POSITION IN SUPPLY MANAGEMENT AS A *PROCESS*, NOT A FUNCTION.

Chrysler maintains platform teams, not siloed technical functions—engineering, purchasing, marketing, and manufacturing, for example—because the new product development process requires simultaneous input from all these disciplines. Hand-offs and internal disagreements impede the creation of their new products, and

Chrysler engineers and procurement executives know that the first step to good design is understanding all the parameters ahead.

When leaders describe their position as part of the company's corporate mission—profit making, market capture, or customer retention—they are demonstrating that they see their role as creating advantage for the entire company. Their best work is understood to enlarge for the greater good; more than being seen as "team players," they clearly communicate purchasing functions and achievements as part of a bigger entity.

3. COMMUNICATE YOUR COMPETITIVE PERFORMANCE.

Let the numbers lead you.

—Dorian Shainin, quality pioneer and Shewhart Award Winner

Why is marketing always well paid and considered so important? Marketing writes the strategic plan, and when purchasing fails to write and deliver its own strategic plan, the advantage automatically slips to marketing, or to whoever is the keeper of the macro numbers. Be aware that you are in a very competitive race internally as well as externally. Internally, supply management is fighting for position, power, and resources; externally, supply management is competing for market share.

Gaining visibility and more resources—bigger budgets, more training, higher salaries and perks to attract professionals, or more resources dedicated to suppliers—is a competitive game internally as well as externally. To communicate effectively, supply management professionals need to understand their relative contribution to the company, because their strongest competition for position, resources, and power is marketing, manufacturing, and engineering.

Learn to think of your company's supply chain and its purchasing professionals as in direct competition with those of other major producers. Competition goes beyond pure benchmarking, which is an interesting and sometimes overused exercise in corporate tourism. Your purchasing professionals are in a race with Chrysler's buyers and managers. If Chrysler's purchasing team, or Flextronics's or Whirlpool's supply managers can deliver better than yours in the key areas of cost, on-time delivery, and quality, your challenge is clear. Use that competitive challenge to justify and publicize, and grow your own department's procurement resources. Make your contribution, and the potential for contribution, clear.

Learn the Language

Unfortunately, most purchasing pros have never learned the data around their competitive contribution—they have no language and no signposts by which they can communicate their value. They cannot, therefore, speak in the language spoken by CEOs and the board of directors. Their gross contribution to the income statement is lumped into a single "Cost of Goods Sold (COGS)" line item that is subtracted from the marketing department's stellar revenue achievements, leaving gross profit—purchasing's contribution is arithmetically a negative one! No wonder purchasing managers find it almost impossible to break that COGS line item down further into the contribution their budgeted spending makes to the total profit picture.

Speaking the language of numbers goes beyond industry's current fascination with benchmarking because purchasing's challenge is to understand and communicate at a very detailed level—the comparative cost of tooling, for example—where and how they can impact the company's competitive position. When leaders describe their position as part of the company's corporate mission—profit making, market capture, or customer retention—they are demonstrating their leadership role to the entire company. Their best work is a solid, measurable contribution for the greater good that cannot be argued away and can be recalculated into a long stream of positive cash flow numbers on the income statement, no matter what calamities marketing or engineering encounters in the marketplace.

It is important for purchasing professionals, planners as well as executives, to study their company's financials and locate the "hot buttons" that become the supply base's leverage points. Each of our

Top Ten organizations understands these levers and has structured the organization, hiring, training, rewards, and daily processes to support the enlargement of these single success points. IBM, for example, under Gene Richter, can immediately impact financials through its aggressive cost management; Flextronics's partnering skills and relationship building make their appearance in product growth and successful acquisitions that grow revenues. Without Flextronics's supply base management of supplier relationships, customer relationships for this subcontract expert fall apart.

Choose Your Words Well

Purchasing managers must learn to use language well, to enlarge or elevate the words they typically use to describe their roles, and to express all their performance as *achievement*, rather than *activity-centered*. Describe what your area *achieves*, not what it *does*.

Bumper Stickers

Adopt a language that emphasizes results. For example, buyer/planners become commodity specialists, thereby raising their level of expertise to cover technologies, global currency issues, and logistics issues, rather than "pieces and parts"; purchasing becomes worldwide supply management; supplier training becomes supplier development; daily performance to schedule becomes quality achievement; purchased price variance becomes value analysis. Ratchet up your performance and objectives vocabulary about two notches to bring it to the same level as the ones executives use.

Use vocabulary to describe your achievement that reflects larger, more competitive goals, rather than activities, because business performance is valued on achievement of macro goals—half the time to market, at half the cost, with twice the quality, for example—rather than how your department spent its budgeted hours last month. Motorola's Six Sigma crusades in the eighties did not win all the objectives the company needed to transition into its next generation

(Motorola is absent from our Top Ten list because it has lost its focus), but its strikingly simple, obsessive drive to higher quality as expressed by Six Sigma changed the corporate landscape and highlighted the importance of supplier performance. Slogans like Six Sigma, 10X, Stretch Goals, and Twice the Value at Half the Cost carry organizations over the rough spots; your extended enterprise needs a three-word expression, a bumper sticker, of its operating objectives.

Speak from Numbers

Numbers show opportunities, and numbers speak across cultural boundaries. Using macro "success" data, like value added, return on assets and return on investment (supplier development or supplier training) to explain your winning position or to seek additional resources will advance your cause strategically.

Several years ago we observed a critical Hewlett-Packard engineering and production project review as a new project launch came closer to deadline. Tension and finger-pointing had marked earlier meetings; the project leader, however, a statistical quality-control

Figure 9.1 Every Successful Supply Management Group Needs a Bumper Sticker

giant, instituted a new rule that eliminated much of the politics and emotion behind the project. Before any meeting attendee could speak, he or she was required to present his issue in numbers; no one could speak without them. Everyone was forced to prepare sound status on quality issues, production process tests and overall units completed.

From this breakthrough approach the group moved easily to more sophisticated problem-solving approaches, including Design of Experiments, because the expectations for the process had been established.

Speaking the language of numbers goes beyond industry's fascination with benchmarking, because purchasing's challenge is to understand and communicate at a detailed level where they can impact the company's competitive position.

This new process focus is particularly productive at the supplier level, where supply management executives can really shine. Improving the comparative cost of tooling is an excellent example, as is the use of raw steel in stampings.

Honda's Maruo

Teruyuki Maruo, the Honda BP methodology guru, was trained, as were all other Japanese manufacturing managers, to preserve valuable resources, most of which were imported by the struggling, post–World War II Japanese economy. He learned that in most auto manufacturing plants, steel stampings could be a big source of waste. The layout of parts on sheet steel was frequently not as well considered as it should have been, and 20 percent or more raw material became scrap.

Machine setups and material movement also contained much wasted time, so Maruo always teaches his followers, most of whom are now in purchasing, to observe and sketch how parts are sequenced and laid out in stamping operations, how material is handled before and after stamping, and how changeovers are conducted. These detailed material processing challenges are not always managed by manufacturing management or by manufacturing engineering, particularly at the level of small and medium-sized suppliers, where the discipline is a new approach. It becomes purchasing's responsibility, therefore, to lead the way; any improvements in raw material usage or machine utilization (changeovers) will belong to the purchasing performance numbers, as will the resulting reduction of scrap and lost machine time.

The 5 Percent Factor, Supply Management's Secret Competitive Advantage

The first general rule of management that all purchasing pros learn is that to contribute 5 percent to profitability, all they have to do is save 5 percent. But marketing would have to see twenty times its projected sales to realize that same after-tax profit increase. Which is the easier task?

Levels of Savings

There are levels of savings that our Top Ten organizations have stepped through, generally over a time span of two to three years. Time spans are not that difficult to pin down; we have seen most supply base managers realize visible, high-impact results in less than one year of focus on low-hanging fruit; sustained savings require organization strengths and new skills that improve processes, and these changes usually take three to five years to implement. Ongoing, predictable savings of the kind that IBM continues to capture cannot be expected with less than a good five years of high-level focus on all the supply base challenges; Gene Richter's leadership is a good example of the successful capture of all three levels of savings—low-hanging fruit, smarter buys, and hard process improvement.

LEVEL ONE—PRICE COMPETITION

Five percent savings for a business that has many suppliers is easily achieved, simply because there is such a wide differential in performance among competing suppliers. Rewarding good suppliers with

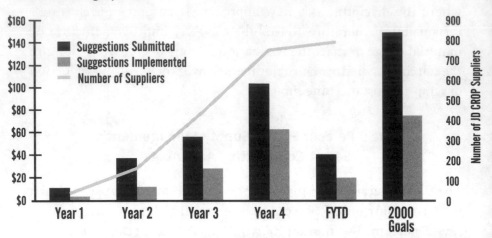

Performance through April 2000

Figure 9.2 J.D. Crop is Deere's Supplier Cost Savings Suggestion System. When savings suggestions are approved, Deere and Supplier share the savings.

more business as the less cost-competitive ones are deemphasized is an easy win.

LEVEL TWO—SMARTER PROCESSES

Five percent savings in an organization that has already narrowed its supply base is still very achievable by paying closer attention to blanket orders, scheduling, or receipts, outsourcing, logistics, and other volume, timing, or material movement issues.

LEVEL THREE—HARD PROCESS IMPROVEMENTS

The next level of savings, process improvement, generally earns better than 5 percent payback, but it requires more focused higher-level attention, such as value engineering experts, process engineering studies, or machine and layout changes. But this level will carry purchasing managers into the next power level. Process improvement is the driver that guarantees ongoing process consistency and resulting cost differentials that clearly identify the process winners.

Level three hard process improvements are the wins that aggressive purchasing pros want to be credited with, the ones that extend beyond the negative "cost of goods sold" contribution. When process improvements fuel time to market advantage, parts move through factory flows faster and cleaner. Typical time reduction results from simple attention to process yields on average 20 percent improvement, but 30 to 50 percent gains are not unusual for high performers like Honda and Toyota.

Five percent savings, especially in low-margin businesses like appliance manufacturing or steel processing, are not unusual, but we believe the true unseen opportunity for purchasing is in the 20 to 25 percent range. Even GM's controversial ex-purchasing head Lopez knew and seized that hidden gain. But not all corporations are geared to reach level three process-generated savings, because reaching this extremely competitive level can get ugly; it's not a friendly, comfortable place for leaders who love routine. Reformation is a nasty, "in your face" business, and it doesn't always pay well.

Not Everyone Will Make the Journey

The poet Robert Penn Warren was once described as a man who looked as if he was about to throw you off his land. The same might be said of the feisty one-time gubernatorial candidate and former president of Boston University, John Silber. Silber's controversial reputation continues, even at age seventy-three, as he maintains his position as Boston's peripatetic thinker, rabble-rouser, and educational reformer. He is commonly disliked among academics and feared by politicians, but he will never be ignored.

> *I don't know. I suppose. . . . there are a lot of people who don't ever want to be challenged with the truth. . . . I think anybody who leads people and has ideas is going to scare some people who don't want to work or who don't have any aspirations. It goes with the territory.* *

*Sam Allis, *Boston Globe,* Dec. 12, 1999, p. A30.

Leveling Up

Silber seems to seek out media opportunities; with three books in process, he continues to "fight the good fight," taking his message to different media, in different dosages. His contrarian positions throw opponents off balance. In an educational system confused by the question of merit, tracking, performance measures, and testing, he makes his position repeatedly clear: "The only time you have equality of achievement is if you cut everybody down to the lowest common denominator. We'll all get down to the level of Down syndrome. Is that what you want? That's equality? Or maybe it has to be worse than that. Maybe it has to be the equality of Alzheimer's."

Silber's is a voice booming from the chaos of another institution undergoing complete transformation, education. Eager to make his mark on accountability, he continues to endure brickbats from all sides—from the threatened meritocracy managers, to teachers faced with bringing thousands of failing students up to passing scores on their high school certification tests. Nothing weakens the reformer's zeal, and every media opportunity strengthens his position.

Purchasing Needs More Publicists!

Although we certainly would not advocate Silber-type behavior in a corporate setting—the ax would quickly fall—we have become convinced that many purchasing managers do not want to be in the limelight. They are not energized by stretch goals and objectives. They are afraid of failure and they fear that they lack the necessary capabilities and training to play in high-demand/high-goal areas. And they are probably right.

Because many of these managers still occupy desks in procurement, when enlightened management looks for new leadership, typical North American executives don't look to purchasing for help; they take their search outside or to other functional areas like engineering or manufacturing.

It's Not a Death Trip, but It Is Death for Linear Thinking

Mike Doyle, CEO of the National Initiative for Supply Chain Integration (NISCI), the leading-edge group of twelve companies and two nonprofits formed in 1997, thinks that purchasing and supply management as we now know them will not survive the journey. Because learning to see how material moves and is processed is not a linear exercise, although some companies persist in diagramming it that way, linear thinking will not take us there. Managers who persist in turning what may be described as a chaotic mess of intersecting flows and loop-backs into their linear vision of linked enterprise map will fail.

Look for Like-Minded Colleagues and Alignment

Doyle predicts that managers who can stand the discomfort of being in unknown territory—indeed of being lost amid apparent chaos—will make the trip. "It's where you should be," says Doyle, "in the discomfort zone." He advises, "Try to make the trip with like-minded colleagues, and you may enjoy the journey."

Harley Works Consensus

We have inherited a gift. . . . a legacy of leadership that
is larger than any of us individually.

–Garry Berryman, 1999 supplier conference

We think one of our Top Ten, Harley-Davidson, is especially skilled at working for common goals and shared values among very disparate partners in their supply base. Harley folks like to ride together, although not everyone at Harley rides a bike, and not everyone in the supply base has the same ideas about systems or schedules. But purchasing leader Garry Berryman accepts that diversity and encourages opinions that move his group forward, because he wants to avoid the "silent partner syndrome"—official agreement that masks silent disapproval or eventual sabotage. For that reason, his supplier advisory council meetings are marked by lengthy discussions around key issues, where his first agenda is to seek consensus and mutual understanding.

Levels of Enterprise Development

In Berryman's 1999 supplier conference keynote, he traces the organization's development of a relationship vision. In 1996 the supplier conference theme, "Growing the Business," reflected an incredible push for Harley's supply management group; production was pumping out one hundred thousand units per year with plans to double that number. By 1997, the conference theme "Relationships We Count On" became Berryman's primary focus because the company recognized that such growth had to be supported by the suppliers. The 1999 conference theme, "Across the Enterprise," brought Berryman's view to the future together, one that he believes truly honors Harley's past—"Growing the Business" through "Relationships We Count On" to "Across the Enterprise".

Not an Individual Vision

A supply management strategy in the making since the middle 1980s at Harley had finally been articulated. Berryman welcomed the progress: "Brick by brick the right groundwork was laid to ensure a future with possibilities that none of us could have imagined individually. . . . A quick look around reveals many skills, backgrounds, and disciplines. But whatever our responsibility for contributing to the future . . . it can benefit from the application of these sound leadership principles. . . . We need to view our leadership roles as interdependent actions . . . not independent actions. Together . . . they will provide the focus to help us achieve our common goals."

One of Berryman's favorite "management texts" is Sun Tzu, *The Art of War*, and despite the contrast between reaching consensus and beating enemies into complete submission, Berryman finds wisdom in the ancient warrior/thinker:

When your strategic thinking is shallow and near-sighted. . . . then what you gain by your calculations is little, so you lose before you do battle. . . .
When your strategy. . . . is deep and far-reaching, then what you gain by your calculations is much, so you can win before you even fight.

Berryman points to specific tactical changes that paved the way for Harley's enterprisewide transformation:

1. cross-functional platform teams that include players from marketing, manufacturing, purchasing, and product and process design and development
2. supplier residencies established to integrate technical product and process competencies that will not be replicated within engineering centers or manufacturing areas
3. new product introduction disciplines from concept through production launch that build predictability throughout the process
4. new system designs that work for better product development and production management
5. continuous sampling of the customer's voice to shape future product designs and processes

Ingenious, Visionary Execution

Berryman's challenge for the next few years will continue to be leadership among diverse interests—suppliers, different consuming Harley plants, executives, dealers, and especially customers. He relates his perspective on strategic planning issues with the following story:

Understanding what's expected is an often-overlooked facet of effective planning. Berryman once asked a friend with military experience how complex operations were briefed—how could everyone on a team know what everyone else was doing, and when they were supposed to do it?

The friend related an incident about watching a young battalion commander working with his field leaders on the eve of a large operation. The young colonel did not tell and retell details that the troops would have already read and digested in a ninety-page order received days earlier. He or his staff did not stand in front of complex maps with overlays and pointers.

Instead, the leader gathered the other commanders around him and rested on one knee, then got "up close and personal" with a replica of the area of operation that the commander had fashioned from dirt and rocks on the desert floor.

After everyone was oriented to the terrain, the leader asked the group to project their minds into whatever time frame he would call out:

"It's first light tomorrow. . . . John, what are you and your people doing?," or "Bob, after John's people secure the high ground around the airfield . . . say about noon . . . how long will it take you to join them on this hill?"

These simple questions had another purpose: the commander wanted to see how well each player understood what the rest of the team expected from him. Berryman takes the lesson in preparation one step beyond this scene. It's not only how sound your ideas are or how well you state them, it's how clearly they are understood by everyone who is expected to contribute.

Berryman speaks directly to his people and to his supply base when he asks them to remember that they will be expected to contribute to the future in ways they have not yet experienced, especially in the area of technical advances. He reminds everyone that a knowledge of their own particular industry is absolutely critical for success. And he tells them not to wait for an invitation but to be clear on how suppliers can deliver because he will certainly not have all the answers.

Among the Top Ten the parallel alignment of purchasing to overall company objectives is shared down to training and experience parallels between top executives. Certainly at Daimler/Chrysler Thomas Stallkamp's rise from purchasing to head the company reflected a parallel alignment between top management and procurement. At IBM, a company whose transformation has moved from hardware to information and idea generation, innovative procurement like Bill Schaefer's completely reflects Lou Gerstner's new directions. Likewise, at Honda, purchasing executives have typically rotated through positions that parallel the president's focus on engine technology and the Racing Spirit.

Learning to Shine

How many purchasing executives have already enjoyed their fifteen minutes in the national spotlight? How many managers can point to at least one mention in leading business publications—*Wall Street Journal, Industry Week, Purchasing,* or *Fortune*—in the past year? Or can any of your supply management professionals claim to be in the Rolodex of CNN network researchers or other media leaders? Yet, business acquisitions, mergers, catastrophes, and new product hits are all directly linked to the power of supply management, so why should these stories not be told?

Honda Purchasing Leadership, Leading the Top Ten

When WEK, Honda of America's main supplier of air-conditioning ducts and other molded plastic parts for the Accord and the Civic, burned down one Halloween night a few years ago, purchasing managers hurried to the site and jumped into the struggle to keep the assembly lines running. They surveyed the damage, knowing that the WEK parts could not be added after-market, and that the cost of an assembly line down situation ran at that time over $26,000 per minute.

The picture was grim; all production at WEK, one of Honda of America's original eight suppliers, was lost, buried under $10 million of rubble, along with tooling and three trailers loaded with parts. The Marysville assembly complex had a one-and-one-half-day supply of Accord parts, and a two-and-one-half-day supply for the Civic.

Within two hours a Honda team moved to calculate inventory in process and in transit, to pull tooling records and process charts, and to strategize. Purchasing manager John Cope called Japan to line up relief sourcing.

Purchasing took center stage as the drama unfolded. Susan Insley, former senior vice president and head of the Anna, Ohio, engine plant, recalls that the first decision was not to shut down but to "juggle production schedules, sequences, shifts." Two Honda Japan suppliers, Nihon Plas and Kumi Kasei, started daily airlifts of some parts to Ohio, working twenty-four hours daily to refill the pipeline.

Purchasing engineers needed to examine WEK molds buried under mountains of debris; though some had melted, two-thirds were salvageable. The normal time to rebuild a mold is five to seven days, but purchasing located a willing supplier that turned out the first, and most critical, mold in fifteen hours, ready for production.

One Week from Disaster to Recovery to Production

The entire disaster became a team recovery effort led by purchasing as Honda, WEK, other suppliers, and even a few former suppliers pitched in to keep the assembly lines running. WEK president Walt Kalberer shifted operations to his second Ohio plant and off-loaded another customer's work, a toy manufacturer, to make room.

By three days after the fire, the first mold was back in production, and one week after the fire, with operations back to normal, Honda assembly lost production time had totaled less than one day.

Cope credited teamwork and Honda's go-to-the-spot philosophy, along with its international sourcing strength, with keeping losses manageable. The final chapter of the disaster included purchasing follow-up on tool trials and analysis of the company's recovery process itself. Honda of America (HAM) performed more in-depth risk management and developed better methods to evaluate supplier disaster recovery plans. Sprinklers, heat detectors, and fire doors, especially in the plastics industry, have become a supplier requirement.

The Leadership Lessons

Just-in-time (JIT) and lean manufacturing networks work, but only with the kind of procurement response assembled by teams like the one in the Honda/WEK fire crisis. JIT is designed, like most production systems, to work well under "normal" conditions. But when labor and transit strikes, natural disasters, and other crises happen, companies learn the value of their supply management professionals. Supply interruptions test the maturity of organizations, as well as their flexibility and reaction time.

Media Management

When your organization tackles a new technology area or achieves record-breaking performance that parallels the stock market's climb, or leads a crisis recovery action, are you prepared to face the public, as well as your internal and external competitors, and tell your story? Honda managers turned the WEK fire into an opportunity for learning and an opportunity to recognize and talk up the benefits of strong supplier networks and purchasing initiatives. Without high-level professionals leading the procurement organization in the Marysville facility—managers like John Cope, well-compensated and hyper-responsible individuals who took personal responsibility for solving the problem fast—production lines would have shut down for more than one day. And without purchasing "telling the story" in a positive and immediate way, the budget for supplier development training and engineering within purchasing would have been an insignificant line item, not the millions that grew with the supply base.

Moreover, the WEK story reached the media and was distributed in the words of purchasing managers who were there. Even with a

About Journalists

1. Journalists are not your enemies, but they are not your friends either.
2. The mike is always "hot," the camera is always "live." Note—this rule applies to in-house visibility events, as well as TV and video clips.
3. Everything you say is on the record.
4. Treat a print reporter the same way you would treat a live mike.
5. Never say "no comment." It makes you look furtive.
6. Any question is a fair one, BUT
7. If you are not prepared to answer a question, don't.
8. Provocation is considered fair play by most journalists. Be prepared to respond to provocation in a nonprovocative manner. Never try to duke it out with the press.
9. When contacted by the media, either return calls or be out of reach, but don't put yourself in a position in which someone can quote you as not responding.
10. Context is a matter of interpretation. It is always OK to ask to have a quote read back, but do it at the moment of the interview.
11. Learn the technique of "Bridging," a key technique for bringing any interview under control, in your favor. There are times when you may have bad news to deliver, and you will want to manage it. Buy yourself time to respond with phrases such as "I'm glad you asked me that," and repeating the question.

The one/two of bridging is important here:

Acknowledge the question, give a brief answer, and shift to another subject.

Example: "I think the Inspector could have responded better, but I think, Joe, that the real issue here is…," or, "First, let's look at…."

Maureen Kelly, *Free Press*, August 1999, "Media Guidelines."

corporate public relations filter in place, purchasing knew it was important to tell the story, and to tell it their way. The lessons of working with JIT, the significance of flexible and lean supply chains, were important for other industry managers to hear about.

Learn to Manage the Media

Unfortunately, many mainstream publications think manufacturing—and, by implication, procurement—is a "black box," a mysterious and unimportant exercise in "thing making" that bears no connection to the things we use or drive or play with. In fact, the exercise of money handling—deal making, real estate, communications, banking, investment services—wins their attention over what they perceive as harder, less glamorous production issues. It will be a challenge for many supply base professionals to take their story public and to be sure it comes out right, but that is exactly what must be done.

The *Wall Street Journal*, for example, has great difficulty covering manufacturing stories; they usually don't get it right, and simple ideas like JIT and lean manufacturing are a challenge that seem to be used as candidates to force fit to particular story lines. Beware! It's a tough time to accurately tell a manufacturing story to the business media. *Fortune* and *Fast Company* have demonstrated more commitment to technology and innovation, as have many new e-zines and TV business talk shows; the *Harvard Business Review* occasionally lands a hit. These media represent safer but smaller distribution channels for marketing procurement.

A November 8, 1999 piece published in the "Outlook" section of the *Wall Street Journal* illustrates the point. Writer Timothy Aeppel is trying to explain "Why Making Things Is out of Fashion," and he attempts to build his case around increased movement to outsourcing (somebody "makes the things," but it just doesn't happen here!). He contrasts the uncoolness of thing-making with subcontract manufacturing's phenomenal growth, unwittingly adding fuel to a devil's advocate position that the whole "movement" out of thing-making is a simple shift. With a dateline of Pittsburgh, this inconsistent and confusing piece unfortunately highlights many common misconceptions about manufacturing that supply management professionals should be ready to counter:

1. Manufacturing and procurement are unimportant and do not impact who wins. Who cares?
2. There are no manufacturing or supply chain heroes.
3. Everything that could be done to improve manufacturing has been done, and "you simply have to move it to China." Labor rates rule all!
4. Just in Time and Lean Manufacturing don't work.

Supply chain leaders must become as adept at telling their stories and handling the media as top executives are. A few rules about media management will help channel the whirlwind of media energies as intrepid professionals take the stage.

Prepare for any public appearance the way you might have prepared for your first job interview by learning the rules:

1. Establish rapport by being clear on how your media contact likes to be addressed; avoid overly familiar use of nicknames, especially with female media professionals.
2. Understand the time limits, the format—Q & A, pre-interview questions, or open-ended—whether your comments will be available for prepublication review or not, and be clear about the role of public relations in a final review of stories, if any. Keep your own agenda in mind and be flexible, but do not try to run the interview. Remember that 85 percent of the discussion will be forgotten in forty-eight hours, so stick to a few basic points and make them memorable with stories, names, and specifics, the colorful elements that the media want.
3. Remember that no interview goes absolutely perfectly, and that if there is a policy of openness and continued information sharing, there will be other opportunities to tell and retell your story. Plan for them. Keep a microcassette recorder in your car to capture immediately the details of an important event; or use your e-mail to send yourself an immediate message for

later release to the press. Build your public relations and media contact file with periodic updates.

Rules for Supply Management: The Next Generation

The proliferation of improvement approaches and change initiatives in supply management can be blinding to outsiders—media, financial gurus, consumers—as well as to any managers serious about change. Your job is to prioritize, plan, execute, and tell the story, again, and again, and again; but learning to set priorities and understanding the resources required to execute each project is a challenge. Implementing the Top Twenty Best Practices requires the same kind of focused effort that North American manufacturing managers faced fifteen years ago when their quality practices were in disrepair.

Plan Your Own Journey to Success

Anyone who has spent time in procurement or manufacturing knows that the production line will eat you up—it will consume all your energy and cause you to forget your strategic focus. There is a certain comfortable state of exhaustion caused by years of crisis management that attracts and retains many traditional procurement managers, even beyond the time to move on. They will not, however, populate the islands of excellence in the extended enterprise, where quality and delivery are a given, and where communications and strategy step to the forefront.

In fact, it is too easy to become safely involved in daily struggles and win—firefighting—and lose the time and energy to work strategic plans and challenges. Yet that is exactly what happens in traditional organizations where daily operations are the reward trigger—making shipments, making the new product launch date, or making micro-cost targets. It is a shortsighted but comforting perspective.

Study and practice the Top Twenty Best Practices in order of priority as to how they will strategically help you win against your best competitors. For example, if your company is racing against a competitor on quality, focus on that very achievable gain. Be sure that everyone, especially executives—suppliers and purchasing personnel—understands the basics of quality management and control—Ishikawa fishbone diagrams, for example, Taguchi and Design of Experiments, Root Cause Analysis, and the like.

Take Responsibility for Leadership in Your Company and Your Enterprise

If your group arrives at the track too late to compete, focus on development speed throughout the supply base. Remember that you have a hidden advantage here because typically North American industry is blind to the potential of good cost savings. By just focusing on the metrics to improve cost-down, you will leverage the other challenges of market share (getting there first), and quality and delivery.

Think of your role as the leader of the enterprise, not just as purchasing manager. Many North American companies, as noted above, fail to include purchasing at the vice president or director level, although almost all Japanese competitors do. The reason Japanese auto companies capture an extremely large market share is that they position purchasing management at a higher level within the organization. They understand that because 50 to 80 percent of the cost of a car, for example, is purchased parts, purchasing can make a major competitive contribution early on. Continuing to train our CEOs to maximize efficiency of their plants and direct labor is pointless; these costs represent only single-digit (and dropping fast) numbers.

Industry leaders who lever their success on supply chain management also manage the capital budgeting process well. They understand the costs of expansion and capital, as well as human resource growth, and they understand what contributions they can easily make to "finance" more product innovation and new technologies. The opportunities lie in their hands.

Be Internally Competitive

The first manager who brings a solution to his or her CEO wins "ownership" of the resources required to manage that area—quality, delivery, cost, development. Being more competitive internally means racing to be the first with the best overall plan to improve your organization's competitive position. At John Deere, for example, manufacturing recognized their next frontier as the supply base, brought a solution package to the CEO, and won the million-dollar budget and support to attack the problem.

Visualize Your Success

Most traditional purchasing managers don't see the big picture; their daily operating mode keeps them working in a meaningless, reactive routine. Degrees and advanced training don't guarantee this type of achievement, however. Instead, develop an awareness of the industry direction and your company's position in the race.

Purchasing organizations typically ebb and flow with company or industry swings. During good times, however, there is more money for buying and training; during downturns, purchasing managers automatically tighten their belts, although they frequently hold the key to maintaining profits.

Expect to Lose Your Best People

When supply base managers make contributions that exceed senior management's expectations, they become targets for other groups. Indeed, after we published the 1998 book *Powered by Honda*, Honda management noticed an increased number of recruiting offers to all its purchasing people. Visibility increased their marketability, and the threat of losing personnel became a strategic concern.

Expect that your best people, the ones who show strong leadership skills, will be promoted into other functions. Although promotions out of purchasing keep the recruiters working full-time, the good effect of this brand of success is that gradually your company will fill key positions with very loyal, knowledgeable professionals who remember their purchasing/manufacturing roots. Their presence throughout the company becomes a political strength as they work to support leadership objectives.

Cost Management Objectives

The three best opportunities for cost reduction lie in maintenance and repair operations (MRO), the cost management system, and supplier development. Although most organizations feel they already understand how to reduce costs, if they don't work with a mature cost management system, they are managing in the dark. Look at the best cost management systems at Honda of America, Toyota, and Whirlpool. All these organizations are struggling with lower margins, global threats, and no time to develop systems. But they have established clear cost management positions within their industries.

It Pays to Develop Suppliers

When suppliers become proficient at new technologies, or improve their quality and delivery performance, they raise the bar for everyone. Per year, the leaders in supplier development expect 500 to 800 percent return on the dollars they have invested in supplier development. They know that each supply management engineer will in a single year have earned five times his compensation. Honda and John Deere have both maximized use of these numbers to expand their supplier support systems.

Contribute to the Society of Purchasing

If your career goal is to be a leader in your company, you must aim also to be a leader in the world of purchasing beyond company walls. George Harris of TRW, Romey Everdell of Rath and Strong, and Hal Fearon of Arizona State each contributed to the professional growth of his own area and was honored for his generosity. Fearon founded NAPM's Center for Advanced Purchasing Studies, Everdell founded the American Production and Inventory Control Society (APICS annually awards the Everdell Prize for the best-researched article on a current production topic), and Fearon continues to model excellence.

Best Practices at Many Levels

We asked 250 top purchasing professionals to name the practices that in their opinion were the most important; their responses, in priority order, were as follows:

1. cost management
2. supplier development
3. value analysis/engineering
4. maintenance, repair, and operating supplies
5. supplier quality circles.

Each of these five top priorities is addressed in the Twenty Best Practices, but the power of these practices comes from applying them at more than one level of the supply chain. World-class purchasing and supply management professionals not only seek out the best today, they seek to know what is coming tomorrow.

At first glance, the definition of "world class" may seem difficult to capture, but over time, we have developed our own understanding of what constitutes world-class supply management leadership. Our top ten world-class leadership organizations share these characteristics:

1. Top leadership understands purchasing's importance and provides needed resources.
2. Benchmarking is used to assess performance and set tough goals.
3. A culture of shared knowledge prevails—collaboration flourishes internally and with suppliers.
4. The view of supply management includes the entire supply chain.
5. Best Practices are institutionalized.

Supply Management Professionals in the Top Ten organizations don't wait for the CEO to get on board. They make sure that supply management's agenda becomes part of the CEO's agenda. And benchmarking doesn't stop with internal and external visits. Benchmarked comparative performance data and procedures from Top Ten companies should be used to establish tough supply chain objectives. It is equally important to reward, rather than punish, risk taking necessary to meet these goals.

We made a presentation to a large group of corporate executives—the board of directors and past chairman of AT&T, a previous secretary of agriculture, the head of Harvard Business School, and the president of Johnson & Johnson. The speaker who preceded us gave a talk on business process excellence—teaming, how to work on specific projects, and so on. This speaker mentioned that if companies do well, the calculation says they will save $140 million per year, what she called "really soft money."

Next up, co-author Nelson delivered his presentation on projected cost-down initiatives, some $200 million over the next five years, at John Deere. We hoped there would be skeptics in the audience, *but no one questioned the calculations or the chart.* Although several members approached the podium at the conclusion of the program, each one of them expressed no surprise at the projected savings: "You will have no trouble saving this money—we know in our companies it's there to be saved, it just takes somebody to step up to it, to lead the initiative." They were already believers! We were amazed—CEOs as well as marketing and manufacturing people believe in the possibilities of the open challenge, but the people who don't believe are the supply management managers themselves.

No individual—and no single partner in a business relationship—has all the answers. World-class organizations share knowledge tapped from the supply chain and their companies to understand and meet customer needs.

Leaders in supply management for the extended enterprise understand the stakes, and they sell their success with the bottom line. Supply executives occupy a powerful position when they understand and communicate that 50, 60, 70, even 80 percent of their company's costs are spent by their own people. It is the responsibility of supply management professionals to use that powerful position to bring real results to their company, to model Best Practices within their profession.

Think strategically and learn to see with the eyes of your CEO. Your vision of a restructured and powerful supply management force, when you express the costs and guaranteed payoff, is your unseen advantage. How can anyone, seeing the hidden profit potential, hesitate? There is money on the table. Take it.

10

BEST COMPANIES, BEST PRACTICES, CONCLUSIONS

Honda of America, John Deere, Harley-Davidson, IBM, Daimler/Chrysler, American Express, Flextronics, SmithKline Beecham, Sun Microsystems, Whirlpool; Honorable mentions for innovation: NISCI and Intellimet

WHEN WE STARTED our search for the Top Ten supply management organizations and the Best Practices among them, we were already in a position of having worked at the extremes of the profession. The three of us had labored in the worst traditional purchasing groups, and eventually we all finally enjoyed rich, comprehensive stays among the very best. In fact, the work we three have done with Honda of America is to a large degree responsible for many of our perspectives on what works best to build a high-performance supply chain, and how far a young organization can go to create an environment of excellence at a greenfield site. For about ten years Honda enjoyed the position of being alone with its very innovative and focused approach to supply chain management; no one in Detroit came close to Honda's philosophies or practices, although the Big Three frequently benchmarked the transplants.

Building Perfect Process

As Honda's Marysville complex assembly production rose, and more vehicles were sourced locally, local supplier capabilities grew, at times not quite fast enough to satisfy outsourcing from Japan. Every year a new group of winners joined the award circle at the annual supplier conference. It was amazing to watch small companies grow and improve so fast that they frequently were overwhelmed with business opportunities and had to be restructured and helped to keep going. Each year the number of suppliers who shipped perfect product perfectly on time increased. Just the concept of absolutely zero defects from more than one company in Honda's supply base—not an anomaly—stunned many U. S. observers.

Honda proved that excellence in the heartland, in a traditional and somewhat mature industry, was indeed possible. As a strange blend of Japanese quality control techniques translated from Deming, Juran, and Shewhart; a native Ohio workforce; Japanese management, and a mix of North American and off-shore suppliers, the company never quite fit what one would have expected of a big automotive supplier. True to the philosophy of Mr. Honda, an underdog, iconoclast spirit pervaded the extended organization.

The purchasing group at Honda was equally blessed with a unique mix of traditional production planning and a spirited approach to solving every problem, meeting every crisis, and winning the race. One could not help but be infected by the satisfying feeling that, being there, we were among true *winners*.

Nothing Is Guaranteed

Not every company that earned a Honda supplier award had a repeat in succeeding years, however. One year Freudenberg/NOK, for instance, arrived at the conference fully expecting to rack up another win but was disappointed to learn that they failed to beat out the competition in any or all categories; needless to say, Freudenberg was back with a vengeance the next year, and won back their confidence with yet another quality award.

Excellence in the supply chain, as Freudenberg and Motorola have both learned, is not guaranteed, especially if management focus is misdirected at the prize and not the process. Every improvement that Honda makes with its suppliers is aimed at two objectives:

1. fixing the problem to keep the line running
2. perfecting the process

Mechanics and Philosophies—Heart and Hands

Honda of America without hesitation was our first pick for one of the Top Ten but not only because the company's particular sharp focus on a few very important supply chain practices allowed them in fewer than ten years to establish a foothold in automotive territory dominated by an American-style Detroit kieretsu. However much a blend of Eastern and Western culture Honda might have appeared to be, it remains a philosophy-driven organization, and we think that has made all the difference.

Transplant Challenge

Mechanically speaking, Honda enjoyed the benefits of a proven arsenal of powerful manufacturing and procurement best practice tools:

- quality teachings based on Ishikawa
- quality circles that quickly took quality principles—problem solving, root cause analysis, organizational learning, and supplier support—to a young, eager, nonunion supply base
- BP (Best Partner, Best Product, Best Productivity, etc.) methods perfected and demonstrated globally to an eager bunch of acolytes by Terry Maruo
- leadership at the top chosen to fit the company's particular needs for the time. When new product competition became the

company's focus, for example, the new president chosen for a few years' leadership was well experienced in R & D. When the company required innovation, stability, or attention to financials, the leadership focus concentrated on that requirement and shifted the organization to meet that overall direction.

Mechanics and systems aside, philosophically Honda was carried great distances fast by a shared understanding and identification with the racing spirit. All Honda presidents have been obsessed with making engines—with the technology, the future, the challenge of focusing on the heart of the machine. From the founder's first few experiences in auto racing that ended in only partial success, down through the company's motorcycle, and then Formula One campaigns, Soichiro Honda's shared obsession continues to influence and fuel the company's growth.

We enjoyed many new experiences while working with and observing the professionals at Honda. From a somewhat uncomfortable attempt to bridge American and Japanese cultures, the contrasts—the benefits and the disadvantages—became clearer.

We learned, for example, the value of consensus decision making. Each important initiative could be executed with no competing agendas, in half the time of traditional American corporations, by using consensus management to build support and finish "the plan."

We were amazed at the company's complete support of procurement's strategic objectives. Understandably, Honda's devotion to its supply base traces back to the founder's experience with motorcycle engine producers in Japan whose commitment to making automotive parts broke through kieretsu barriers and grew a new company. Co-author Nelson's prime-time opportunity to grow his organization into a multitalented unit that sourced materials, funded suppliers, improved supplier performance and worked to support company new product and growth objectives was a valuable lesson for anyone in a traditional automotive landscape.

Further, Honda's workforce policies in production as well as procurement, especially around safety and compensation/incentive systems, were influential models for raising the performance levels of many small and medium-sized suppliers. It is impossible to measure accurately the impact of these practices on the workplace generally, but in Ohio the changes the company made as it built the Marysville complex transformed what had been a depressed Rust Belt into a hopeful, growing economy.

We all started our careers when purchasing and manufacturing were relatively untouched by technology, and very relationship-oriented. When we started out, these areas were not the most influential or the most favored places from which one could build a career.

We have traced the incredible steps that supply chain has taken along a continuum that has positioned industry to take advantage of integrated quality improvement and cost savings beyond leanness and flexibility. The Twenty Best Practices, the core of good habits, assume expertise in the quality function, but more broadly, upper management dedication to good workforce development through training and conferences, and additional focus on visibility devices—good PR, benchmarking, public events, being good members of supplier communities, and growing one's reputation.

Other organizations noted among our Top Ten list have worked especially hard to perfect these less measurable attributes and to build a winning spirit around sound practices and a philosophical unity. John Deere, for example, has a surprisingly rich heritage of innovation, from the founder's creation of a billion-dollar industry from the self-scouring plow, down to the company's quiet application of leading-edge information technologies—like genetic algorithms—to manage production.

"For Amber Waves of Grain. . . ."

John Deere enjoys and protects the benefits of a committed workforce, supported by enormous worldwide market opportunity. Some observers have commented that unlike Deere's lesser competition—Harvester, Allis Chalmers, Oliver, who fell to bad strategies around unions and pricing—"it's their business to lose." With that potential, it would not be difficult for a 150-year-old Midwestern organization to be complacent and slow. And perhaps that is an accurate description of Deere's early manufacturing and supply chain practices.

Some Deere sites carried all the attributes of traditional production practices, pre-JIT. However, as company founder John Deere knew when he made the monthlong journey west, there is money in opportunity, and growth in new products and better processes. Deere's supply chain machine is working to harvest a different kind of product—higher profits from healthy growth in an established business.

10X Opportunities and Investments Justified

Supplier management and development at Deere, unlike at Honda, is growing because the company has made a 10X commitment to making its supply chain more efficient, and therefore more profitable. Each supply base engineer's multiplier of ten guarantees savings and increased profits for within one year of an approximate $100,000 investment.

Deere supply base management has also proven that their investment in data gathering and information analysis yields profits—typically through consolidation and leveraging of supply—also in the 10X range. Similarly, the Deere investment in information technology, although it has always resulted in immediate process efficiencies, demonstrates daily visibility and worldwide supply chain power that continues to support a 10X machine.

Harley-Davidson's Next Generation

Another Midwestern institution, Harley-Davidson Motorcycles, has a taste for colorful innovation and thinking that is just different enough to fuel a very profitable, older industry. Harley-Davidson has become passionate about new products, and with the addition of young ideas from Buell, the Milwaukee-based giant is exploring renewed growth in its supplier base as it pushes technology.

The MIT Crowd

We must admit to a strong bias for anything out of the Dome, including Tom Gelb's recruitment of a passel of MIT engineers to bring product development and information technology courage to the organization. The results have been exciting to report. The power of Greg Smith and company's work on the new Softail was confirmed by an exhilirating run down San Diego's main drag—it don't get any better than this, she said.

Harley has always been a manufacturing innovator—one of the founding, charter members of the Association for Manufacturing Excellence. The company now finds its market position challenged by a host of nameplate revivals and new competition. Consider it a gift. Iron Horse, Excelsior Henderson, even Kawasaki in its 1980 Nebraska plant have all offered this very American company the opportunity to kick it over again and enter a new race, a new generation sparking its fourth life.

Big Blue

What can we say about IBM? It's been several lifetimes of severe ups and downs for this living survivor of everything good and bad that has ever been written about corporate life, about how to manage and lead a company. From its gray flannel organization-man image, to unchallenged domination of automated business equipment and all the arrogance that position brought to the market, to near starvation and rapid comeback, IBM seems to have proven that at its core, Big Blue has the heart of a survivor—not a machine at all.

We have tremendously enjoyed talking with IBM's new leadership, and we continue to be impressed by its worldwide, extremely rational approach to supply chain management. If it is indeed possible to see the character of an organization's leaders in the reflection of daily operations, it is clear that Gene Richter has made his mark on the entire company.

IBM's supply base management group is remarkable because it remains a complex layering of many organizational charts and objectives over a market that periodically shakes out and changes direction. Richter knows that no thin and shallow group would work well here. Experienced and very smart professionals take a relentlessly focused approach to commodity market management and leveraging what IBM continues to preserve despite its many transformations—enormous leverage—over a scattering of disparate supply sources.

Out of Richter's assembly of a new supply base management organization, Big Blue has created some surprising innovation. Certainly Bill Schaefer's global procurement group will be counted among the first to every new service opportunity. This kind of market leadership wins admirers, as well as customers and profit. Even more remarkable, the innovation is growing out of procurement, of all places.

Word from Detroit

We can't admit to the kind of prognostication skills that will tell the future of Daimler/Chrysler. Unfortunately for some professionals, as a merger of two companies that are really not true equals, this linkage may prove to be extremely unsettling, and many will chose not to continue on the joint journey. However, with every well-considered merger of innovation, market reach, and financial strength, new muscles emerge. It's almost Darwinian, and we predict equally impressive results from the Daimler/Chrysler union. Certainly not a union of equals, but a joining of talent and potential, backed by presence and funding. And in the tough automotive marketplace predicted by David Halberstam in his book *The Reckoning* twenty years ago—four buyers for every five vehicles—innovation and money may win over "goodness of ideas." This is also Darwinian.

Watch for Chrysler to continue to leverage the supply base that Thomas Stallkamp's team worked so hard to rebuild. And watch for Chrysler's Auburn Hills design center to migrate previously expensive technology features out of Mercedes into a mass market for vehicles that will redefine mass market needs. With all these market-climbing changes, Chrysler's supply chain should find itself further and further away from GM, Nissan, Mazda, and perhaps even Ford business, because winning suppliers will align themselves even more completely with winning original equipment producers.

American Express, Money-Movers

When we first looked at American Express, we expected to find a financial institution—a bank, faster and more plastic—but still, a bank. Instead, we found an innovation machine, service-driven, backed by innovative ideas about exactly what supply base management does. We think that is what has allowed American Express to be the most innovative of our Top Ten companies—their products come in so many different packages.

Valuing Human Assets

Like most service-based organizations—and service organizations should be models for hard manufacturing companies—good employees, or human capital, are hard to find, hard to keep, and a challenge to compensate and grow. American Express's entire information structure, however, is based on human databases; for that reason we think Joe Yacura, whom we profiled as AMX's supply chain thinker, is so important as an example of the innovation leader whom supply chain enterprises desperately need to grow. Yacura's product is ideas. His approach to implementation of bold new strokes in his organization takes big steps beyond even what he might easily settle for simply to maintain American Express's current market position.

There are many other service institutions from which manufacturing can learn much about locking in customers and about money pipelines. Indeed, most hard production operations understand that their business objectives go far beyond marketing, selling, and general push methods. Dell Computer's split between selling hardware and harvesting cash—both on-line—continues to warrant benchmarking and replication; Fidelity Investments' worldwide growth and market support is a lesson in access. Amazon.com is unfortunately showing us that not all good ideas pay off in profits; behind their on-line showcase of available products lie costly warehouses and distribution networks badly in need of rationalized supply chain pros. Their competitor niche booksellers, companies like Fatbrain and CEORead, combine access, smart logistics, supply chain, and customer lock-in that most manufacturing pros already understand. Prepare for another shakeout.

Flextronics

We have been fascinated by subcontract manufacturing for years, but now companies like Flextronics, Solectron, and SCI, which might once have been labeled second tier organizations because of their position in the food chain, have proven that they can beat their own customers at efficiency, quality, delivery, and supply chain expertise. In fact, we chose Flextronics as one of our Top Ten because their group continues to be small and smart, and much lighter on their feet than organizations of similar or larger size. Flextronics has "grown up" with the pressures of feeding big, high-visibility customers like Apple, Hewlett-Packard and 3Com. Consequently Flextronics, among others, never had time to build superfluous organization flows or systems. These subcontractors' growth was envisioned early and translated by a series of visionary business leaders—Winston Chen and Ko Nishimura of Solectron, and Michael Marks, the current CEO of Flextronics, planned and succeeded in pushing their organizations into new opportunity areas.

Movable Expertise, a Global Weapon

What also surprised us was that the best companies in supply chain typically bring their own structure and philosophies with them to new markets—in effect, supply chain organizations on wheels. Honda and the other North American transplants did this, although Nissan and Mazda continue to struggle; their systems and people are quite transportable across geographic, language, and cultural barriers. That is another innovation lesson that slower organizations would do well to study.

SmithKline Beecham

Pharmaceutical companies have a reputation for making profits, but not necessarily making them well in manufacturing or procurement terms. With complex distribution networks and abundant warehouses, and typically led by marketing thinkers rather than operations experts, many pharmaceuticals still miss opportunities for cost savings in their supply chain. But we were convinced by SmithKline's Willie Deese and his managers that Deese, having come from a series of rough-and-tumble manufacturing groups, understood there was money out there, and believed that if his people were smart enough and focused enough, they would find it.

Not that Deese concentrates purely on individual effort to win big victories—his pioneering approach to internal information sharing sets a model for learning and sharing, and learning some more. We would bet that his organization would be well positioned to adapt to any difficult market or organizational challenges—such as a merger or consolidation—just because of the resilience and learning capabilities Deese has nurtured, and rewarded. Deese finds much of his strength in selection and growth of good professionals, armed with very good systems; we think that other functions in pharmaceutical production groups can learn from his example.

Sun

In the computer industry, Sun started out strong in supply chain and has only continued to improve. Both Dell and Sun have created new outsourcing and logistics models. Their early work on purchasing metrics paralleled the growth of outsourced businesses, and we think that as outsourcing grows bigger and more focused on narrower niches, what Sun crafts for its delivery system will be exemplary. Sun's supply management professionals are veterans of numerous other computer companies, but they tend not to apply tired methods to a parallel problem.

NISCI

Adding the National Initiative for Supply Chain Integration (NISCI) as an adjunct honorable mention to our list of Top Ten supply chain leaders was a bit risky. From its inception barely three years ago, this group of powerful leaders—the top executives of the supply chain leaders—companies like Intel, IBM, Chrysler, and Hewlett-Packard—enjoyed the unique opportunity of a blank slate and good funding. NISCI also enjoyed strong commitment among its founding members and a shared hope that sooner rather than later the group would hit on the magic wand to fix supply chain relationship problems.

But NISCI has not located or created that magic device; instead, a few of its more powerful leaders have taken the group in a new direction, toward systems solutions that go far to enable information sharing among competitive enterprises. These problems of simulations and interenterprise communications and exchange of intellectual property—schedules, designs, data files and even architecture—have been custom-solved by other industries before—specifically aerospace and automotive.

NISCI's continued challenge is to bridge and translate a set of working tools for other transaction-oriented industrial environments, and they are not far from finding that solution. With the continued good leadership of Mike Doyle, strong member support, and a politically unfettered laboratory agenda, we think NISCI will continue to be supply chain leaders asking the right questions, and finding some of the correct answers. We continue to wish them luck, hanging out there on the precipice, hoping for a rescue team to arrive in the morning.

Whirlpool

The appliance business has always been a messy mix of metal bending, electronic features, quality issues, and cost challenges. Many early competitors have fallen to mergers, quiet acquisitions, and nameplate buyouts. We think among the top three or four worldwide appliance giants—GE for price, Maytag for innovation, and Whirlpool for affordability and quality—Whirlpool has a good shot at continuing to be around as its own entity in twenty years, because Whirlpool management has continued to keep their eyes on the target. This is a tough business where slim margins are easily destroyed by any number of systemic problems, including quality and materials costs, and appliance manufacturers have always been pulled in opposite directions by cost targets and logistics questions about producing in the consuming markets.

Again, forays into appliance manufacturing by managers from other industries have not seemed to work. It's hard to introduce "foreign" brain matter; Raytheon's acquisitions of Glenwood and Caloric were "problematic." That's one more reason why we were so impressed by our talks with Roy Armes and his people, who were so thoroughly appliance people.

Supply Chain Link to Financials

Financials tell the same story of high expectations and successful execution. *Industry Week's* "Stock Performance of the IW 100 Best-Managed Companies" (January 10, 2000, pp. 39, 40) ranks our supply chain leaders in these positions:

	1-year return (%)	*3-year return (%)*
1. Sun Microsystems	273	499
2. Flextronics International Ltd.	228	321
3. IBM Corporation	89	297
4. Harley-Davidson, Inc.	69	136
5. SmithKline Beecham PLC	7	99
6. Honda Motor Co. Ltd.	35	64
7. John Deere	30	-2
8. Daimler/Chrysler	-13	(N/A)

The Two Short-Term Supply Chain Challenges:
Lean and Technology

Companies that embrace lean manufacturing principles reap visible, immediate direct benefits in manufacturing efficiencies as well as improved employee morale. Lean manufacturing ideas have been around in various incarnations and under different names since Henry Ford, but in the past two years more organizations at different levels in the enterprise have begun lean initiatives.

Outsourcing Lean

Still, few companies have actively extended lean techniques into their supply base. Thirty years ago, most manufacturers incurred most of their product costs—typically 65 to 85 percent—in-house. As companies moved their focus more to asset management and horizontal processes, they began to rely on others—"outside experts"— to supply parts and processes that they had once produced themselves. Now it is common for only 20 to 30 percent of the costs of manufacturing products to come from inside. The other 70–80 percent come from the supply chain.

In fact, high-growth companies like Cisco Systems have recognized, according to Barbara Siverts, manager of supply chain management, that the company could not have grown so big so fast without pretty much complete dependence on outsourcing. Cisco sales in 1995 were $2.2 billion but four years later they had climbed to $12.2 billion."In the early 1990s we were having 100 percent a year growth and realized that we could not sustain that every year without doing things differently. *We could not have built manufacturing plants or hired and trained enough people to staff them.* It wasn't an option. We chose to extend our system processes and networks to a few key suppliers."*

In fact, one of Cisco's major contract suppliers, Flextronics, is on our Top Ten list because of their ability to serve Cisco and other

*Purchasing Magazine, Dec. 16, 1999, p. 75.

high-growth/high-flexibility customers' needs, while still growing exponentially. There is no room in this supply chain for inflexible legacy systems and extra links in the chain. We think that the key to these performers' winning financials is a combination of leanness and technology; the system simply won't work without both of these approaches. Cisco's "leanness" across its supply chain is estimated to have saved "$175 million a year . . . through cost avoidance, head-count avoidance. A lot of that is direct cost savings," says Siverts.*

E-Enabled Cash Farming

Technology enablement is of course clearly accountable for time to market and cash harvesting, along the lines of the Dell model. In fact, about 56 percent of Cisco product is built outside and shipped directly to Cisco customers; purely electronic, technology-managed transactions at the front end trigger the build, and at the back end, or simultaneously, collect the cash.

Developing Perfect Process

Cisco, Flextronics, Sun, Deere, Honda, IBM and others continue to prove the importance of shifting the focus of resources from the 30 percent or so of costs that occur in-house to the incredible payback to be captured in the supply base. Teaching lean manufacturing concepts to suppliers—what we call in our list of twenty Best Practices "supplier development"—is a good investment, in some chains a 10X return. So incredible is the supply base potential that producers invest in supplier development engineers to bring Best Practices and lean techniques to the supply chain the same way they invest in manufacturing engineers to improve processes in their own factories.

Good supplier development is not cheap, but neither is reengineering and rebuilding manufacturing processes. When supplier development projects are chosen carefully, they provide immediate returns. But effective supplier development is more than getting cost

*Ibid.

TWENTY BEST PRACTICES OF TOP TEN SUPPLY CHAIN LEADERS

1. cost management
2. supplier development
3. value analysis
4. MRO (maintenance and repair, indirect materials and services, nontraditional purchasing) management
5. supplier quality circles
6. training
7. supplier information sharing: supplier study groups, supplier seminars, top management meetings
8. supplier conference
9. supplier performance reporting
10. supplier surveys
11. delivery improvement
12. tool and technical assistance centers
13. supplier Support (SWAT) teams
14. loaned executives
15. early supplier involvement
16. new model development group
17. written strategy for every supplier, every part/commodity
18. strategic planning and administration
19. career path planning and academic outreach programs
20. purchasing systems

reductions for a particular part, the green eye shade syndrome; it is helping a supplier take costs out of their *processes*. Effective supplier development looks at *all* of a supplier's processes to eliminate waste and gain improvements in quality, delivery, cycle time, and costs.

This kind of development requires supplier integration at the earliest stages of new product development: shared information, resources and savings, and dedicated resources to identify and close performance gaps. In other words, best practice in supplier development requires the manufacturer to treat suppliers as if they were a department within the manufacturer's own company.

No two companies will approach supplier development exactly the same way, and no two supplier development projects take the same path to produce parallel results. However, the most effective projects follow the same general steps taken by both the manufacturer and the supplier:

Twelve Supplier Development Project Steps

1. review performance gaps
2. explore project analysis and execution methods
3. work to align mutual agreement—narrow down—on project focus
4. identify processes that result in waste (mapping and data gathering)
5. compare performance gaps with the desired state
6. establish project metrics and baseline metrics
7. gather and analyze data
8. develop improvement strategies
9. create an implementation plan
10. calculate the return on investment
11. create and review a project proposal with suppliers' management
12. execute

Step 4, mapping to understand processes and locate waste, is one of the most productive exercises an individual company or enterprise can perform to locate opportunities. (We recommend the Lean Enterprise Institute's *Learning to See* [www.lean.org] and its sequels to begin the complete map.) These steps and development of skills in most but not all the Best Practices, overlayered with technology skills and courage, we think are the combined factors that have taken our Top Ten companies into hypercompetitive zones of profit and market growth.

About Technology . . .

From the day this book was conceived and proposed, to the day the first copies are delivered to book stores, over two years will have elapsed, a lifetime in technology terms. Yet each of the Top Ten companies and their supply chains has consistently leaped ahead on technology gains. Yesterday it was EDI, today it is E-Manufacturing℠ and E-procurement; tomorrow it will be e-money and e-design.

However, among our evaluation of Top Ten capabilities we tended to avoid big, expensive software solutions. This was not because we felt that big systems would not eventually link extended enterprise networks, because eventually they will. Instead, we were captured by the innovation and creative problem solving we saw in smaller, sometimes off-the-shelf, and sometimes homegrown systems and technology solutions. Buell Motorcycle's project/parts management system is a prime example, as is SmithKline's Spendtrak and Deere's use of Evolver and Microsoft Excel to rationalize supplier operations.

Right now, and for the next three to five years, we expect that enterprise technologies will make bigger, more important advances from smaller, creative, but not permanent technology ideas. In five to ten years, however, we expect that big software providers will have caught up—at least we hope so, for the sake of continued market growth and profitability. Yet we can't guarantee that their vision will extend to creativity over short-term profit taking.

Every Best Practice tenet, every supplier development twelve-step program, and each progressive improvement in the Top Ten companies we think has succeeded because management has taken a closed-loop approach to improvement. Our approach to improvement can be reduced to three important criteria:

1. expectations
2. performance
3. rewards and recognition

Making Performance Goals Real

Leaders like Harley-Davidson's Garry Berryman, SmithKline's Willie Deese, IBM's Bill Schaefer, and Flextronics's Michael Marks combine daily operations issues with an eye to the numbers that count. That is, we believe, what allows them to set expectations, step number one. They understand in macro terms where they want their supply operations to be in the marketplace and how they need to communicate their targets and results to management and shareholders that also speak the language—numbers, financials—of the marketplace.

Organizational Performance and the Language of the Market

Second, with an eye to the marketplace and set standards in hand, these Top Ten leaders have an easier time than others establishing clear performance measures in terms that translate into their own particular organization's performance trigger, whether that trigger is set to go off at customer satisfaction performance ratings, cash flow targets, or new product introduction goals. The best managers find a way to bridge macro market goals to everyday organzational and supplier issues.

Rewards and Recognition

When managers like Willie Deese set up exhibitions of associates' breakthroughs, he is telling the organization that each idea counts, and that particularly for important ones, employees will be credited with their achievements. In big organizations, that approach is truly innovative.

Other managers have evolved other methods of acknowledging excellence that meets and exceeds expectations. Honda of America uses its annual supplier conference to highlight and reinforce supplier performance, and to funnel creative energies to internal improvements.

Harley-Davidson showcases its products daily and brings the "Harley experience" to an extended network of dealers and suppliers by trips, conferences, and real exposure to the products they make, a unique opportunity that not all manufacturers can so colorfully exercise. IBM and Daimler/Chrysler have chosen to go public carefully with their innovation work, and the leadership position that the media continue to afford them reflects well on IBM associates. Employees have sustained Big Blue's reputation of being the smartest. Flextronics' stock performance and continued expansion offers great financial rewards to a very energetic and generally young workforce that has developed an unusual loyalty to the company in an area marked by job hopping.

Procurement Ten Years Out

The word is global, and the medium is the Net. John Deere and all our other Top Ten procurement groups plan to expand their global expertise with technology that works globally. Deere, for instance, whose strategy includes doubling its size within fewer than ten years, will do it through global expansion and acquisitions, all outside North America.

India boasts four brand new Deere plants; the company recently bought out the remaining 50 percent of a Brazilian joint venture, and the largest forest equipment company in Finland ($650 million); there is a new tractor plant in Turkey, a new combine plant in China, and a new engine plant in Mexico. Because Eastern Europe will likely be the center of new growth in agriculture—it is the most newly freed breadbasket—Deere just bought a large Polish grain storage company to support alternative currency—grain. Clearly, the company is establishing a network of global production.

With multiple global plant sites, Deere understands its next challenge as finding a way to expand equally well its global supply chain infrastructure, through technology and data analysis. The company needs a global ability to examine different kinds of parts in each of these producing countries, to compare the relative competitiveness of each country through its enormous parts variety. Deere strategic planners already know, for instance, that low-cost countries, particularly Mexico, have an unbelievable ability to make wiring harnesses; Turkey is recognized for its forgings and machined castings; so each global area hosts an exportable expertise that can be exported for global price and market advantage if the infrastructure and intelligence is there.

Technology

Deere continues to enjoy a reputation for technology leadership, and planners currently completing a design spec blueprint for next-generation business-to-business systems hope to create an integrated ERP/purchasing and logistics system that will raise the bar for other big enterprises. Forty full-time professionals are dedicated to this project, which is expected to further enhance the $7 billion spend. As most companies eventually learn, thirty-year-old legacy systems die hard, not without significant planning and financial investment, and with not absolutely 100 percent satisfactory replacements. First implementations will roll out by the year 2003; the remaining sixty-nine production centers will implement two to three years later.

Notably, indirect and direct material management will continue, even under these leading-edge technologies, to be handled by separate systems; indirect material control will be executed via a software package, and direct and logistics will be executed through an in-house software system design, driven by an SAP engine.

Simulation

In Chapter 8 we covered John Deere and supplier applications of genetic algorithms, primarily through Excel and Evolver. Deere is making an important step forward in technology planning by its unique application of a simulation routine from Rajan Suri of the University of Wisconsin. We have long held simulation as a parallel technology well understood in aerospace but neglected in other equipment manufacturing. Finally, we are seeing the technology cross-over of this powerful tool into manufacturing. In this Deere application, which will be followed by others, simulation software designs and tests production layouts of equipment in cells, thereby allowing traditional factory designs to be changed to lean cells, without interruptions and layout mistakes. Perfect process simulation has become an easier exercise for any manufacturer, even small suppliers, to achieve.

Global Outsourcing Trend Continues

Supply management will continue to achieve larger recognition for its contributions to aggregate processing dollars. Although many companies seem to be in a catch-up mode about dedicating resources to increased outsourcing management of material flows, universities like Arizona State and Michigan State continue to turn out students well prepared in undergraduate and graduate supply chain studies, and the rate at which they are being snapped up is an indication of the rapid rate of change in the profession.

Business-to-business commerce enablers have extended beyond the initial hype into procurement leaders participating in dot.com start-ups, a true indicator of the technology's rapid advance. The ability to perform comparative analysis is not unlike what consumers learned two years ago about the auto and homeowner's insurance industries—when a consumer within ten minutes can receive competitive rate quotes on dozens of companies, on-line, and complete processing of applications, it is clear that procurement of other, bigger items can be handled with equal dispatch.

Prediction: Thirty Percent Cost-Down in Ten Years

In ten years winning companies will have combined all their Best Practices and technology assists to achieve absolute reductions of purchasing costs in the 25 to 30 percent range—absolutely. Quality performance that is at some organizations in the Six Sigma range will have uniformly achieved near perfect quality (where and *if* it is required by the market); and delivery and logistics performance will enjoy similarly high performance levels.

Twenty-five or 30 percent cost savings represent productivity gains, not leveraging of costs, the Lopez approach—or paper transactions—most of which is initially achieved by attention to lean practices and waste elimination, but also greater visibility to the best companies through the worldwide technology networks.

Prediction: A Different Kind of Growth

The kind of market growth that opened seemingly unlimited opportunity for traditional organizations cannot be the basis for procurement's continued healthy advances. Growth will be sliced into different layers—markets, niches, geographic areas, technology segments, logistics groups—which enable creative thinkers to improve revenue retention. Focus on growth is a change for strategic sourcing pros because it will allow them to think about customers, as well as product makeup, and it will allow procurement to make and publicize strategic contributions.

Prediction: Design It Yourself—
Translation: More Variety, Not Less

Customers designing on-line—even products designed in transit, customers designing on-site, third-party design services—all sorts of "misplaced design" efforts will have two effects on procurement's job:

1. Supply chain pros will have even less time to lose in the pipeline.
2. Intellectual property issues—who owns designs, who transfers designs and technical specs, what about licensing, and how much money can we reasonably collect—all become specialized issues beyond the current purview of layers. Supply chain managers who previously owned and outsourced materials will become experts at outsourced ideas and royalty schedules, an added benefit to becoming process experts.

Prediction: Lock-down

This is a tough prediction, with tough implications for anyone holding utopian images of the extended enterprise. In our book *The Technology Machine,* we predicted that there would be winners and losers in the manufacturing world of the year 2020. Small and medium-sized suppliers will become—either by choice or by necessity—more integrated members of large producers' enterprise structures. The giants will find a way to lock in desirable supply chain members, legally and through corporate intellectual property rulings, much the same way Microsoft, pharmaceutical giants, and various media mega-mergers have consolidated entire markets and changed technologies.

Prediction: Data-Driven Decisions

Data and intelligence about markets, technologies, personnel, and pricing, are gold. Excellent companies like IBM and SmithKline have developed their data collection and sorting capabilities in supply chain beyond what even marketing analysts of twenty years earlier could do. Data on which markets, which countries, for how long, sources of components, and logistics help will become valued, tradable intellectual property mined and packaged for sale by third-party sources. Although much of this information may appear at this time to be free over the Internet, available for the cost of dedicated research help, next-generation Web management will buy into packaged data services, like membership in stock and commodity exchanges. Cross-enterprise data theft—industrial espionage—takes on new implications for the extended enterprise.

Prediction: Common metrics, like common software protocol, will further "lock in" supplier-partner cooperation. Indeed, the science of encryption is moving so quickly that within ten to fifteen years, metrics and performance data that are not offered for sale will be encrypted and tagged for use among specific alliances—Ford and its supplier partners in raw material buying consortia with Deere, Dell, and Ariba, for example.

The next ten years will be the most exciting years yet in the purchasing profession, and we hope you will be coming along on the trip—it's going to be a helluva ride!

BIBLIOGRAPHY

Allis, Sam. *Boston Globe*, Dec. 12, 1999.

Arkin, Herbert and Raymond R. Colton. *An Outline of Statistical Methods.* New York: Barnes and Noble, 1950.

Bartholomew, Doug. "Lean vs. ERP," *Industry Week,* July 19, 1999, p. 24.

Carbone, James. "Reinventing Purchasing Wins the Medal for Big Blue," *Purchasing,* Sept. 16, 1999.

CAPS Research Study. "The Future of Purchasing and Supply, a Five- and Ten-year Forecast," Center for Advanced Purchasing Studies, Tempe, Arizona, 1998.

Clausing, Don. *Total Quality Development.* New York: ASME Press, 1994.

Fingar, Peter, Harsha Kumar and Tarun Sharma. *Enterprise E-Commerce, The Software Component Breakthrough for Business-to-Business Commerce.* Tampa, Fl.: Megham-Kiffer Press, 1999.

Fitzgerald, Kevin R. "The Profile of the Purchasing Professional," *Purchasing,* July 15, 1999.

Ford, Henry. *Today and Tomorrow.* Portland, Ore.: Productivity Press, 1988.

Grief, Michel. *The Visual Factory.* Portland, Ore.: Productivity Press, 1991.

Galsworth, Gwen. *Visual Systems.* New York: AMACOM, 1997.

Henderson, Bruce and Jorge L. Larco. *Lean Transformation.* Richmond, Va.: Oaklea Press, 1999.

Ishikawa, Kaoru, *What Is Total Quality Control—The Japanese Way.* Englewood Cliffs, N.J.: Prentice Hall, 1985.

Laraia, Anthony, Patricia E. Moody, and Robert W. Hall. *The Kaizen Blitz.* New York: Wiley, 1999.

Laseter, Timothy. *Balanced Sourcing.* San Francisco: Jossey-Bass, 1998.

Moody, Patricia E. "Two in Twelve," *Target,* Fall 1995.

————. *Breakthrough Partnering.* New York: Wiley, 1993.

Moody, Patricia E. and Richard E. Morley. *The Technology Machine.* New York: Free Press, 1999.

Moore, Geoffrey A. *Crossing the Chasm.* New York: HarperBusiness, 1995.

Moroney, M.J. *Facts from Figures.* New York: Penguin, 1978.

Nelson, Dave, Rick Mayo, and Patricia E. Moody. *Powered by Honda.* New York: Wiley, 1998.

Nelson, R. David. "The World-Class Organization," *Purchasing Today,* August 1999.

————. "Manufacturing Solutions," *Automotive Engineering International,* August 1999, p. 68.

Paulsen, Gary. *Zero to Sixty, The Motorcycle Journey of a Lifetime.* New York: Harcourt Brace, 1999.

Reid, Peter C. *Well Made in America: Lessons from Harley-Davidson on Being the Best.* New York: McGraw-Hill, 1991.

"Stock Performance of the IW 100 Best-Managed Companies," *Industry Week,* Jan. 10, 2000.

Teresko, John. "Driving Success at New Blue," *Industry Week,* Dec. 6, 1999.

Tsu, Sun. *The Art of War,* trans. Thomas Cleary. Boston: Shambhala, 1991.

Womack, James and Daniel Jones. *Lean Thinking.* New York: Simon and Schuster, 1997.

Yates, Brock. *Outlaw Machine: Harley-Davidson and the Search for the American Soul.* New York: Little, Brown, 1999.

ACKNOWLEDGMENTS

Creative minds have always been known to survive any kind
of bad training.
— Anna Freud

JUST AS WE NEARED the completion of this manuscript, we learned of the death of an old friend, one of the founders of the Association for Manufacturing Excellence, a real supply chain pro, the survivor of many years running a GE Indiana lexan plant, and more recently, a happily retired author, Dave Riggs. Too seldom we stop, take stock, and reorder our reflections of life's opportunities—gifts—and we were reminded of the dozens of individuals—welcoming, difficult, demanding, charming, brutish, tired, brilliant, and occasionally generous—and hundreds of companies that each of us has experienced in our long professional lives.

Reciting the list of contributors to our book, we sincerely hope we don't miss too many. We would like first to recognize the many contributions of our dearest partners—the companies and organizations that offered us the opportunity to "actively explore" excellence and mediocrity in action.

TRW, Honda of America, Nippondenso, Freudenberg/Nok, Matsushita, John Decre; Simplex, Digital Equipment Corporation, Data General, Rath and Strong, Johnson & Johnson, Glenwood Range (which became a division of Raytheon), Motorola, Solectron, Cisco Systems, Schering-Plough, Fairchild Republic, Briggs and Stratton, World Color Press, Association for Manufacturing Excellence, National Association for Purchasing Management, American Production and Inventory Control Society, Council of Logistics Management; *Target* magazine, *Sloan Management Review*, John Wiley and Sons; Jim Womack and his Lean Enterprise Institute; TBM Consulting and CEO Anand Sharma.

And we of course recognize the lively contributions of many individuals who supported this book's mission—to uncover and recognize the best of the best—and patiently shared their time and expertise on this very long and windy road:

Thomas Stallkamp, former president of Chrysler Motors

Gene Richter, VP of IBM procurement

Jeff Trimmer, Director of Strategic Sourcing, Daimler/Chrysler

To our most favorite red, white, and blue organizations, the Harley-Davidson Motor Company, and Deere and Company, we appreciate all your spirited help and loyalty to the project. It was truly a fun ride:

Garry Berryman, Nicole Gruber, Doug Hevner, Gregory J. Smith, Harley-Davidson

Erik Buell, John Oenick, Buell Motorcycles

Dave Meyer, Bill Butterfield, Mick McCleery of John Deere

Mike Ouellette, pipe fitter and proud Harley rider, deserves special thanks.

Also, for nerdish inspiration, Joe Yacura of American Express, Dick Morley of the Barn, and Dave Coteleer of Harley-Davidson, Lori Frantzvé of Intellimet, and everything and everybody under the Dome; Alicia Hills Moore and Gene Bylinsky of Fortune.

And for keeping us on track and well prepared, Cindy Sackett of John Deere, Nicole Gruber of Harley-Davidson, Diane K. Filstrup of Whirlpool, Manuella Solomon of Flextronics International, and Dave Schaefer of Honda of America. For telling me to get out of the damn car and get the degree, Doug Glasson. For being more patient than any kid I know, Lizzie Glasson. And for daily trips to the beach, sun, rain, blizzard, or hurricane swells, Nikki, the wild-eyed American Eskimo.

INDEX

ABOUT THE AUTHORS

DAVE NELSON is Vice President–Worldwide Supply Management for Deere & Company, and a world-renowned authority on supply chain best practices. At Deere, Mr. Nelson oversees a supply management organization that annually purchases more than $7 billion in materials and services from suppliers worldwide. His focus since joining Deere in December 1997 has been to create a cross-divisional supply management organization and a common set of global sourcing strategies designed to make Deere's supply base the most competitive in the world.

Before joining Deere, Mr. Nelson served for ten years as a corporate officer of Honda of America Manufacturing, Inc., where he led the growth of the company's purchasing division from $600 million to $6 billion in annual North American purchases. That purchasing division has been the subject of a number of benchmark studies by industry analysts and in 1995 was the recipient of the Medal of Professional Excellence from *Purchasing* magazine. In 1998, Mr. Nelson co-authored *Powered by Honda*, which chronicles the division's role in Honda of America's rise to American automotive leadership and a key part of Honda's global operations.

Mr. Nelson began his career with TRW, Inc., headquartered in Cleveland, where he spent 17 of his 30 years in various purchasing and supply management capacities and manufacturing roles, including plant management, quality control, metallurgy, materials, sales and marketing.

Mr. Nelson has long worked to advance the purchasing and supply management profession and holds a C.P.M. certification. From 1999 to 2000 he served as president of the National Association of Purchasing Management and is a member of the Board of Trustees of The Center for Advanced Purchasing Studies.

Mr. Nelson is a founding member of the Board of Directors of the National Initiative for Supply Chain Integration, Ltd., a public/private partnership supported by the National Institute of Standards and Technology to develop and enhance manufacturing supply chains. He also serves on the Board of Directors of the Purchasing Round Table. A native of Pike County, Indiana, Mr. Nelson attended Purdue University. He lives in Bettendorf, Iowa.

PATRICIA E. MOODY is a veteran manufacturing management consultant and writer with about thirty years of industry, consulting and teaching experience, and a client list that includes such industry leaders as Cisco Systems, Honda, Solectron, Motorola, Johnson & Johnson, Mead Corporation, across a range of industries—from high tech to aircraft and steel. For twenty years she was always "the first woman"—the first female master scheduler, the first female import/export manager, the first female material planner, the first female business planner, the first female senior consultant—until she gave up being the first in favor of being the best.

As editor of *Target*, the magazine of the Association for Manufacturing Excellence, she created and developed breakthrough work on the future of manufacturing teams, kaizen, new product development, supply management, and now e-commerce and e-manufacturing ^{SM}.

She grew up in a mill town, the descendent of generations of factory workers, engineers, entrepreneurs, managers and innovators, including Paul Moody, the brilliant engineer who integrated the textile industry and created the mill city of Lowell, Massachusetts.

In 1967 she co-founded an underground newspaper called, you

almost guessed it, *The Mother of Voices*, in Amherst, Massachusetts, a mostly profitable start-up that for a time rivaled Boston's *Avatar*. She enjoyed the various roles open to such a young and wild and crazy enterprise—selling ads, writing copy, editing copy, and overseeing printing of the final unblemished product.

Fond of multitasking, she is a prolific author who always has at minimum three books in process. Her more recent books include *The Perfect Engine*, with Anand Sharma, (The Free Press, Spring 2001), *The Technology Machine*, with Dick Morley (The Free Press, 1999); *The Kaizen Blitz* with Robert W. Hall and Tony Laraia (Wiley, 1999); *Powered by Honda, Developing Excellence in the Global Enterprise*, with Dave Nelson and Rick Mayo, Honda of America (Wiley, 1998); *Breakthrough Partnering* (Wiley, 1993); *Leading Manufacturing Excellence*, (Wiley, 1997); *Strategic Manufacturing* (Dow Jones/Irwin, 1990). Her next book, *Mill Girls*, about women executives, engineers, and shop floor workers, features the stories of one hundred revolutionary manufacturing women. She has authored dozens of features for the *Sloan Management Review, iSource, Target* magazine, *Production and Inventory, Business Horizons, Executive Excellence, Electronic Buyers News, Total Quality, Manufacturing Asia*, etc.

She is certified by the Institute of Management Consultants, and is a frequent keynote speaker, usually in English. She has been profiled as a "Woman Manufacturing Hero" by *Fortune* magazine and was featured on CNN's "Manufacturing 21st Century" series with Bernard Shaw. She is a member of the Sloan Management Review, Editorial Advisory Board. She holds a BA from the University of Massachusetts, and an MBA from Simmons College Graduate School of Management.

She is a founder, trustee, incorporator and former treasurer of Massachusetts' first public charter school, the Marblehead Community Charter School.

Ms. Moody is a fortunately undiagnosed dyslexic who struggled with Dick and Jane until the letters suddenly made sense—she has the same grind-followed-by-an-epiphany experience for every other new subject she tackles—tennis, accounting, motherhood, finance, even book writing. Academically (BA/MBA), she holds a spotted record punctuated by many A's, a few F's, and not much in between; she is a self-described experiential learner who has consistently failed at most first attempts—tennis, accounting, book writing, husbands, typing, and driving tests.

Around the neighborhood she is recognized as a workaholic who is seen occasionally on the back of a Harley, or sitting in complete silence on her prized stone wall. Her current hobbies include forgetting how to cook ("that's why God created restaurants"), moving shrubbery ("hey, you, yeah you, the Magnolia rosacea, step two feet to the left"), poetry, singing random bits of opera, including clips from "La Somnabula" and "La Donna E Mobile." For Christmas and birthdays she treats her special friends and mere acquaintances to well-rehearsed recitals of "God Rest Ye Merry Gentlemen" and "Lo, How a Rose E'er Blooming," in a well-preserved mezzo.

Her unrealized dreams are few—she's done a lot in five decades—but she has yet to learn to play the cello, speak fluent non-restaurant German, play "Johnny B. Goode" on her spinet, or own a pasture bounded by maple trees and stone walls. She no longer holds a passion for sailing, partying or obscure Persian poets.

Ms. Moody lives with her MIT engineer husband and beautiful red-haired daughter, an old cat, and one annoying white dog on Boston's North Shore, seven miles from the spot where her predecessors dropped anchor in 1634. She can be reached at PEMoody@aol.com.

JONATHAN STEGNER is Director, Supply Management Strategic Sourcing at Deere & Company and a 20-year Supply Management practitioner.

Mr. Stegner's responsibilities include strategic sourcing of corporate direct and indirect materials, service, and non-traditional purchases. He leads supply management recruiting, workforce planning, and development programs. He also is editor of Deere's supply management newsletter, "Linkages."

For three years before joining Deere in June of 1998, Mr. Stegner filled a number of important purchasing roles at Honda of America Manufacturing, Inc., participating in many of the initiatives regarded as integral to the Purchasing Division's rise to benchmark status. Among the positions he held at Honda was Manager, Purchasing Planning and Administration. In that capacity, Mr. Stegner was responsible for strategic studies and analyses of strategic business issues. He led preparation for Supply Management ISO 9002 conformance registration, prepared forecasts of purchases and local content, and coordinated activities in supplier performance reporting. His responsibilities also included purchasing communications, preparing purchasing information for release to media and other external audiences including acting as Project Manager for Dave Nelson's *Powered By Honda* book.

From 1991 to 1995, Mr. Stegner was Director, Purchasing, for Bush Industries, Inc., of Jamestown, New York, where he was responsible for centralized procurement of $90 million in raw materials and $5 million in maintenance, repair, and operating supplies and services. Before that, he spent 12 years at TRW, Inc., in Cleveland, Ohio, where he was selected to participate in the Purchasing Management Development program, resulting in responsibilities in several factory locations and corporate staff assignments.

Mr. Stegner is a native of Olean, New York, and a graduate of St. Bonaventure University, where he earned a bachelor's degree in economics in 1976 and a master's of business administration in 1983. He is a member of the National Association of Purchasing Management and the American Production and Inventory Control Society. He lives in Davenport, Iowa.